# Men and Popular Music in Algeria

Modern Middle East Series No. 20
Sponsored by the Center for Middle Eastern Studies
The University of Texas at Austin

# Men and Popular Music in Algeria

## The Social Significance of *Raï*

*Marc Schade-Poulsen*

UNIVERSITY OF TEXAS PRESS, AUSTIN

Printed in the United States of America
First edition, 1999

Requests for permission to reproduce material from this work should be sent to Permissions, University of Texas Press, Box 7819, Austin, TX 78713-7819.

∞ The paper used in this book meets the minimum requirements of ANSI/NISO Z39.48-1992 (R1997) (Permanence of Paper for Printed Library Materials).

LIBRARY OF CONGRESS
CATALOGING-IN-PUBLICATION DATA

Schade-Poulsen, Marc.
Men and popular music in Algeria : the social significance of raï / Marc Schade-Poulsen. — 1st ed.
p. cm. — (Modern Middle East series ; no. 20)
Includes bibliographical references (p. ) and index.
ISBN 0-292-77739-6 (alk. paper). —
ISBN 0-292-77740-X (pbk. : alk. paper)
1. Rai (Music)—History and criticism. I. Title.
II. Series: Modern Middle East series (Austin, Tex.) ; no. 20.
ML3503.A4S33 1999
781.63'0965—dc21 98-29603

# Contents

# Acknowledgments

I would like to express my gratitude to the Danish Research Council for the Humanities, which financed this project; the staff of the Institute of Anthropology at the University of Copenhagen, who helped me formulate my experiences in Algeria as a scientific discourse; and the Centre for Development Research, which financed the rewriting of my thesis as a book. I thank Susan Whyte and Michael Harbsmeier for their fruitful comments during the initial phase of the project, and Åke Norborg for supervising the thesis on which this book is based. Michael Gilsenan, Hassan Nissar, Vered Amit Talai, and Helena Wulff have provided valuable comments at different periods of the development of this work. Nidam Abdi, Bouziane Daoudi, Rabah Mezuoane, Hadj Miliani, Amina Ben Salah, Brahim Hadj Slimane, and Marie Virolle have been a constant source of inspiration during my research, not to mention Fanny Colonna's hospitality and comments on my work. I thank Majid Allaoua for helping me check the Algerian words and Robert Parkin for correcting my English. I would like to thank "my family" in Algeria for their great hospitality. Although raï music was not to their taste, they showed profound respect for my work. I chose to show them the same respect and did not take field notes on their family life. Back home—between Italy and Denmark—Fabrizia Forieri has endured the most difficult moments of writing and "creative fear." My love goes to her.

# Men and Popular Music in Algeria

## Note on Transliteration

I have tried to use a correct scholarly transliteration system while at the same time making exceptions so that the text can be read as smoothly as possible. I have used the transliteration system of the *International Journal of Middle Eastern Studies* because it is the most familiar to English-speaking scholars. However, using a transliteration system designed for literary Arabic is not without problems. One is caught between what one sees written and what one hears said, and even what one hears sung. With the Oran dialect the problem is mainly related to the vowels. Thus, the short *-a* in the text, when not placed at the end of the word, is most often read as *-e* in *painter.* I have represented most words only in the singular, with plurals indicated by *-s* except for the song lines, where I have kept as close as possible to the sung words. No distinction is made between the *-d* and the *-z*.

Place names and personal names are not strictly transcribed. The former are rendered as one is likely to find them represented on maps. The latter are rendered in a form that can be recognized by readers in English without straying too far from Algerian transcription practice.

Terms that occur commonly in Western languages, such as *cheb, raï,* and *Ramadan,* are presented in their Western form. All translations into English are mine unless otherwise specified.

# 1

# Introduction

This story is based on my experience in Algeria from 1990 to the middle of 1992, a time of political turmoil that led to the tragic present-day armed conflict. I was living in Algeria frequently during this period, studying music, love and men's relationship to women.

Before going to Algeria, I had read and written about the major Islamist ideologues whose works were the basis of the present-day quest of Islamist movements to set up "God-given law" as the guiding principle in their different postcolonial nation states. I found that their texts were filled with arguments aimed at "converting" Muslim readers to a particular interpretation of Islam, that they were implicitly putting forward a sociopolitical analysis of their societies which continually returned to notions of greed, the abuse of power, egoism, lust, and amorality. These were Western attributes that had invaded the Islamic world, surrounding the Muslim, attracting him to the same behavior and making him feel it was impossible to live as a good Muslim in such a non-Muslim environment (see Schade-Poulsen 1988).

However, rather than entering the current debate among Islamists and other Western commentators, who are often engaged in the mutual confirmation of frozen images of Islam, I wanted to look for a more differentiated understanding of the then-current changes in Algeria. The conflict between the Islamic ideologues and their opponents was clearly the basis for intense feelings. I looked for a way to study the nonverbal, emotional aspects of this debate, and I ended up focusing my attention on raï music, the music of Algerian youth.

Music has always been an important part of my life. As a boy I was trained in music and particularly in the European classical choral repertoire. I grew my hair long and played the guitar. I studied African rhythms and Greek bouzouki, and began to explore the range of my voice. I experienced how music could provoke moods and release emotions, how it could be used as a form of therapy, and how it seemed that musicians possessed a language that reached across social borders. It struck me as paradoxical that the musical language in left-wing demonstrations did not differ much from the harmonies of bourgeois concert halls. And in Tunisia it seemed equally ironic that in the cafes, male arenas par excellence, it was women's voices—such as the great Umm Kulthoum—which defined the musical mood.

I felt that deeper, nonverbal messages and meanings were alive in music, and that a more profound and humanistic understanding of social life could be discovered in it. I was naive in this construction and I do not subscribe to so simple an understanding today. Nevertheless, at the time I was seeking to integrate my early private interests into my professional life, and as time passed, I became more and more eager to leave the square four beats of Western rock to become involved in music that fused elements from different worlds.

I remember the first time I went to Algeria, in 1978. On the boat, between two songs by ABBA, I heard Idir, a singer whose Kabyle songs, set to an instrumentation inspired by Western folk and protest songs, were having a profound effect in Algeria. The next time I returned I was again carried away by the richness and variety of modern Algerian popular songs. Finally, in 1987, when visiting Souk Ahras in eastern Algeria, I became aware of the importance of raï. My friends there knew and enjoyed listening to at least a dozen raï singers, even though the musicians came from the other end of the country. I subsequently read that raï seemed to contradict the basic approaches of the Islamist movement (my first sources were Benkheira 1986 and Lefevre 1986). Yet it was clear to me that both raï and Islamism appealed to the young, and I decided to look for means of enquiring into that musical form.

As I became more focused on the purpose of the study, it became clear that I was not going to undertake a traditional ethnomusicological project. Instead, I wanted to approach music as a means of answering nonmusical questions; rather than asking questions in Algeria about issues such as Islam, economics, and politics, I would ask questions about music in order to reach an understanding of those aspects of life.

This meant that I began to break not with my naïveté (a state of mind recommended to students of music by Seeger 1987) but rather with the notion of music as pure and deep emotion. Although music can be said to be descriptive of emotions (i.e., it is "different" rather than "deeper" or "more profound" than other forms of expression), I began to favor the idea that from a logical point of view music and songs cannot be verbalized because—as a category of art forms—they are of a nonverbal nature. This goes even for words set to music, since lyrics are sung and not spoken.

This approach led me to investigate raï as "a total social fact," to study it in as many of its aspects as possible in order to circumvent its unspeakableness. This does not mean that I consider a musicological understanding of music useless. One must venture into music, its production, and its form in order to acquire a precise understanding of the ways it reaches from "pure" sound into social life and how the latter in turn reflects back on music. In seeing music as total social fact, I had to follow it from production to consumption in order to understand the processes that are embedded in the making and reception of a musical form such as raï. This is what I have attempted to do in this book.

## Sources of Inspiration

Raï is a popular musical style from Algeria which uses Western instruments and mixes local popular songs and rhythms with American disco, the songs of Julio Iglesias, Moroccan wedding tunes, Egyptian preludes, and other sources. It came into being in the late 1970s and early 1980s. It is sung by young singers called "chebs" (or *chabas,* young women), most of whom come from Oran (Wahrān), the second largest city in Algeria. Since it began, raï has produced hundreds of songs and spread over a much wider territory, becoming known worldwide.

In studying raï, I have found an invaluable source of inspiration in writings on games and plays such as those by Bateson (1972), Bromberger (1995), Caillois (1958), Geertz (1973, 1983), Hammoudi (1988), Huizinga (1970 [1949]), and Mead (1934). But because raï emerged in a contemporary context of mass-produced luxury goods and transnational cultural expression, current anthropological debates on cultural production are also relevant. Increasingly, the classical approach to societies as self-sustaining communities has been questioned. Culture can no longer be seen exclusively in terms of a discrete geographical territory (if indeed it ever could) because of increased worldwide interconnectedness through systems of cultural communication. Popular culture, pop music, youths' gaze toward the outer world, can no longer be seen as "noise" to be filtered out in order to expose a "purer cultural reality."

Thus writings on Western youth cultures and their relation to music are also useful in the study of raï.[1] However, it is important to recognize that although since the 1970s young people, as a distinct group, have expressed part of their identity through music (Malm and Willis 1984, Robinson et al. 1991), Western concepts of youth or leisure time cannot be transferred to other cultural contexts, such as the Arabo-Muslim world. Indeed, one of my main preoccupations in this book is to avoid indiscriminately using Western social concepts in describing the Algerian situation with respect to raï, and to instead focus on how apparently worldwide homogenizing tendencies within music can nevertheless result in specific musical and sociopolitical realities.

Gender relations constitute an important part of such specific social worlds. My decision to focus on men reflects the fact that foreign male anthropologists in a Muslim country are not allowed much access to the female world. I realize, of course, that it is impossible to represent a whole society only through men's eyes. Recognizing the importance of gender relations in any society, I have tried to take gender seriously while focusing on men and not to mistake them for the entire social world. Nor does my concern with men mean that women will disappear from the text. When dealing with music and its relation to male youth, I found women standing at the center of male attention. Raï is a form of popular music[2] which, like most mass-produced music, mainly deals with love. Wherever I went in Algeria, when discussing raï I inevitably found myself involved in stories of love and men's relations with different categories of women in a society undergoing rapid change. It is in this way, in a male mirror, that women will appear in this story, and clearly the Algerian male world as it is expressed through raï certainly has sociocultural as well as political consequences for women.

In fact, this book can be seen as a narrative which moves from the production of raï to its consumption and then to an analysis of men's views on and relation to women in Algerian public life. It is in public life that the male anthropologist will most easily meet young men in Algerian society—outside of working hours—where many formulations are made and remade about what work activities should ideally lead to in terms of patterns of consumption and social mobility. This is particularly interesting because the most potent political force in Algeria today, the Islamist movement, has as one of its major preoccupations the separation of men and women in precisely these spheres of work, consumption, and social mobility. Thus, though this book is concerned with music, love, and men's relation to women, it situates itself in a precise historical, political, and economic context.

## Algeria and Islam

In the last thirty years, Algeria has developed from a colonial, agricultural exporting area to an independent, rentier state based on the exportation of gas and oil.[3] It has experienced a modernization of agriculture that never "took off" and an *industrie industrialisante* that was never completed. Although economic investments succeeded in creating an increase in earnings from wage labor and a parallel rise in the number of wage labor jobs,[4] the 1980s experienced a severe recession particularly after the fall of oil prices (from $30 a barrel in 1982 to $12 in 1988). Foreign debt rose from $1 billion in 1970 to $24 billion in 1988 (see Addi 1990). In 1992, 70 percent of foreign currency earnings were being spent to finance foreign debt at a time when the country was in acute need of productive and social investment.

These changes have been accompanied by one of the world's most rapid demographic growths. In 1966 there were just under 12 million inhabitants in Algeria. In 1989, there were 25 million, of whom 80 percent were under the age of 30 (*El Moudjahid,* September 19, 1990). This growth was accompanied by a massive influx into the cities. Whereas 31.4 percent of the population was urban in 1966, 50 percent of the population lived in cities by 1987 (Office national des statistiques [ONS] 1988).

These changes have been acutely felt in daily life.[5] In 1989 only 4 million out of the population of 25 million were officially employed, and 1 million were officially unemployed. Of these, 80 percent were between 17 and 27 years of age (*El Moudjahid,* September 19, 1990). In 1992, 1.2 million were officially unemployed (*Le Matin,* August 24, 1992). The most catastrophic development, however, has been in housing. In 1994 the population of 27 million lived eight persons per unit. To make this average fall by just one person, six hundred thousand units would have to be constructed immediately. To reduce the crisis, two hundred thousand units would have to be built every year for ten years, an impossibility given the actual capacity of the system (see Lesbet 1994).

At the same time, significant structural changes have taken place in Algeria with regard to the young. First, the system of education has been democratized. In 1991, 81.5 percent of those aged six to fourteen were enrolled in school, 96 percent of them in the large towns (*Horizon*, September 11, 1991). Second, the period of adolescence[6] has lengthened considerably. In 1966, the average age of marriage was 18.3 years for women and 23.8 for men; in 1987, it was 23.7 and 27.6, respectively (Sari 1990:28). Third, for the first time in its modern history Algeria has witnessed a significant entry of women into the public sphere. Although out of a potential female workforce of 4 million women only 365,000 were employed in wage labor in 1987, this number nevertheless represents an increase of 164 percent in ten years. Furthermore, the majority of the female workers were young, unmarried women living in the cities (ibid.:37). Eighty-five percent of the girls in large cities were enrolled in primary education (*Horizon*, September 11, 1991), and 30 percent of the students at the secondary level were women (ibid.:45). Finally, the creation of wage labor jobs in the 1970s, the population influx into the cities, and changes in youth conditions also seem to have changed the structure of the Algerian family.

The departure of the French in 1962 in itself left a large number of vacant houses and apartments for the Algerians to move into. But even without this event, the general trend has been for the extended family as a unit of production and consumption under the guidance of a patriarch to diminish in importance (see Boutefnouchet 1982; Kerrou and Kharoufi 1994). The extended family as a unit of consumption has gained importance, and there has been a shift from the extended family to the nuclear family.[7] The couple has emerged as a central social unit, weakening the foundations of patriarchal control. An example of this change can be seen in the Family Code of 1984, which, although conferring a dependent status on women, detached itself from the classical Muslim definition of marriage, which implies contracting for a wife in order to gain access to licit sexual relations. While remaining silent on the subject of marriage, the Family Code instead mentions the founding of a family on the basis of affection and mutual aid (see Dennouni 1986:712). However, as Boutefnouchet (1982:154) has noted, the nuclear family is not necessarily a stable unit. It may develop into an extended family, depending on individual family norms, housing conditions, and the job opportunities of family members.

Algeria has also witnessed the rise of Islamism. The factors involved in the growth of this form of Islam are too complex to discuss at length here.[8] However, it is appropriate to point out that the origin of this form of Islamist thinking must be traced back to at least the beginning of the century and that it grew in importance mainly at the time of the national awakening of the 1930s (see Carlier 1995; Colonna 1974, 1995; Merad 1967). After independence, it was continually present on the political scene. The ruling party itself promoted a policy of "arabization" and made diverse attempts at national islamization. For example, in 1976 it introduced Friday as the weekly day of rest and in 1984 adopted the Family Code, which severely restricts women's rights.

At the same time, Islamism grew in strength as a force of opposition. The introduction in the early 1960s of teachers primarily from Egypt with a background in the Muslim Brotherhood was of importance to this development. The politics of arabization were even more important because outlets for arabophones were not created in the state apparatus, the language of which remained French. The lack of social mobility among major groups within the postindependence generation is a prime factor in understanding the success of an activist form of Islam whose main political (utopian) goal seems to be the installation of a moral, uncorrupt state of justice. This must also be combined with the fact that since independence, Algeria has been ruled by an authoritarian elite which has left little room for popular, democratic experiences and whose backbone has been the army.

In the early 1980s (the years of the raï breakthrough), Islamism started growing into a mass movement, gaining further strength during the revolt of October 1988. This revolt was the result of both popular dissatisfaction with worsening economic and social conditions and of disagreements among factions within the ruling elite. As a result, for some years the country experienced an intense democratic period with a change in the constitution, the temporary withdrawal of the army from the political scene, and freedom and proliferation of the press. It also experienced the unification of major Islamist groups into the FIS (Front islamique du salut), which in 1990 won the first free city elections to take place in the country since independence.

However, after 1990 the political situation grew increasingly complex. In 1991 a branch of the FIS decided to challenge the government by launching a general strike and agitating for (among other things) progress toward direct presidential elections. In June 1991, the movement was broken and parliamentary elections were postponed until December of the same year. In the elections, the Islamists won a major victory, with 54 percent of the votes cast in the first round of the elections. Shortly afterward, President Chedli was effectively deposed and the army took control of the country. The installation of Boudiaf as leader did not succeed in legitimizing the government. After his murder in June 1992, it became increasingly clear that the country was moving rapidly toward a tragic armed conflict.[9]

## Fieldwork

I carried out my fieldwork on raï in the intense period between the nationwide city elections and Boudiaf's murder. Inspired by Marcus and Fischer's recommendation (1986) to study communities as parts of larger systems, I began my fieldwork with an initial six weeks in Paris in 1990, where I contacted journalists, promoters, bars, discos, and local radio stations involved in the dissemination of raï music. I soon lost a large number of illusions in regard to what musical activities were about. It was obvious that in France, raï could in no way be seen as pure art. At the time, it was being incorporated into the World Music concept[10] and was being cultivated by a chain of middlemen who were necessary for the mass dissemination of raï to take place.

With these experiences in mind—and with a collection of press articles in my files—I went to Algeria for three months in the autumn of 1990. My idea was to broaden my personal knowledge of Algeria, and since raï was a mass-produced product, to try to obtain an impression of its wider impact in the country. My journey took me to Algiers, Oran, Tlemcen, Sidi Bel Abbès, Bejaia, and Souk Ahras. I contacted journalists, raï studios, and raï singers. I had formal and informal encounters with fourteen cassette dealers and did twenty-four structured interviews with young men involved in raï. It became clear that except in the Kabyle area, raï was the most popular music in Algeria.

One of the most notable results of this experience was the realization that whenever I looked for agents who were supposed to have played a central role in the creation of raï—singers, producers, and others—they were difficult to reach, and when I did reach them, I did not obtain much more information than I had already read in the press. One reason for this was that those involved in the raï business were busy people in constant demand. Another was that dozens of journalists had been there before me. A story had already been told which—I gradually realized—did not exactly correspond to the reality of raï music for the singers, and which did not necessarily bring them positive returns.

I also knew that an overt interest in Islamism had to be played down. Two months before I arrived, the Islamists had won the local elections in the major cities. As a consequence, almost every public music concert in the Oran area was stopped by the Islamists, who were ceasing to fund nonreligious cultural activities. Only after the army crushed the Islamist general strike in June 1991 and arrested the main leaders did some concerts and festivals timidly reappear. The political atmosphere in the country was extremely tense. I did succeed in meeting a few regional leaders of the FIS, but otherwise it was obvious that any systematic inquiry into raï and Islamism at the same time would not be advisable.

Thus, although Islamism was an initial interest, the subject had to be excluded formally from the project. I did not tape sermons in the mosques. I did not systematically associate myself with active members of the movement. And I did not want to merely reproduce what was already known from other writings. The Islamist movement is thus filtered through the "lens of raï" rather than being approached directly.

I returned to Algeria in the spring of 1991, shortly after the end of the Gulf War, in which a majority of Algerians had been pro-Iraq and during which photos of Algeria's former strongman, Boumedienne, appeared side by side with photos of Saddam Hussein. I planned to stay in Oran for six months and then complete my field research with another two months in Paris in 1992.

My basic idea was to follow the performance, production, and consumption of raï in as many of its phases as possible, using a qualitative approach. During my first trip it had become clear to me that any quantitative approach to raï would have to be abandoned given my time schedule. Such an approach would be of little use anyway without an initial qualitative understanding of the factors involved in the success of raï.

Thus, I looked for young men with whom I could reach a level of confidence. My friends turned out to be between twenty and thirty years old, most of them unmarried. Thus they had been teenagers during the development of electric raï. The young men and youths who people the following pages belong to this group of friends and their numerous acquaintances. When I discuss young men's problems, I refer to theirs, and not to the even worse problems of today's teenagers in Algeria.

I also spent a good deal of time in the recording studios and tried to reach the best known singers for interviews, though my initial plan of playing with a group of musicians met with several problems. First, it turned out that the notion of a group was no longer current in Oran. People met for performances only as a consequence of being hired by the one with the performance contract. Second, the rising conflict between the FIS and the government meant that very few weddings had live music.

Finally, in the beginning of July I hastily had to leave Oran. Three months had passed, during which Denmark had introduced a requirement for visas for Algerian citizens. Algeria responded by demanding the same for Danish citizens. With the acute political crisis, no one in Oran dared to take the responsibility of giving me a visa, and I was consequently forced to leave by the local authorities.

Back in Denmark, I succeded in obtaining a two-month visa in the autumn with the help of the Danish Embassy. I arrived in Oran in time to take part in a number of weddings and a raï festival with second ranking singers, which took place under the auspices of the army. By then I had decided to go back to Algeria during Ramadan in 1992 and spend in all two months in Algeria and then one month in Paris. By then I felt certain that it would be of greater interest to concentrate on a study of raï in Algeria, for it was only described in writings to a limited degree, and my understanding of it was only just beginning.

In 1992, I returned to Oran a few months before the murder of Boudiaf. During Ramadan I had the opportunity to take part in a number of live performances in town, mainly in cabarets and restaurants. The arrests of thousands of leading members of the FIS had provided a temporary if uncertain breathing space for secular leisure activities. I spent the last month talking with young men about raï in restaurants and bars, attending weddings, and visiting with friends. I succeeded in contacting a good number of singers and also conducted intensive interviews with my friends on how they perceived a number of raï songs.

Thus during my last stay in Algeria, several elements which until then had run separate courses began to come together. I began to realize that most of what I had read about raï until then (mostly in the press) and a lot of what I had been told, while factually correct, had not uncovered the basic principles of raï. In particular, I found that the performative aspects of raï and the consumer's and producer's awareness of the raï format had been neglected. I began to understand that my own approach had been biased in similar ways, and finally, that this bias not only had to be corrected, but also had to be taken into consideration as an important part of the whole complex of raï. In this sense, my investigations in Algeria stopped just when they began to bear most fruit.

The following pages will take readers into my interpretation of the raï universe. In chapter 2, I start with a formal history of raï and then show how the music became integrated into the media and subsequently translated into a Western discourse. The latter version of raï, which prevails on the global scene, is not necessarily the most enlightening one.

In chapter 3, I break with the Western media version of raï. In order to do this, I start with the basics of raï, the live performance, and gradually show how raï is transferred from live performance to the recording studio. I describe how the songs are reproduced on cassette tapes for a wider audience.

In chapter 4, I venture into the social life of seven raï listeners I met and describe the context of their lives in the city of Oran. The chapter is intended to be a wider introduction to the discussion in the next chapter of how raï songs extend from cassette tapes into social life. Chapter 5 then takes the form of a dialogue, with intensive interviews I conducted with the seven raï listeners on their perceptions of songs I played for them.

In chapter 6, I move from individual cases to the wider society, describing the context of the songs' origins in the cabarets of Oran and discussing their impact on Algerian society. The chapter thus situates the songs with regard to Algerian family life, moral codes, and power relations, as well as placing raï in the present-day context of Algerian society, with the rise of Islamism.

Finally, in chapter 7, I leave the cabarets and the family to venture into public Algerian life, into the spheres where young men and women meet. Raï songs are discussed in relation to young men's experiences with women. Topics of national politics are expressed in raï in terms of women and love, and raï gives a clue to the understanding of two major movements among Algerian youth: one toward the mosque, the other toward the West.

All in all, the study follows "the social life of raï" (see Appadurai 1988). It looks at what people have done to it, and what it does to people. As such it highlights not only raï itself, but also Algerian cabarets, weddings, recording studios, family life, and street culture, particularly in relation to men.

The study claims only a qualitative insight into raï and to conditions of life among male youth. When I write about what "people," "a number of listeners," or "youngsters" "say," "state" or "do," this must be understood not as statistically representative, but as behaviors that I observed in (primarily) the city of Oran in the early 1990s. Events occurring after 1995 have not been included in this book.

I have chosen to preserve the anonymity of all my informants. Due to the situation in Algeria it is impossible to know the purposes for which a book like this might be used. Since my departure, two of the people I knew, the top singer Cheb Hasni and the producer Rachid Baba, have been killed, and most other singers have sought refuge in France.

I dedicate the book to my friends and all those who helped me. Many are today in an extremely difficult situation as citizens of a state in armed conflict and economic crisis. The Algerians I know want a state of justice and prosperity in which their overwhelming creativity can be expressed.

## Basic Raï Terms

Several terms that are essential to understanding the story of raï are explained here.[11]

*What Does Raï Mean?*

Raï (*rrāy*) literally means "a way of seeing," "an opinion," "a point of view," "advice," but also "an aim," "a plan" and even "a thought," "a judgment," "a will." In Orania it is widely said that in the past people went to a *shīkh* (see below), a poet of *malḥūn,* to ask for his raï, his advice, expressed as poetry. Many, even raï musicians and singers, will say today that this is the real raï.

But the word also appears as a stopgap expression in a number of songs of a more popular kind, as one finds "*amān, amān*" in Turkish songs, "*ya līl, ya līl*" in Egyptian songs, and "*dān dāni*" in the poetry of the *shīkhs* (see Virolle-Souibès 1988a: 203—all of these expressions are also found in raï), or the "oh no, oh no" or "yeah, yeah" of rock and blues lyrics.

Raï's rhythmic and tonal universe originates from western Algeria, with its center of gravity lying between Relizane, Saïda, Sidi Bel Abbès, Oujda (in Morocco), and Oran. The emergence of raï is generally associated with the migration into the cities of western Algeria (Miliani and Belkhadem 1981, Comité 1985, Miliani 1983, Virolle-Souibès 1988a), starting with the world depression in the 1930s. Other sources, however, mention elements which are associated with the raï music of today, such as the "repetitive" musical form, improper forms of expression, women entertaining men, and games of competition, indicating that raï as a genre goes much further back in history (Azza 1979; Daumas [1869] 1983; Delphin 1886, 1891; Gaudefroy-Demombynes 1901; Rouanet 1920).

One important element in raï has been that it is danceable, with simple but characteristic lyrics. It also uses the local dialect, with noticeable influences from Spanish, French, literary Arabic, rural, and city dialects (Virolle-Souibès 1988a: 192). This has been true of popular local poetry since the middle of the nineteenth century (Azza 1979:15, Tahar 1975:43). Another important element in raï is the incorporation of Western instruments into a local repertoire. This is not a new thing either, since it has been reported throughout this century (Bureau 1964, Rouanet 1920, Safir 1949, Yafil n.d.). In fact raï relates to a multitude of sources, which can be best understood by looking at the cheb, the *shīkh,* the *shīkha,* the *maddāḥa,* and the *wahrāni.*

### *What Is a Cheb?*

Cheb (*shābb*) is the title given to male singers of the new musical style. The women are called *chabas* (*shābbas*). Cheb means young man (*chaba,* young woman) and must be seen in relation to *shīkh* and *shīkha,* which designate experienced or older singers. The fact that a great number of singers use the word in their artistic names has been seen as a novelty and as a self-conscious label expressing a rising youth identity in Algeria. But not all raï singers use it. It is as much the creation of publishers as of singers, and the expression is not new. As early as 1957 a songwriter of the light versions of *wahrāni* (see below) presented himself as Cheb Mohammed Benzerga.

### *What Is a* Shīkh?

The title of *shīkh* is generally accorded to a learned man to suggest that he is an educated, mature, practicing Muslim, but in relation to raï it is associated with poets or interpreters of *malḥūn,* sung poetry in the local dialect which has existed in the Maghreb since at least the sixteenth century (see Comité 1985, Virolle-Souibès 1988a:179). The poetry is a highly elaborate art form which takes years to learn through an apprenticeship, and it consists of thousands of verses and *qaṣīdas* (poems) dealing with historical events, satire, religion, heroism, and love.[12] It exists all over the Maghreb, and in the Oran area is associated with the *badawi* (Bedouin) styles of recitation accompanied by at least two *gaṣbas* and a *gallāl.*[13]

As noted, many in Orania consider the *shīkhs* to be performers of the true raï.[14] The Algerian press in general, as well as a number of scholarly commentaries, have described raï as a degenerated form of the *malḥūn.* But as we shall see, this is not true, even if parts of the *shīkhs*' poetry and style of declamation are found in the raï of today. In Oran the *shīkhs*' poetry was highly esteemed in general, but seldom listened to by the young, and in many cases it was not understood, even among raï singers who recorded extracts from the *shīkhs*' songs.

### *What Is a* Shīkha?

While *shīkh* is a title with a positive connotation, the feminine *shīkha* is more ambivalent. The *shīkha* performs with male instruments, the *gaṣbas* and *gallāl,* sometimes also with other female dancers. Her art is built on a spontaneity appropriate primarily for men, and this in a Muslim society constitutes an act of moral transgression. The places of performance have been *wa'adas* (religious festivals), weddings, *maḥshāshas* (taverns with hashish), taverns, and pleasure parties (*baṣṭas*). Historically, *shīkhas* are associated with brothels and prostitution. Their names and recordings have been an inspiration for the raï singers of today.[15]

### *What Is a* Maddāḥa?

The expression *maddāḥa* comes from the root word *madḥ,* "to praise, celebrate, sing religious poetry." The *maddāḥa* is a woman versed in religious as well as profane songs, who sings at different ceremonies such as weddings and circumcisions. In the early 1990s, the *maddāḥa* performed with a group of female instrumentalists; one was a violinist and the others played percussion instruments such as the *ṭbīla* (a small clay drum beaten with a stick), the *darbūka,* the *gallāl,* or the *banndīr* while singing response choruses. Like the *shīkhas,* they play in a generally spontaneous style.[16] Their reputations, however, are more positive than those of the *shīkhas* since they play exclusively for women; as such they are considered less transgressive. Some are known to have been poets in their own right, for example, Khaira Es-Sebsajiyya and the *bināt* (girls of) Baghdâdi (Belhalfaoui 1982a, Mebarki and Naceri 1983). Many female raï singers started their careers as *maddāḥas,* and they still perform in the acoustic genre at female gatherings.[17] They too have had an important impact on the male raï of today.

### *The* Wahrāni

The *wahrāni* (Oran music) is associated with the music developed in the city centers of Orania, mainly Oran, from the mid-1930s through the flourishing period of the 1950s. Broadly speaking, the *wahrāni* is an adaptation of the *malḥūn* to city instruments (such as the *'uud,* the accordion, the banjo, the piano, etc.), to the melody and rhythm of the Oran area, and to a tone universe relating to the mass-produced music of the Arab world and to Spanish, French, and even Latin American songs.[18] It has provided present-day raï with a repertoire of instrumental sounds, melodic patterns, and combinations of rhythm. However, raï must not be confused with *wahrāni.* Raï musicians do not possess the same finesse of musical approach as is found in the *wahrāni,* and the poetical ideas are not nearly as elaborate. On the other hand, electric raï has adopted and recorded *wahrāni* songs and given new texts to *wahrāni* tunes, while composers of *wahrāni* have created songs for raï singers.

This brief overview of the main elements in raï shows that this musical genre does not have clearly demarcated lines. When I was in Oran, however, people frequently referred to the first records after independence—on which the "spontaneous" form of raï was adapted to the instrumentation of the city—as the beginning of raï. The best known was a 1965 recording by a twelve-year-old, Bouteldja Belkacem, of two songs by Cheikha Ouashma: "Zizīya" (Ziziya told me to have a party at her place to night, Ziziya told me to spend the night with her) and "Sīdi l-ḥakim" (Mister judge, where are they taking me?). So there are considered to be definite origins.

One important early raï musician was Bellemou, a trumpet player who before independence played in the local marching band of Aïn Temouchent. After 1962 he expanded his repertoire by combining trumpet and saxophone with local percussion instruments, thus replacing reed flutes with brass; he performed at events such as football matches and wedding processions. A third notable development took place in the raï groups of Sidi Bel Abbès, who replaced reed flutes with the electric guitar and the wah-wah pedal. The earliest name associated with this genre is Mohammed Zargui, who died in 1981.

At the end of the 1970s, the key instrument of raï in Oran was the accordion. Western music, Hindi film music, and Moroccan music (such as Nass el Ghiwane and Jil Jillala) were popular. A great number of musicians were also versed in the popular songs of the area. They would meet with musicians like the Nawi brothers, the Qada brothers, Mokhtar the drummer, and later Hocine the keyboard player, who were all playing Western pop and rock, and they became among the first to introduce electric instruments to raï. Violinists like Kouider Berkane and Abdallah Rerbal and the *drabki* player Hocine, on the other hand, contributed to maintaining continuity with *wahrāni* music.

Another important musician was Mohammed Maghni, one of the few in raï to have formal musical training and practical experience as a keyboard player in the pop group the Students. He created new arrangements in raï—with feel-ins and riffs from rock, disco, and sometimes jazz—within the Oranian style of phrasing. The best known "electric" musicians, however, were Rachid and Fethi, the Baba brothers, lovers of Western pop and music technology (with some ability to invest) who were the first to introduce the complete synthesizer and drum-machine sound into raï in 1982. Later, they invested money in the best multi-track studio and recording facilities in North Africa and were clever enough to employ trained musicians like Ben Ali and Samir. Rachid is now dead, shot down in Oran in February 1995 by people who never publicly acknowledged the act.

But in the early 1980s it was not yet apparent that Algeria would experience its present-day tragedy. It is here that the story begins.

# 2

•

# A Story of Raï

This story begins in the late 1970s in the second largest city of Algeria, Oran, or *Wahrān*.[1] At that time a number of groups—the Students, the New Clarks, La Main, Les Welcomes—versed in European pop and rock (the Bee Gees, Led Zeppelin, the Beatles, French Johny Halliday, Adamo, Charles Aznavour, etc.)—were playing at concerts and amateur contests in cinemas or rented halls, as well as in the numerous cabarets in the city and along the coast, which was known for its pleasant beaches.

At least two orchestras performed in the cabarets, one playing Western music and the other playing Egyptian, Moroccan, or *wahrāni* styles. In the late 1970s the Arabic part of the program seemed increasingly to consist of the acoustic raï genre, played with combinations of percussion such as the *darbūka,* the *ṭbal* and the *qarqabu,* and with melodic instruments such as the accordion, the trumpet and the violin. Musicians say that during this period the two groups would often fuse, creating such a success in terms of people coming on to the dance floor that it became the standard pattern in the clubs.

This trend coincided with the appearance of a new generation of singers, Sahraoui and Fadela, Houari Benchenet, Kouider Bensaïd, Cheb Hindi, Zargui, and the most well known today, Khaled. They were all born around the time of independence (in 1962) and can thus be said to represent the first generation of Algerians not having experienced the colonial period. This musical phenomenon also coincided with the "death" of the vinyl record in Algeria, which around this time finally was ousted by the cassette tape. Since the latter is a cheaper and easier medium to handle in terms of production and distribution, it opened up possibilities for an unprecedented wide-scale musical production in Algeria and for a more widely extended consumption in space and time.

This "more democratic" medium also allowed a new generation of producers to enter the music business. Quite a few of them were regulars in the cabarets and they got the idea of recording their performances on cassette. One result among many was the first raï hit at the end of 1979, "Ma ḥlali n-nūm" (Sleep doesn't come easily to me), first sung by Chaba Fadela and soon after by Cheb Khaled. These two versions have only a few lines in common (a peculiar characteristic of raï that I return to all through this story), but the chorus is the same and is said to originate from local prisons. The two songs also contain a joking sentence, reflecting a kind of popular wisdom and the atmosphere of the cabarets: "*Birra ʾarabiyya w wiski gawriyya*" (The beer is for the Arabs, whiskey for the foreigners). At that time, a bottle of whiskey was worth sixty-seven beers (Benkheira 1982:15) and a few Europeans still frequented the cabarets.

Over the next three or four years, the new raï style spread with a speed and success which indicates that it expressed elements of acute concern in Algeria and that it was a genre reflecting sociocultural change from a passive to a more active position among the young, who already at that time represented the largest group within the Algerian population.[2]

At the beginning of the 1980s, raï was still absent from national radio and television. After independence, Algeria had been endowed with national institutions by the ruling elite, such as the Institut national de musique (1968) and ONDA (the Organisation des droits d'auteur), which was established to protect authors' and composers' rights. A number of official festivals featuring different musical styles were held all over the country, and music became an integrated activity in the party-controlled youth centers. In 1964, *andalus* was declared the national classical music of Algeria, an elaborated genre mostly enjoyed by the elite in the traditional cities of Algeria, such as Tlemcen, Constantine, and Algiers, the roots of which can be traced back to the classical Arabic empires via Muslim Andalusia (see Guettat 1980).

Raï's syncretism did not fit at all into official national politics, and even less did its association with the tradition of the *shīkha*. However, in 1982, a commercial radio station, Medi 1, owned jointly by French and Moroccan private interests, started releasing raï songs on the airwaves from Tangiers. In December 1984, the French-language Channel 3 in

Algeria began doing the same, partly, as I was told, to compete with Medi 1. About the same time the French-language *Actuel,* a Parisian left-wing magazine for the young about lifestyle and travel, sent a reporter to the cabarets of Oran, who, as we shall see, mispresented raï as a subversive and semipornographic movement that was rapidly gathering momentum.

This presentation did not at all please a number of people in Oran, who were increasingly aware that it was worth trying to manage the meanings of raï, whether for the sake of the money, the truth, or the regional pride involved. It also happened that raï was closely followed by a large number of the members of Front de libération national (FLN's) youth organization. An alliance was subsequently formed between members of the local bourgeoisie, radio officials, and musicians whose songs had been ousted commercially by raï. They included university academics who had been engaged in the Ciné-pop movement, bringing high art films to the people, and government officials with close relations to Chedli, who had been in charge of the western military region before becoming president of Algeria. Out of this came a festival in Oran in August 1985 which attracted the press in Algeria and France as well as Riadh el Feth in Algiers. The latter was a new, Canadian-built, billion-franc center which included a weapons museum, a memorial to the war of liberation (including a huge monument dominating the heights of Algiers that was baptized *hubal* [an idol] by Algerians), a shopping center, a nightclub, and discotheques. It represented the new face of a liberal regime in which money could be extracted from state resources and put into private pockets. Here cultural activities were to take place, including a youth festival in June 1985 with top groups from Africa and France, and it was from here that the further official promotion of raï was organized.

Two concerts took place in Paris at the beginning of 1986 which were sponsored in part by *Actuel* and the French daily *Libération.* The same year, an Algerian cultural week was held in France in cooperation with the French Ministry of Cultural Affairs, at which raï was cast as the dominant representative of Algerian musical life.

All in all, these events, in which raï was given official recognition and brought to the concert stage, meant a decisive breakthrough in Algeria as well as in the West. In the years that followed, raï spread to the whole of Algerian territory as well as to Morocco and Tunisia and to the North African communities in the West. New cassettes and singers emerged constantly in this period. Names like Cheb Hamid, Cheb Mami, Cheb

Tahar, Gana el Maghnaoui, Cheb Zahouani, Cheb Abdelhaq, Cheb Hasni, and Cheb Nasrou appeared throughout the second half of the 1980s and the beginning of the 1990s. A number of public concerts were held, and in 1989 the raï stars Sahraoui and Fadela performed at the meeting of the five leaders of the Maghrebin states, and one of the groups Boudiaf consulted in Oran before being assassinated in 1992 functioned as the local association for the promotion of raï.

However, the story of Algeria in the 1980s also concerns the catastrophic growth of economic and social problems, which in 1988 led to the October revolt. In 1990, the Islamist party took over the major cities of the country and stopped funds for nonreligious cultural activities. Not until the army crushed the Islamists did the concerts revive. By that time, the radio orchestra of Oran had not existed for four years, the local conservatory was closed, and in Algiers the main conservatory was used to house families whose homes had collapsed due to lack of maintenance. Raï, the main pop genre of the country, became one of the few important spheres of popular creativity. We will never know if this was why Cheb Hasni was assassinated in front of his house in October 1994. But it is obvious that by that time raï had become an important site for discussions on the identity of Algerian society.

When I started my fieldwork, the debate had already been going on for years, especially in the press, in which a major discourse had developed. It is necessary to venture into this press story in order to approach the complexities of the relationship between raï and social life in Algeria. It is through the press that raï became officially recognized. The following pages tell this story and show how raï subsequently proliferated in the West. My account is based on a collection of over four hundred press articles, mainly from the Algerian, French, British, American, and Scandinavian presses. I focus on some of the more important articles in the next few pages.[3]

## The Press Story

One of the first articles to mention the phenomenon of raï was written in Algeria *(Algérie Actualité,* April 2–8, 1981). It concluded that raï had become extremely popular and listened to by all family members, though not in each other's presence. At the same time, raï was said to have provoked fierce opposition. The article reported how the critics of raï viewed it as a destructive deviation from the Bedouin *shīkh* poetic tradition, drawing its substance from a noxious and vulgar jargon signaling the emergence of moral decadence. However, the article also claimed that raï had to be seen as a social phenomenon with its initiates, detractors, unscrupulous merchants, and large audience. It argued that for those who were more informed and prepared to analyze it, raï could be seen as a cry of revolt, a quest to break down taboos and prohibitions.

The article also showed how the Bedouin tradition had been modernized musically in Oran in the 1950s, leading to other innovations in the 1970s. It mentioned that raï had been inspired by apparently immoral and subversive interpreters such as the above-mentioned *shīkhas*. It proceeded to describe how in the 1960s raï grew out of the social environment of a rural population coming to the cities, impoverished and crowding together in poor housing, where illiteracy, unemployment, and a debased culture created an atmosphere of violence, criminality, and a lack of sexual inhibition. It mentioned the town of Sidi Bel Abbès, known for having been the headquarters of the Foreign Legion in colonial times and for its brothels—the center of a marginalized society with its own codes and secrets. The article then analyzed a selection of raï songs transcribed from cassette recordings. The songs appeared to be interspersed with dedications to people termed as "marginals"—from whom the identity of potential raï consumers was deduced: single men of poor origin, nostalgic immigrants, psychologically disturbed and divorced people, urbanized peasants in quest of supernatural solutions to their problems, and subproletarians expressing a crude male machismo in which women were portrayed as sexual objects.

Raï was thus represented as the main, ambiguous, fuzzy expression of the most deprived people in Algeria. At the same time, it was put on an equal footing with the gypsy music of the European cabarets and the blues of New Orleans. The famous Cheikha Remitti was compared with Edith Piaf, and the expression of the young Fadela with the hard rock of Janis Joplin. Finally, the article concluded that raï was changing from being emblematic of a social condition and was becoming the expression of a popular state of mind.

Two years later, a second important inquiry appeared in the same weekly newspaper, with three articles entitled "The Maquis of Raï," "All We Need Is Raï," and "Raï, Blues and Psychoanalysis" (*Algérie Actualité,* March 1, 1983). They confirmed much of the information in the article just summarized and also stated that raï had its opponents, for whom the lack of proper texts was the main problem. However, the journalist added that the subjects raï touched upon were no more immoral than in many a classical Arab poem, and that the lack of good texts might be due to the fact that it was the rhythm and atmosphere in raï that mattered.

Raï was also presented as being the music of the young, and the title of "cheb" was even considered to be in opposition to the older generation. It was a way of saying that the young were conscious of their age while they languidly watched a seventeen-year-old neighbor's daughter, looked jealously at the car of a cousin or the villa of a careerist—and regarded the future with perplexity.

The 1983 articles continued and expanded on the story of raï that was evolving in the press, going a step further than the 1981 article, by referring extensively to two academic essays (Miliani 1983, Miliani and Belkadem 1981).[4] These were the only academic commentaries available at the time, and they were quoted extensively in the Algerian press throughout the 1980s. In them, although singers and producers were described as having a marginal status, it was argued that they were not in conflict with Algerian norms. Rather, their songs were using bits and pieces, clichés from a variety of sources, which was why raï could be seen as a symbiosis between destructured forms of cultural expression and ways of mass producing cultural goods. In its own composition, raï—with passages from the sacred to the secular or from the conventional to the prohibited—was using complex and contradictory cultural codes and references expressing an ambivalence in the singer's personality. Raï presented an inarticulate narrative, a puzzle for the informed listener to solve. It was not possible to define any unified and coherent theme in raï. The songs could not be apprehended as a structured system. They constituted a partially acculturated medium, which, because of its lack of formal rules and its marginal position in relation to the legitimate culture, allowed a number of different representations to be formulated ideologically.

However, not being completely convinced of Miliani's analysis, the journalist in 1983 ventured into a personal analysis of raï, seeing it as a (self-) expression of sexual forces in which the notion of the scream—as in 1981—was central: ". . . but you may ask yourself if it [raï] doesn't signify 'being,' a being which has surrendered to destiny by means of its weakness or by the forces of desire. . . . Certainly, most of the texts in raï are interspersed with apostrophes, similar to the scream or complaint, where the singer is referring to his own raï" (*Algérie Actualité,* March 1, 1983).

These articles led to the first interview with a singer, Khaled. Impressed by his personality and popularity, the journalist described the singer as "a monument of sympathy. . . . It was as if I was in the local cafe, with an old friend of the local area" (ibid.). The singer did not know anything about music theory, but "he throws himself into a genuine interpretation of the quarter note, which is unknown in European music" (ibid.). Khaled's life was then sketched: how he found school suffocating, how he loved music, how he started his career by playing Moroccan music, and so forth. Questioned by the journalist, Khaled apologized for having no good texts. If raï was to widen its popularity, it needed proper words. He knew, being a member of a family, that some words could not be heard in its midst, but he said this was not so of all raï songs. He said that he thought raï was successful because it offered a style different from the one played on the radio. He himself had been rejected as a musician by the radio and subsequently went into raï. The article concluded: "You come to raï as you go up in the maquis—a maquis of music without iron collars" (ibid.).

The third major inquiry into raï was published in the program of the raï festival in Oran, August 1985 (see Comité 1985). It constituted what can be seen as the official legitimization of a history of raï and would be used in numerous future press features and articles in Algeria and the West. Here, the roots of raï were traced all the way back to pre-Islamic, post-Islamic, and later classical texts derived from Muslim Andalusia. The program described raï's passage into colloquial Arabic, the famous *malḥūn* of the Bedouin poets, and stated that in colonial times the latter became the lot of the rural indigenous elite, many of whom had close relations with the colonial administration. The *shikhs'* poetry was simplified by shepherds and market singers, and then brought by the *shīkhas* to the public bars and brothels created by the colonial powers. In the 1920s and 1930s, raï began propagating the themes of social misery created by the colonial regime. This tradition became musically modernized in the 1970s, a period when the Bedouin poets had run out of ideas, constrained, as it was said, by their mercantile egotism. The program concluded that with the rise of a new generation of singers in the late 1970s, the advent of cassettes, and the introduction of the synthesizer from rock, disco, and reggae, raï imposed itself without any official help over the whole of Algerian territory. It had become an independent musical genre, a form of youthful expression. Not being patronized, it ought to develop an adequate framework and themes free of taboo subjects.

## The Narrative

These three journalistic inquiries represented sophisticated attempts to describe raï and present factual elements concerning its antecedents and its actual state of being. In so doing, they broke with the previous ideological consensus about a coherent and healthy civil society based on sound peasant values (Virolle-Souibès 1989: 58). The raï articles put forward social and sexual problems, the existence of brothels, and social tensions in the life of the population, especially in the daily life of the young. Thus the journalists broke new ground in creating a biography of raï which included nearly all the topics that would be debated in the Algerian press in the years to come.

Up to and during the time of my fieldwork, one element in the Algerian press was also the idea that raï has a disruptive effect on its consumers. In the course of its spread to the West, a further argument has developed from this that raï is an instrument for politics or occult cultural imperialist forces attempting to destabilize Algerian society and secularize the second generation of immigrants in France.

A more dominant line, however, has been concerned with defining the debate as "for or against" the words in raï. In this discussion the problem of vulgarity in raï has constantly been at issue as well as the problem of the simplicity of texts and the absence of poetic ideas. A good deal of well-meant or paternalistic advice has been given to raï performers, along with extremely harsh attacks on the music producers.

Since 1985 several articles dealing with raï have criticized the negligence of the state in terms of its cultural politics. Other articles have portrayed raï as a vital representative of Algerian youth and of national cultural vigor, endangered by rising Islamist forces. Both tendencies have been strengthened by the cultivation of raï in the West. One series of articles has reported on raï singers' success abroad; another has compared opportunities for artists in Algeria with those in the West (though not without a critical perspective on Western "showbiz"); and other articles have involved raï singers (valued because of their success in the West) in the struggle against the Islamists. Even my own work sometimes became a topic in the ongoing debate: "In our country raï is returning to its status of being half underground, while it is simultaneously reaching out to become universal and has even become an object of anthropological studies in foreign universities" (*Algérie Actualité,* July 26–August 1, 1990).

Low culture versus high culture, commercialism versus self-expression, poetic eloquence versus lack of proper words, vulgarity versus the family, youth versus experience, Algeria versus the West—all have been mediating words in the debate surrounding a musical form in which Algerian identity was seen to be at stake. But precisely how music and identity were related to each other remained unclear. Rather, in the media the central elements of the three news inquiries have persisted, placing raï in the context of tension between the (acculturated) oppressed and the oppressors.

In the 1981 version, raï became a scream of revolt by a poor and uprooted peasantry confronted with the postindependence politics of the Boumedienne regime and the sexual taboos of Algerian society. In the 1983 version, raï became the expression of youngsters protesting against forbidden sexuality, against the older generation, against the newly rich of the Chedli regime, and against the national media, with the latter story being "headlined" by a powerful association with the war of liberation (i.e., "the maquis of music"). In the festival story, raï, as part of the national cultural heritage, proved its vitality in opposition to the colonial regime, mercantile *shīkhs,* and a cultural invasion from abroad.

All in all, what Bruner (1986) has called a heterophonous[5] master narrative was established in the sense that raï became a heroic expression with a past of oppression and a present of resistance. The future, however, was not explicit. The end of the story was unknown. But this master narrative was the one brought to the West. Here, the singers had already been performing in Oriental clubs and weddings before 1986, and the tape cassettes had been available for a long time among North African communities through an informal marketing network reaching across the Mediterranean.[6] Furthermore, before 1986, another "raï link" came to exist between Algeria and France.

In the early 1980s the French government allowed some local radio stations to transmit on the national airwaves. One of these was Radio Beur, which became a center of communication for young, upwardly mobile, second-generation immigrants and for young French people involved in antiracist marches, both groups being involved in a struggle for recognition of the cultural presence of North Africans in France. It was here that raï was played on the airwaves for the first time. Furthermore, through the network of people radiating from this milieu, relations were created among the raï festival committee of Oran, British record labels, Algerian producers, fashion magazines, and local promoters, the latter of whom were involved in both French show agencies and in concerts with the local Algerian immigrant community. A number of people became known in the French press as the only voices with knowledge of raï. They took the politicized Algerian story of raï to the French press, where, in connection with stage performances, it was polished and transformed into a distinct discourse. As we shall see, this did not improve understanding of the relation between raï and Algerian society.

## Raï in the Western Press

A key example of raï as presented in the Western press is provided by an article in *Libération* published on the occasion of the first raï concert in Paris, which summed up all the previous elements in the Algerian press and added new factual information to the biography of raï. However, the interesting fact is that it was accompanied by an editorial headline proclaiming "Raï: The Enraged 'New Wave' of Oran" (*Libération,* January 22, 1986), plus a column referring to the liberation war (and introducing "flip machines" in raï):

> Born at the start of the 1980s, raï is much more than a rhythm; it is a way of being. . . . While distancing themselves from classical lyricism the chebs rehabilitate sex, alcohol and realism by singing about flirts, flip machines and cars. . . . The kids of the Mazda . . . make a symbol out of raï. The censorship is ready and still active today, but there is nothing to be done. Raï keeps moving. The chebs know they have won their Battle of Algiers. (ibid.)

And finally a review of the first long-playing record in the history of raï:

> [Khaled] often spends his nights in a very chic nightclub. . . . He is a nighthawk: he never sings before . . . four o'clock in the morning, and this record only brings forth a prudent testimony of the "folly of Khaled" confronted with his audience of crazy people in love. . . . The piercing complaints of this inspired singer and pleasureseeker recall the great moments of blues or Salif Keita's psalmody, but Ray Charles has also gone by. The instrumental accompaniment of the synthesizers and the drum machine, the accordion which blends with the synthesizer, the heavy sounds of the electric bass and the arabesques of the electric guitar backed up by traditional percussion, give a sound which cuts through all you might have heard before. It's a universal music like rock and reggae. . . . (ibid.)

Obviously, once the master raï narrative moved to Europe, it was transferred into another field of knowledge, interest, and perspective than that found in the Algerian press. The most revealing accounts of what took place are three articles in the monthly French review *Actuel.*

In the first article Khaled was not described as just a guy from the local cafe, but as the representative of an underground movement deemed licentious and pornographic by the national radio. The author also described the music as follows: ". . . a song of broken love, a complaint, a *fado*. It is inspired by andalousian singing and by local music, the Oranian rhythm mixed with an electronic sauce. . . . With a sound as cheap and beautiful as a Colombian *cumbia*"(*Actuel* 50, 1983). The story also explained that the words "of raï are raw; when it speaks about love, it goes on, it sings a kind of blues, joyous though and sensual. . . . an assertion of sexuality" (ibid.).

The major part of the article, however, dealt with the growing Islamist activism against women and described in length the economic, demographic, and political problems facing Algeria as a result of the Boumedienne era. The article asserted that things were slowly changing under the Chedli regime due to the latter's politics of anticorruption, democratization, and liberalization. Raï was seen as a central aspect of all these changes.

Young girls were now seen dancing in the cabarets—marginal girls perhaps, but nevertheless something unthinkable under the Boumedienne regime. The author told how he had spent two years in Algeria as a teacher in solitude and boredom, which were only sometimes lightened by secret passions. Now things were changing: "I saw a couple kissing. Even if the man hurried away, with a look of guilt, it was an earnest anticipation of freedom" (ibid.). Two years later, some of the same topics were repeated in another article: "Raï is at one and the same time Algeria's punk, blues, reggae and funk. . . . Oran is the Kingston of this underground, secret, lyrical explosion. Cheb Khaled is the Bob Marley, but he is considered too beastly a person, so there is nothing on television" (*Actuel* 68, 1985).

The article also described the instrumental changes that had taken place in raï since its beginning as an acoustic song form—how the music was recorded without finesse and how family members did not listen to raï in each other's presence. It included another "fascinating" description of the cabarets of Oran and told of an encounter with Khaled—the first to be published in the Western press—which differed radically from the first encounter described in *Algérie Actualité*. In *Actuel* Khaled became an oppositional figure, a bohemian: "Two years before, he was driving dead drunk with a whore in a stolen car. They had just been fighting, they were mad, they drove a guy down and Khaled was taken to prison for three months" (ibid.).

The article concluded with a description of the time the journalist spent with Khaled, which, he reported, ended with a night in an apartment with the singer, his "real" girlfriend, two musicians, an officer in the military police, and some merchants, all listening to Khaled's latest cassettes while watching an x-rated film and consuming a huge quantity of wine.

In 1988, *Actuel* published a third article entitled "Raï—Algeria Wants to Make Love, the Arab Blues against Fundamentalism," which was later translated in the *The Face* (June 1988) under the title "Sex and Soul in the Maghreb." It began: "In the year 2,000 there will be thirty million young North Africans. With whom will they be? With fundamentalism or with raï?" (*Actuel* 115, 1988). Obviously inspired by the *Algérie Actualité,* raï was described as the scream of desire of Algerian youth. France had waited a long time for a break in the Arab-Islam-veil-Koran-fundamentalism image of the Arab countries. The article proceeded with an analysis of Arab sexuality, demonstrating how Algerian society hides its fantasies and sexual frustrations. It ventured into a detailed analysis of the ways the taboo subject was circumvented among North Africans. It presented a list of the secret signs used by the young to have sex, covert techniques employed in their lovemaking and related matters, and it proclaimed that raï was consciously reacting against this state of affairs: "Tired of masturbating, raï is claiming the right to fuck when you want, where you want and how you want" (ibid.). As such, the conclusion was that raï could be compared to nothing else but the reaction of the 1968 generation against the morality of Catholic France.

With this background, what, then, took place in the *Libération* article? The answer is that the master raï narrative was guided into a new field of understandings in which drinking and rock were associated with the notion of a liberal, modern Islam and opposed to an intolerant, archaic Islam and the totalitarian state. The whole construction was seen as the homologue of a situation in which the possibilities for the consumption of leisure goods like "sex, drugs, and rock 'n' roll" opposed the morality of parental, authoritarian, middle-class, Western society.

Raï was made recognizable by means of a trans-Mediterranean network of people with a basic background in the French left-wing intellectual tradition, sharing a worldview opposed to totalitarian cultural tendencies in Algeria as well as in France. The singers were made "good Arabs" and were pitted against French racist tendencies. From the gatekeeping media, who were also involved in the practical promotion of raï itself, the *Libération* and *Actuel* interpretations of the raï narrative continued to spread through the Western media, on record sleeves, and other forms of advertising, partly because journalists tended to use previous French press articles as a main source of documentation and partly because the press material sent out to journalists by record companies and concert promoters tended to consist of the same press articles.

Headlines such as "Rock against Islam" (*Nouvel Observateur,* July 1985), "Rather Elvis than FIS" (*L'Evènement du Jeudi,* March 5, 1992), and "He talked to Paul Sweeney about Fundamentalism and Fun" (*The Independent,* September 3, 1992) are examples of how raï, endowed with a touch of exoticism,[7] was (and is) associated with the myths of youth and subculture in the West. References to Liverpool, Elvis Presley, Jim Morrison, Detroit, the Bronx, punk, and reggae have surfaced regularly. "Rebel" is another code word, referring to James Dean. Finally, with the Islamist takeover of Algerian cities, raï has become the main representative of a liberating opposition to Islamism, and the singers have become the latter's main victims.

All the doubts and uneasiness with which the raï story was created in Algeria disappeared in the West (with the exception of some more thoughtful articles in *Libération*) and the vulgarity discussed in Algeria became a virtue. Miliani's statements about the conformism in raï were forgotten. I myself had the mixed pleasure of seeing a "sober" article about raï in Paris headlined "Sex, Alcohol, and Islam" by a serious and progressive Danish monthly music review, however.

Other French–Algerian differences became noticeable. First, in Algeria, the press rarely went into a detailed description of the singer's personal life, in accordance with a general public norm to which I will return (see chapter 6). The singers are described "front stage" as conforming to Algerian codes of normal family life, as loving sons who respect their parents, and as artists engaged in serious work. In the West, the press has focused on the milieu of the cabarets and the leisure life of the singers. Second, what the Algerian articles considered to be the low artistic input of the texts has not been discussed in the West. The texts—if translated and consequently understood—have been regarded and valued as factual statements of self-expression. Third, the commercial aspect of raï has been heavily criticized in Algeria, and a dividing line has been drawn between the singers as the creators and the producers as the profit seekers. In the West, the tendency has been for no critical inquiry into Algerian or Western promotion strategies. The French press has shown a good deal of interest in the musical recording process in Algeria, but only as a sociological fact of Third World conditions.

In the Western press, raï as a music has slid out of the Arab and Middle Eastern landscape and become integrated with syncretic musical styles such as New Orleans blues; Argentinean tango; West African *jùjù;* Greek, Turkish, and Flamenco melodies; Portuguese *fado;* and reggae. After 1987 many of these musical genres were increasingly labeled "World Music," a notion rarely used in the Algerian press, which has described raï mostly as a success story in the West.

Finally, the musical aspect of raï has rarely been described in the Algerian press basically because the readers have already had direct experience with the music. In the West, a verbal introduction has been necessary, an exotic one indeed, mainly focusing on the voice,[8] but also portraying raï as having a dual character—modern and traditional, Bedouin and rock, recognizable and unknown.

## The Mediascape and the Singers

Despite the differences it is undeniable that a musical "mediascape"[9] appeared in connection with the propagation of raï. Within it was found a transnational point of view, fluctuating between considering raï on the one hand as the screaming of pain of uprooted peasants, and on the other as the scream of the rebelliousness of James Dean. This mediascape has confronted the singers as if they were self-expressing, stage-performing, politically conscious artists.

In Algeria, it is a long-standing fact that singers tend to avoid the press. When finally "caught," they have adapted to the press's expectations and recounted small stories of how they created and wrote songs based on their personal lives or from observing their social surroundings. When confronted with questions about the vulgarity of raï, they have been quoted as answering that raï is not about debauchery, but deals above all with realities of life—social problems like love, sorcery, and divorce—in a language everybody understands. They repeat arguments that have appeared in the press that vulgarity can be found not only in raï, but also in other Algerian genres, and abroad in the songs of Brel, Edith Piaf, and others. Finally, even if some words in raï were "unclean" and unsophisticated, this was not the fault of raï but of other singers' abuse of it. A variant of this would be to state—as Khaled did in 1983—that in raï there is good and bad, and the singer himself regrets the "bad." As regards Islamism, the singers are evasive: for example, they sing about the concerns of Algerian youth, which is why they cannot agree with the possible prohibition of raï. Some singers have simply expressed their wish for a peaceful and prosperous Algeria. With the increasing political crisis in Algeria after 1992, they have tended to answer in a neutral way to Algerian journalists interviewing them in Algeria, but to make statements critical of the Islamist movement to journalists interviewing them outside Algeria.

There has been a greater interest in interviewing the singers in the international press than in Algeria, and they have been more accessible to this press through official interviews arranged by their promoters. The singers have not had to defend themselves regarding the quality of their songs since the matter has basically not been problematized—rather the contrary—and gradually the top names seem to have learned how to manage their interviewers.

Thus although Khaled, in a series of interviews, has not made any fuss about being described as a heavy drinker or being asked about his drinking habits, no story like the one presented in *Actuel* has ever appeared again. Another singer stated in 1986 that he had nothing against an Islamic republic in Algeria and that he would stop singing raï in public if required. To the inevitable questions about their view of Islamism in Algeria, they all today regret the situation and the violence of the Islamist armed groups.

However, with the release of the record entitled "Khaled," the singer did have to resolve a difficult situation. In an interview in *Le Monde* (February 20, 1992), he was asked why he represented France in a concert on July 14, 1991 in New York and was asked to comment on the release of his album in Israel. He replied that he was born under the French flag in 1960, that his godmother was French, that his bass player was Jewish, that his group members were Jewish, Arab, and French, and that Jews and Arabs were cousins. These conciliatory, pliable answers by a "liberal Arab" representing multicultural French civilization did not please many people in Algeria, and headlines appeared in the Algerian press until Khaled disavowed his statements in an interview in *Le Matin* (March 18, 1992): "Me, I am not an intellectual. I talk, as they say, in Arabic French." It was a wise answer by a singer involved in a game for which his voice has not been trained, as the story of the record 'Khaled' will show.

## "Didi, Didi"

The fact is that if raï has had positive press coverage in the West overall, this did not exactly make it a commercial success. When it arrived in France in 1986, it was perceived by some as the successor to reggae on an international level. Numerous journalists flocked to Oran (among others the BBC and the French channel Antenne 2). In Paris, leading singers like Cheb Khaled and Cheb Mami were taken up by experienced managers, and a local immigrant, Cheb Kader, was launched as a raï singer. In London, Island Records signed a contract with the studio of Rachid and Fethi mainly to promote Sahraoui and Fadela; and before 1990, the four top names in raï had given concerts in Europe, North America, and Japan. Out of this came a number of records and CDs intended for the Western market. Most of these were retakes of master tapes from Arab cassettes, but several were also produced directly with a Western audience in mind.

However, when I started my work in Paris in 1990, raï's expected breakthrough to a wider Western audience had not happened. There was a division between the large cultural commodity supermarkets like Fnac and Virgin and the local retailers in the unofficial North African community market such as Barbès, who mainly sold low-quality cassette tapes for half the price asked in FNAC and Virgin. Again these were selling mainly raï and CDs classified as "world music." Here the (unofficial) sales figures for raï were extremely low, rarely above twenty thousand copies, and the "international" records had not met the large audience expected, except as Hebrew remakes in Israel.[10]

In 1991, *Libération,* raï's main press promoter, dropped its monthly review of raï cassettes and replaced it with a "world music" review. In 1992, Mami, Kader, Sahraoui, and Fadela were not in the international record business, but instead were performing in Western towns and suburbs with a high concentration of North Africans or at concerts featuring World Music. The market in France, though important enough to support a milieu of raï music, seemed primarily to consist of weddings, local community concerts, Oriental clubs, some discotheques, local community and World Music radio stations, a few larger concerts in Paris, and occasional features on state radio channels.

In France, raï's lack of commercial success was thought to have been caused by hidden French racism and the subsequent de facto absence of raï on commercial radio and prime-time television. All in all, it did seem difficult to "sell an Arab" to a Western audience, as was the case, for example, with Cheb Mami's U.S.-recorded album "Let me raï," released during the Gulf War.

Another reason, however, lies in raï music itself. From the beginning of raï's appearance on the Western stage there have been musical problems in "crossing over." Raï uses complex rhythms and styles of singing which are easy for Algerians, but difficult for Western listeners to grasp. In Western pop, for example, it is important (as it is in raï) to have a refrain to sing along to, but Arabic is not the ideal language for a Western audience. In Western pop, it is also important to be able to use the body in order to dance. However, raï is based on a rhythmic principle which deemphasises the four beats to the bar of Western pop music. In raï, the bass tends to stress triplets, which are related to the popular form of dancing in Algeria in which the hips are the leading part of the body (following the triplets) rather than the feet (following the four beats). This use of the bass, therefore, tends to make Western dancers lose the "feeling," as they are used to letting their feet be guided by a bass stressing a four-beat rhythm.

Overall this tends to put listeners out of time with the singer, and thus they have "no body" to use in identifying with images of sex, alcohol, raï, and youth. This means, for example, that the emblematic song of raï "Ṣḥab al bārūd" ("The people of the gunpowder"), which always brings a crowd of Algerians to the dance floor, has the opposite effect in the West, making people stop dancing. Finally, for raï musicians—who are, as we shall see, party entertainers—the major necessity is to communicate with the audience, and in so doing they do not always respect time sequences (the number of beats in a bar), as is the rule in the West.

Algerian styles of playing can still be found on the first recordings made by minor labels for a Western market. However, one of the things raï managers did in Europe was to hire musicians to form steady backing bands, thus in a way disciplining the singer. This was done in international studios, where only the Algerian singer, the musicians involved in phrasing the melody lines, and the percussionist participated. Here all those rhythms undanceable for a Western audience were replaced by more accessible ones. The only elements taken from Algerian music were those which were a rarity in Western music: a certain sense of rhythm, of singing and phrasing, the whole of which was subsequently put into a better known body feeling.

Thus in 1992 the record "Khaled" was released after the singer had signed a contract with Barclay, with distribution through the multinational Polygram. On the record produced in the United States and Belgium, the only things left of Algerian raï are textual formulas from the raï stock of sentences, the sense of phrasing of some instruments, and above all the voice of Khaled. The top hit formula is "Didi," an easy singalong chorus. Many tunes on the record are accompanied by a heavy funky bass; polyphonic background choruses (never heard of in raï before) have been added, and the informal atmosphere of Algerian raï recordings has completely gone.

However, Khaled's record company did more than this in seeking to remove the remaining barriers to a crossover of raï to the Western scene. With a budget of two million francs, it appropriated the songs Khaled recorded for Algerian producers and registered him as a writer of several hundred songs with the French copyright authorities.[11] With multinational Polygram, it succeeded in obtaining press coverage for the album on a scale then unknown for raï. In addition to this, the record company bought a substantial amount of TV time for a video of "Didi." The record cover shows Khaled photographed from the same angle as Stevie Wonder on one of his records. For the first time in the history of raï, the words were printed on the inside sleeve, though in Arabic and without translation. Finally, the company introduced a change in Khaled's image and concentrated promotion efforts on liberating him from "all practical purposes" (see Langer 1953: 53)—that is, all political contexts—except that of creating art.

In a filmed interview, Khaled is thus seen explaining his career as a musician in a Parisian museum of art, while his American producer is comparing him to Bob Dylan. A Magritte-inspired headline occurs in the press material: "Ceci n'est pas un Arabe," and the words of raï can be read: "We indeed owe to him beautifully surrealistic poems . . . which neither the French poet Apollinaire nor André Breton, the founder of surrealism, would disown" (press release, Barclay, 1992).

With "Didi," Khaled became the first Arab singer to enter the French top ten, after which raï and Khaled passed into what are apparently the *most* disparate contexts—a background voice in readings of Rimbaud and in erotic video clips, and a representative of La Francophonie in cultural exhibitions abroad! In 1991 he represented France at a large open-air concert in Central Park, New York, and in 1992 he was made Chevalier de l'ordre des Arts et des Lettres in Paris. He has had huge successes in Egypt and India. "Didi" has been played and translated in Spain, Israel, Turkey, Sri Lanka, and other countries. The press story mentioned above is now promoted and naively repeated verbatim in Bombay, Tokyo, New York, Copenhagen, and even in the recent *World Music: The Rough Guide* (Broughton et al., 1994).

Whether Khaled will continue his rise to world fame is not clear, however. Among other things, this depends on whether the returns from record sales will be satisfactory compared with the investment in the singer's promotion. After "Didi" came another CD, "Nsi-nsi." Here Barclay and Polygram record companies included songs from the *wahrāni* repertoire (claiming Khaled to be the composer) to the accompaniment of twenty Egyptian violinists, obviously an effort to promote Khaled in new markets with consumer potential in Asia and the Middle East.

"Musics do not have selves, people do" (Waterman 1990:6). The world of today must be seen as involved in a constant process of creating and adjusting musical performances, embodied habits, and meanings to one another. When I arrived in Paris and Algeria, this process had been going on for a decade.

In Algeria, the concept of World Music was not current at the time. The most popular viewpoint was that raï had, as it were, "conquered" the world. Among the raï fans I knew, it was as if part of their personality had been accepted in the West in the same way that the singers had been taken out of anonymity to become names on a world stage. Only rarely was it perceived that the success of raï was due first of all to the important North African communities outside the Maghreb and to the World Music stage. That Khaled had been to Japan, and Mami to the United States, seemed to be sufficient evidence of a successful Algerian presence in the West. Indeed, the promotion of raï in the West had made it even more incontrovertible social fact in Algeria. In addition, there had been subtexts to the main narrative of raï, seeing it as a result of artists' self-expressive, univocal, creative activities.

Commercialized raï had been caught up in easy dualisms where static links were made between the songs and their audience, for whom both the form and performative background of raï had been obscured. A lack of awareness of these elements among the singers and producers was also apparent. In addition, the economic basis of the songs and the singers had been separated from the outcome, the songs themselves. In short, few had asked questions about the ways in which raï was related to non-musical spheres as a musical activity.

For a long time in my fieldwork, I too was caught up in the main narrative of raï. With time I reached a point at which a number of loose ends crystallized into an awareness of the necessity to break with the official narrative and incorporate it as an element in my own version. In pursuing that version, it is necessary to continue with the basics of raï, the live performance.

# 3

# The Raï Performance and Studio Recording

When I was in Oran, raï songs could be heard everywhere, sometimes from the voice of a boy killing time with his back against a street wall or from a group of children walking through the narrow streets of their local neighborhood on their way to a football game. More often, raï burst out of loudspeakers in cassette dealers' shops, the amplifier turned up to maximum in order to impose the latest hit on passersby. Raï could be heard coming from the open windows of apartments when women were having a moment of rest or doing their cleaning, or from the windows of cars cruising the town's main streets between five and eight in the evening, the main time of day for meeting girlfriends and chasing women.

In summer raï songs could be heard even more often, as this was the wedding season. On a Thursday night, the day before the weekly day of rest and prayer, the town was like an enormous disco. Wedding processions drove to the center of town to the accompaniment of rhythmic hand clapping, and trumpets and orchestras and cassette tapes played the latest tunes at open-air parties.

If one drove out of town, toward the airport but mainly along the coast, one could see cars parked outside buildings that seemed to be closed; after listening for a while, one could hear raï playing inside. These were the cabarets where electric raï was heard for the first time in the late 1970s and subsequently transferred to the recording studios.

Generally, studios, weddings, cabarets, and the streets were the main places from which raï extended into the wider society. Like all music, raï is interweaved with social activities. For me, following raï from production to consumption meant discovering the importance of these places, not only because they had raï in common, but also because they all turned out to be spheres of men's relations with one another and with women. In the pages that follow, I will emphasize the importance of these spheres and describe the elements of a raï performance. Then I will describe how the performance is transferred to the recording studios, how songs are made, and how the cassettes reach consumers. I will start with the cabarets and weddings, continue with the production of cassettes, and from there venture into public life.

First, let us visit a male performance, an evening in La Guinguette club in the month of Ramadan, 1992, where the public announcer (the *barrāḥ*) conducted the show. This account may seem confusing at first, but it is the key to understanding the places and spaces where raï was performed in the city.[1]

> In honor of my God, there is no one but Him to make beings prosper,
> Before the Prophet and his holy companions, before the parents of nobility and of the ancestors,
> I ask of you, oh God, the example of guidance, to approve my words before these distinguished people,
> Before this assembly, who came from all over the country, approve my words with blessing and guidance.

> Friends, may peace be with you, may your dinner have pleased you well and may you all be welcome at our place, at La Guinguette. Houari B. told me to make praises in honor of friendship and brotherhood and of the people gathered who "eat" big as well as small cars. And welcome to our friends, welcome to our friends, in honor of the gathering of those who know the art of living and of being well in this earthly life. There is another dedication in honor of the town of Cheraga and of the people of Cheraga, in honor of the Arabs [i.e., men] from the town of Chlef, of Miloud and Djelloul. The song requested is the poem "I will love that woman till I die."

The music begins, and people go on to the dance floor while the *barrāḥ* collects money from the people in the audience as well as their requests and dedications. As soon as the *barrāḥ* reappears on the dance floor in front of the orchestra, the dancers return to their tables and listen to his words.

In honor of this meeting of friends, the cars of whom are large and small. There is another dedication in honor of the Arabs of Mostaghanem, the people of Aïn Tèdeles, Nono and his group, and one in honor of Mustapha, Mohammed, and Noureddine and Nono, and those with large and small cars, and another in honor of the Arabs of Oran and the people of Mostaghanem and Yahiya, the Arabs of Aïn Tèdeles, in honor of friendship and brotherhood and the people gathered here, whose cars are big and small. There is another dedication from Abdallah the baker from Aïn el B., long live the 16 [the registration number of Algiers], in honor of his group, those who spend the evening with him and who are near him. In your honor, my brother Boualem, says Abdallah, in the same way as you give us consideration, may God increase your importance every night. We pray for a long and prosperous life for you. In honor of Kamel and Busnad, of Samiah and Amina Sghir, in honor of friendship and brotherhood and the people gathered here, whose cars are big and small, may God keep your attention.

The virtue of differentiating good from bad comes step by step, and the *jinn* [a spirit] though it may get milder, is not of its habit,
And the man knows by whom he has been raised and what his responsibilities are which increase his problems, but he does not escape from them.
Every grain brings its fruits to its owner, And the virtues of men are endless.

May God not diminish their prosperity. Kada, the dealer of old iron, asked for a dedication in honor of his group, of those who spend the evening with him and who are around him; may God not diminish their prosperity. Abdelkader, the son of Z., told me to give a dedication in honor of Nono, he told me that this is an invitation to Toumi, and in honor of Mohammed and his group and Noureddine T.—may God not diminish their prosperity—and also Houari the grocer and the group that is with him and showed us consideration; and the people who know the art of living and of being well in this earthly life. In honor of Abdallah, Abdallah the baker from Aïn el B.—who has given us consideration the whole night—he told me to offer a dedication in honor of Boualem and the whole of his group, and the people of friendship and of brotherhood—he also told me: "Now, tell Cheb Hindi, I tell you, do you know my song? I tell you to sing 'This day is a blessed day.'" This is also requested by the people of Cheraga—and it will come after the song "That woman." In honor of the group of friends and the men who came here in large and small cars, may God keep your attention.

(The music begins, and people go on to the dance floor.)

From the children of Aïn Tèdeles, the Mostaghanem people, in honor of the Tizi R. family, in honor of the Tizi R. family, in honor of the Hassani family, in honor of S. the taxi driver from Aïn Tèdeles, in honor of the friendship and brotherhood and people assembled here with large and small cars, to Nono and the people assembled with him and the handsome warriors. As they give us consideration may God give their house consideration. We have one other dedication from the Arabs of the town of Hassi Mamach in the department of Mostaghanem close to Mesaghlal, in honor of friendship and brotherhood and the group assembled here that upholds its duty—and the poem asked for is "I don't have a mother, I don't have a father" . . . the poor orphan. In honor of the group of friends who came here, tall and small:

Do your deeds, do your deeds without asking,
The dastardly, the dastardly cannot bring you evil,
If you pass by and go in the direction of Saïda with a message,
If the dastard speaks, do not pay attention, his words are not stories worth listening to.
A man is a man, do not worry on his behalf. Where he goes he leaves glory behind him.

The father of the Arabs of Mammach, the people who know the art of living and of being well—may God not diminish their prosperity—in honor of friendship and brotherhood and the poem "I don't have a mother, I don't have a father," may God keep your attention.

(The music begins, and people go on to the dance floor.)

In honor of the Arabs of La Guinguette, the duty is upon us all, all of us tall and small, the people gathered; as they give us consideration may God give their house consideration, the handsome warriors, the people who know the art of living and of being well. The ways of men are to show one another consideration. There are one hundred thousand Francs from Abdallah, the baker from Aïn el B.;

he told me it is in honor of friends from between the towns of El Awuna and Cheraga. He told me it was for El Awuna and Cheraga, in honor of the children of Mostaghanem, the people of Aïn Tèdeles and Hassi Mamach and the whole of his group, in honor of Kada, Kada the dealer of old iron and the group that is with him, the people of friendship and brotherhood. He told me it was in honor of Fayza, Fatiha, and Fatima—there are three of them—in honor of friendship and brotherhood, of the people assembled with their large and small cars; in your honor Boualem take care of Fatiha, and God is great. In honor of Busnad and the people of friendship and brotherhood and all the groups, large and small. Do not forget the songs of the people of Hassi Mamach. Here comes the poem "I do not have a mother, I do not have a father." And still we have left the Arabs of Chlef and of Cheraga, who want "That woman," and the poem "This day," and the poem "I didn't expect the news that came to me by telephone."

(The music begins, and people go on to the dance floor.)

In honor of the groups of friendship, may God keep your attention. In honor of friendship and brotherhood and the people assembled here, in honor of the men who show one another consideration. First there are one hundred thousand francs from Kada, the dealer in old iron, he told me it was for the Arabs of Petit Lac and in honor of R. Castor, he told me it was in honor of Hammeto and Houari and in honor of Toumi. He told me it was against Mohammed until the Day of Judgment, he told me it was in honor of Nono, in honor of Abdelkader the son of Z., he told me it was in honor of Noureddine T. and the whole of their group, in honor of the Arabs of La Caserie and Rashid of Petit Lac, Rashid of Petit Lac and the people of Castor, he told me to say to Abdallah the baker from Aïn el B.: "As you showed me consideration, may God show you consideration, take care of him on my behalf." To Boualem, in honor of the group of friends gathered here and the men present here tonight, in honor of the Arabs from Mostaghanem, the people of Aïn Tèdeles. He told me it is in honor of Marc, Marc and the group that is with him. He told me, "Listen Cheb Hindi," he told me that after the poem requested by the people, he wanted the poem "I didn't expect the news that came to me by telephone," he told me: "This one I dedicate to Fayza and Fatiha and Fatima," in honor of the men present—all of them tall or small. There are one hundred thousand francs from Abdallah, Abdallah the baker from Aïn B., long live

> the 16. He told me it was in honor of Kada, the dealer in old iron. As you show us consideration, may God show your house consideration; he told me, may God take care of his soul. He told me, may God take care of his soul. In truth, he told me, "May God take care of the soul of the children of the Arabs of Mamachi. May God take care of the soul of the children of the Arabs of Mamachi and may God take care of the soul of Houari who was here, may the people present tonight die in glory; the people cry for him because of his disappearance; the man in power has to be proud."

(The music begins, and people go on to the dance floor.)

This was the scene at La Guinguette, a cabaret outside Oran known as one where the electric raï formula appeared in the late 1970s. The room was not yet full, but it became so in the course of the evening. Among the guests were at least Abdallah the baker, Houari B., Houari the grocer, Nono and his group, Abdelkader Z., Noureddine T., Boualem, Rachid from Petit Lac, and R. from Castor; the latter are both parts of Oran which kept their colonial names in daily use despite state arabization efforts. Finally there was Mohammed, whom Kada, the dealer of old iron, challenged for fun.

All the guests appeared to have cars, lots of cars. In Oran people identified others by their cars. If two had the same surname and one or both owned a car, people would say, "Isn't that Mohammed with such and such a car?" There will be even more cars in the course of this story, for they were markers of social climbing in Algeria and allowed people to move in and out of different social contexts. For example, that night people had driven from the village of Hassi Mamach and even as far as from Chlef and Cheraga, attracted as they were by Oranian club life and its dance hostesses, like Fatiha, Fayza, and Fatima.

Only tea was served because of Ramadan. Those attending respected the prescriptions of the holy month. They did not drink alcohol, but a number of them would have a couple of joints after supper before coming to the cabaret, an especially prominent practice during Ramadan among men who otherwise enjoyed the pleasure of the bottle.

The guests were seated around the dance floor, which was situated in front of the stage, on which a group (consisting of synthesizer, electric bass, drums, bongos, and *darbūka*) was accompanying one of the early singers of electric raï, Cheb Hindi (who got his name because he started his career singing Hindi film songs). Later in the evening he toured cabarets on the coast, being replaced by two lesser known singers, Cheb Youssef and Chaba Amina Sghir, in La Guinguette.

Right beside the stage was placed a *snī,* or a tray, in which the *barrāḥ* placed the money he was collecting from the audience while the music was playing, well in sight of the audience and musicians. A *barrāḥ* is a public announcer or party entertainer, a well-known figure all over North Africa (see Azza 1979, Gaudefroy-Demombynes 1901, Westermarck 1972 [1914]).

The whole evening continued as it had started. Before I left the cabaret with my friends at 2 A.M. we had counted at least forty thousand dinars on the *snī* to be divided among the *barrāḥ,* the musicians, the singers, and the cabaret owner (the minimum wage at that time was around three thousand dinars a month). The show that night was the center of the male raï performance and took place elsewhere as well, such as another cabaret where late in the evening a belly dancer aroused guests with a floor show and a dance on their tables. We might also be in an extremely expensive restaurant with three top singers collecting money from the audience, though lacking the verbal finesse of the *barrāḥ.* Or we might even be at an engagement party or a wedding *en famille,* where a well-known cheb introduced the evening with a religious song while the *barrāḥ* used his verbal art without the collection of money being involved.

We might also be at a large public wedding with hundreds of men gathered in a parking lot in a newly built area. Here, the raï group would add a violin to the electric instruments, and there might even be two *barrāḥs* present. We might be in the garage of a private home; again, it is men only—the women stay inside the house. Elsewhere, a party of music lovers was held with several experienced chebs, some new talents, several *barrāḥs,* and a band with synthesizer, accordion, *darbūka,* electric bass, sometimes saxophone, sometimes *nāy,* and sometimes violins, *banndīrs,* and bongos. The solemnity of the evening might be marked by an "overture" consisting of a religious song or a song from the repertoire of Farid el Atrache, the great Egyptian singer and movie star.

Or we might be in a narrow street where friends of the groom's brother found an amplifier that was even more distorted than at other parties. Local amateur poets and singers would entertain the dancers from the neighborhood, while the groom and his friends enjoyed a significant quantity of red wine indoors. We might be on the roof of a five-story house, under a tarpaulin with another group of amateur players, or in a crowded three-room flat, with the guests sitting all the way down the staircase. A singer here made people dance, not minding the sound system, which long ago lost everything except the high notes.

Finally, we might be at a party without any live performers, but with cassettes of the latest Western rock or disco hits, to which the most talented youngsters could show off steps they had just learned. But mostly they danced to raï. Even there, however, on the raï cassettes, the performative setting of male raï would not be forgotten, as we shall see.

Thus, the performance of raï was "staged" in very different places—at cabarets and at weddings. There were differences between the two settings. Characteristic of the first—and I will deal with this in more detail in chapter 6—was that as a rule it was open to all, men as well as women. This "openness" was indicated by the fact that the women's names might be called out publicly in the cabarets, which was not the case at weddings.

Weddings were also frequently open to all, since the tradition of the countryside was to invite the whole village to a wedding. But in these cases men and women were segregated. If men and women did mix at weddings, it was when the guests were personally invited. The wedding was then said to be *en famille,* as it was called in French, as opposed to having strangers present.

Generally, wedding parties take place against a socially more elaborate background, as the culmination of a much longer and more planned meeting than those that occurred in the cabarets. A wedding is the celebration of a union between members of two families who on this occasion are entering adulthood. Among other things, information about the qualities and defects of the groom, the bride, and their families is collected before the wedding contract is concluded.

Of course, there are differences among marriages, in terms of the nature of the contract, the habits of the families, and their social and economic positions. Ordinary weddings involve agreements covering at least the groom's financing of jewels, a furnished bedroom, and the wedding party. Larger weddings might include a demand by the bride's parents that the groom provide his own apartment, a car, a television, and a refrigerator.

There are also differences in the timing of celebrations. However, in Oran it is most common for the festivities to occur within three days of the wedding party. The first day, often a Wednesday, is for the groom, his friends, and his family. Friday is the day of the women's party, for which a group of *maddāḥa*s is often hired to play. There, among other things, a dance is performed in which a child (often a boy) gives the bride a belt to wear as a sign of her womanhood. However, the second day, Thursday, is the most important day. On this day the groom or *mulāy el sulṭān,* the king of the party, retires to a quiet place with close friends and prepares for the evening, bathing and dressing himself. A *wazīr* accompanies him in his preparations throughout the day, acting as minister and advisor to the groom. He is a married man who knows from experience the things a man could face on such a day and the conflicts that might arise at the party. In Oran, it was said that all the *sulṭān*'s wishes should be fulfilled. It was most important to give him a pleasant day, since it is also a tense one. A duty awaits him in the evening, namely the defloration of his bride behind closed doors while the guests are waiting and partying outside. Some grooms go to a doctor to get a sedative. Others, who do not pray in the bridal chamber, are advised to fortify themselves with alcohol (sometimes even more than one drink).

While the groom gets ready, his family brings the bride in a procession to the sound of car horns and perhaps a group of musicians. Later, the groom meets his friends in an apartment, restaurant, or the like, and from there the procession proceeds to the waiting family and his bride, also with the cars sounding their horns. Two trumpets and two *ṭbal* drummers frequently accompany the procession. At more expensive weddings, a group of members of the *Sīdi Bilāl* brotherhood plays in front of the procession and fires a blunderbuss. Often a white stallion—capable of "dancing" with its rider, the groom—is hired, but just as often only a large group of youngsters follows the groom, beating a rhythm and shouting, "*Jbadh w ʿaṭay*" (Shoot and give it) while the groom approaches the bridal chamber. Shortly before entering the house (*dakhla*), the groom might cover his face with a hood. A jealous woman might seek to bewitch him by catching his eyes and at the same time locking a penknife or padlock while murmuring magic words, which might make the groom incapable of completing his act of virility.

In wedding parties segregated by sex, the groom often leaves the bridal chamber soon after deflowering his wife and after his brother has danced in public with the bride's blood-stained underwear. The groom joins the men's party and is received with kisses and congratulations. He stays for a while, enjoying the entertaining and dancing in his honor. Mostly, however, this practice of dancing in public with proof of the wife's virginity (and the husband's virility) has tended to disappear in Oran. At most weddings the underwear is shown only to the respective mothers of the couple and to the women close to them. At sexually mixed wedding parties the practice of the groom leaving his wife has also tended to disappear; bride and groom both join the family party and entertainment. In mixed wedding parties held in restaurants and hotels, the practice is for the couple to stay with the guests the whole night, only then leaving the party for the bridal chamber.

The wedding party, however, remains a most important ritual and event in the life of a young man as a threshold to adulthood. In Oran in the early 1990s, it was usually an extremely costly affair. The cheapest wedding I heard of (a marriage between cousins) cost twenty thousand dinars. A normal party is considered to cost between sixty and eighty thousand dinars, including food, jewelry, and bedroom furniture. Music, singers, musicians, and *barrāḥs* are also integrated into the economic circuit of the party.

## Entertainment, Money, and Emotion

The job of the entertainers is basically to enter into the distribution of words and money, with music as a background medium. It is a game of *tabrīḥas* or dedications. The formal idea of the party is that the audience offers money to the *barrāḥ* and asks him to praise the family of the groom and a number of persons present, and to have the musicians play a favorite tune. The *tabrīḥas* are formally given in order to help the groom pay for the music. In this sense, they are a continuation of earlier North African ceremonies where a sum of money (*ghārama*) is offered or a collection (*tāwsa*) is made by the invited guests to the bride or groom, to be reciprocated on another occasion.

To encourage the collection of money, the dedications might also take the form of a competitive game. This is basically a game for fun in which people offer a sum and ask for a tune "against"—*kūntra*—one of the guests. This leads the opponent to raise the offer as a counterbid. The competition revolves around having a favorite tune played, the idea being "to burn" the bid of the opponents. It can develop into a long sequence constantly alternating between two songs. It sometimes takes place between supporters of the two first-division football teams of Oran, and is particularly elegant if there are two *barrāḥs* present in a *rsās l-bard* (cold bullets)—a competition between the two parties in terms of poetry. This game, too, is closely connected historically with the North African concept of *rishshq,* which etymologically denotes "to plant," "to drive in," "to thrust," and in which the money is pasted (with saliva) on the forehead of a dancer. In this sense, the game is invested with the praise of (or competition with) people present at a party.

In Oran in the early 1990s, the practices of *ghārama, tāwsa,* and *rishshq* were mostly concerns of women's parties. On the male side, the practice of giving has been emptied of its earlier meaning. Nevertheless, a number of negotiations are conducted, mainly before the wedding party. For example, sometimes the groom and musicians decide to share the money put into the *snī*. But the groom might also choose to pay the group in advance if he knows that wealthy people will be present in the audience. The risk here is that the group and the *barrāḥ* might not work as hard to get people to offer money. A hierarchy also exists at the level of the party organizer and the musicians. The wealthy can afford better known names, who attract more money for themselves and more money and prestige for the party organizer. The lower the income level of the party organizer, the more likely it will be that the wedding party does not have live music.

Most musicians work for a fixed price, with the cost of a group ranging from three to thirty thousand dinars, depending on fame and quality. Sometimes they make other arrangements which create tensions: the top name in the group (usually the singer) might be paid in advance and invite musicians to play with him for a share of the *snī* only, or the top name might take the *snī* and give the musicians a fixed payment. The musicians, the party organizer, and people in general therefore experience directly the fact that entertainment and business are hard to dissociate from each other. But the result is a performance, sometimes even a good performance if properly carried out.

From the point of view of the public, the role of the *barrāḥ* and the musicians is to create a good atmosphere and to be at the service of the audience for the whole night. A good evening is one in which the *barrāḥ* and the musicians know their jobs, have a wide repertoire of songs and words, and know how to balance an evening without letting the game of *kūntras* become serious. Fights break out quite often, mainly in the cabarets where guests are strangers to one another and the *barrāḥ* is less likely to know them than at a local wedding. Furthermore, bets laid in the cabarets are closer to the logic of calculated exchange than the logic of the disinterested gift (see Bourdieu 1980).

From the *barrāḥ*'s and the musician's point of view, a good evening is one with an atmosphere propitious for the rich circulation of music, words, and money. The *barrāḥ* and the singer form a team working to create this: a good *barrāḥ* is one who knows the psychology of partying. He watches his audience and notices who has been drinking and who is well dressed. A good *barrāḥ* knows which people in the audience will be patient and which will be impatient waiting for their songs to be played. He can also judge who among the audience would support a competitive game. This is what occurred one evening at La Guinguette when my name was mentioned in a *tabrīḥa*. At that moment none of the guests knew my name, only the *barrāḥ* and Cheb Hindi, whom I had met previously and interviewed. The *barrāḥ* thus introduced my name to flatter and encourage me to enter the competition, asking for songs and dedications.

Early in the evening, at weddings, he says "proper" *tabrīḥas* when older members of the respective families are present. Late at night, he tells more daring jokes. When he is on unfamiliar ground, a good *barrāḥ* is one who learns people's names easily. He makes *tabrīḥas* praising the courageous man; he trys a *tabrīḥa* of love, and if someone starts laughing he knows that some people present might be emotionally touched by the subject. He does not allow himself to be provoked by people looking for trouble, but instead knows how to passify them with a particular poem, how to say things indirectly so that they will be understood without causing offense.

In the course of an evening, one might hear dedications to individuals called by their nicknames, geographical origin, or attributes, such as Muḥammad Jzīri (Algiers), Muḥammad ʿAnnabi (Annaba), or Muḥammad Yamaḥa. One might also hear dedications to colleagues, the PTT (postal employees), *les taxieurs, les réfrigérateurs, les mécaniciens, nās de l'université* (people of the university), *la famille* "x," and to football clubs (Mouloudia, ASMO), local areas (*nās* HLM, St. Eugène, Hippodrome, *les Zalumit, nās* Ançor), and cities (*nās* Jzayr, *nās* ʿAnnaba)—not only in Algeria, but also *nās* Valencia, *nās* Toulouse, *nās* Marseille, and even *nās* Boston. Everything happens as if what is going on is a naming of social relations, a mapping of the social and geographical networks of people present. It is as if they are involved in a series of alliances, of duties and obligations formulated in relational attributes such as occupation, origin, or residence (*nisbas;* see Bourdieu 1980:202, Geertz 1979:142, L. Rosen 1984:19). It is as if in public the individual interprets and designates the system of relations in which he finds himself, as if he uses his resources and position to forge a network of affiliations in a wider range of personal, contractual, and ad hoc ties to others.

Everything also happens as if the people present are mentioned without attention being drawn to social distinctions. No hierarchy is expressed, while at the same time, individual scheming, intrigue, and manipulation take place through gifts of money mediated by the entertainers (Crapanzano 1980:78).[2] Nonetheless, a constant insecurity exists that the bonds of reciprocity might dissolve in the face of power differences. Thus while money, momentarily turned into gifts, serves the search for face-to-face relations of equality, the games of the *kūntras,* by contrast, highlight differentiation and distinctions. This game of one-upmanship is like the potlatch (see Jansen 1987:191, Miliani 1983), where there is a constant threat of fights.

The *barrāḥ* is at the center of this tension. He is in control of the word (*kalma*), which is used in mediating positions of power, prestige, and autonomy, and in assertions of personhood.[3] He uses *kalma* as a rhetorical device and adopts a calculated, relativist attitude to truth in order to secure the relationships among those involved in the game.

However, he is not alone; the singer is also present. In Oran, a singer has to follow the *barrāḥ*'s instructions when the *barrāḥ* is present. In my experience, not all singers would do so, but in a good team there was a close understanding between the musicians and the *barrāḥ*. For example, if the singer was well known and had had a recent hit, the audience tended to ask for that song repeatedly throughout the evening. The singer and *barrāḥ* had to know how to delay things just enough to maintain the expectations of the party. Otherwise, when the time came for a song to be sung, the singer might bring in his personal compliments by sending messages in songs to dancers or those who had offered money for the song. It might happen—and there were stories that it happened often in the cabarets in the early 1980s—that the singers made up new song lines while singing. In the 1990s, however, this was rare; the singer most often limited himself to singing the key phrase of the song and a couple of verses, waiting for a new round of dedications to be offered.

When there was no *barrāḥ,* the singer took over the responsibility of the games of competition and the dedications, but I did not hear of raï singers being able to command poetry in public as could the *barrāḥ*. Basically, then, the singer did nothing but sing what he was asked to sing. Even the best known chebs, the greatest names, sang what they were asked to sing, whether songs they had made famous themselves or the latest hits of other singers. They therefore had a different role from the *barrāḥ,* much less powerful in the prestigious world of words, being rather voices expressing emotions through songs people already knew.

However, the *barrāḥ* and the singer were professionals in a game of entertainment in which they were both marginal in the sense that they did not participate as guests but as paid professionals. This was not always true, since singers were invited to weddings as guests by a host hoping that in the course of the evening they would entertain and bring prestige to the party. Male guests did sometimes stand up and show their skills as singers and *barrāḥs*. But as regards the circulation of money, the singer and *barrāḥ* were outside the circle of equal relations because they were excluded from the reciprocity of the gifts (see Jansen 1987:191).

The gifts were their pay, for which they did, however, give something back: the *barrāḥ* offered words, the singer songs, so as to create emotion. They showed that words and music in the right place could make money, and that money could be exchanged for emotion.

It gave people pleasure to have their names mentioned in public. It gave pleasure to have a favorite tune played, and it was aggravating when it was stopped because of another bet. It gave pleasure to move in time to the music, both index fingers raised to the sky, and to play with kinetics in time with the music. It gave pleasure to coordinate one's movements with a partner or to provoke the other to make an original movement. Outside the weddings, in restaurants and cabarets, it gave pleasure to offer money and to outbid others present in attracting a belly dancer to one's table and to watch her dance. In the cabarets it could give more than pleasure to move in time with a person of the opposite sex or to use money and words to send messages to a person of the opposite sex without others realizing it. All in all, it gave people pleasure to watch others experience pleasure, people being "light," *khaffīf,* in such a way that they became a gift to the party, without calculation, strategic purpose, or the negotiation of truth.

## Recording Raï

The raï performance had one additional effect. Rarely was a song sung to its full length. In general, in raï, a song rarely had a "full length." This shows a basic feature: the music was embedded in a social relation which began and ended according to the money involved. Relations such as these, as well as the exchange of money for emotions, is of course at the heart of all commercial entertainment and mass production of cultural goods. It is nevertheless often overlooked in discourses on music, as shown in the press accounts of raï.

However, each musical genre articulates the relation between money and emotion in its own peculiar way. This will become even clearer in this section, where I deal with how the live performance was transferred to the recording studio. Here, although the *barrāḥ* disappeared, the structurally weak position of the singers was nonetheless reproduced.

When I arrived in Oran, the first places I started visiting regularly were the recording studios. This was not only to become acquainted with the production of music as such, but also to obtain interviews with the singers, who were generally extremely difficult to meet for such formal purposes. On one of the first occasions I went to a recording studio, I actually met one of my favorites from the records I had back home in Denmark. I felt a sincere wish to tell him how much I appreciated his style and songs, but he looked at me as if I came from another planet and hurried out of the studio as soon as he had finished recording.

One day, later in my stay, I went to one of the smaller studios and found the door locked, as was usual when a recording was being made. There was great tension in the studios then because the publishers feared that their ideas would be pirated by others. Sometimes I was not allowed to stay in certain studios because some publishers knew I was visiting others. But that day I was allowed in, although under great suspicion from the publisher and his friends, advisors, and co-investors.

Behind the pane of glass of the recording chamber, I recognized one of the early singers of raï who I knew had recently returned to Oran after divorcing a barmaid in the south of France. He was now trying to reenter the raï scene and had found a publisher to finance a master tape. The song being recorded was called "Katbīli" (Write me) and consisted of three short verses and a refrain. It dealt with a divorce, the touching scene of a man longing desperately for news of his wife and children. A great argument was going on between the singer and the keyboard player. The singer wanted to use a tune from a tape of Julio Iglesias, and the keyboard player could not make the accompaniment fit the text. I could see the problem. The text was written for only half the song plus the refrain, and to the great relief of the singer I was able to accompany him on the keyboard. This meant that the people present began to show a greater interest in me. Cheb Mami's U.S.-produced "Let me raï" was having great success in Algeria at the time, and it inspired in those present the idea that I could join in on the refrain with a response line in English, "Write me please." This I did, and when the publisher and the singer left the studio, the keyboard player asked me to add an acoustic guitar accompaniment.

At that time, I hoped to have won direct access to the milieu of the musicians and publishers, since I thought rumors would spread about the recording. However, it was only published six months later in Paris; until then it was kept secret. But the publisher did start showing an interest in me. We had a couple of private meetings, at which he proposed that I bring some Western disco tunes that he would then have translated into colloquial Arabic for me to sing. Eventually, I kindly refused the offer, but my relation to the singer had changed. He did not hurry away when he saw me, as the first singer had, since I had helped him without asking anything in return.

Generally, the transfer of raï to cassette recordings involved an intriguing network of alliances, strategies, and power games among the publishers, singers, and studio staff, in which the former were the dominant figures. Out of twenty-two publishers (an estimated two thirds of the Oranians in the business), seven had been in the business of raï music before the advent of the cassette. Four had been publishers in the record business, and another three were market or itinerant record dealers. Seven others had been in small or poorly remunerated jobs before entering the cassette business.[4] Two others were successful merchants who seemed to have widened their commercial activities by investing in the cassette business. There was also an alliance between a singer who had invested in a publishing company and a restaurant owner from Oran. Finally, there was a former court clerk, now a car dealer, plant owner, and *barrāḥ,* with two wives, one of them a well-known *shīkha.* There was only one woman in the business, a former hairdresser who was divorced from a publisher. Few of them could be said to come from the higher strata of Algerian society in terms of educational or occupational background. Only one had a degree, and several were illiterate. Three seemed to have had a different course in life—one a jeweller, one a university student, and one a former official in the higher echelons of the public sector—all having entered the music business through a passion for Western rock music. Thus, although most of the publishers were from lower class backgrounds, the business did develop links with higher society. Some who had moved up the social ladder were associating with politicians and the more important industrialists of the town. They also maintained relations with the most important publishers in Algiers, who in turn associated themselves with these circles.

The publishers relied mainly on family members in conducting their affairs. Often, a brother or several brothers managed a retail store while the eldest took care of the recordings, distribution, and contacts. Older publishers had sons helping them. Others worked together with cousins, brothers-in-law, and so on, who were either in the business of duplication and distribution or were engaged in similar activities outside Algeria, in France, Morocco, Belgium, or elsewhere.[5] In this way the production process stayed within a circle of mutual confidence or, as one publisher said, "When we are cheated we prefer it to stay within the family."

Everything happened among publishers as if production was carried out in a market that was regulated only insofar as the official system was the common enemy, in spite of which production continued. As mentioned earlier, after independence a number of institutions in Algeria were created for the "nationalization" and regulation of musical activity. In 1973, the National Copyright Agency (l'Office national des droits d'auteurs, or ONDA) was created in order to take over the protection of author and composer rights in Algeria from the French SACEM (Société des auteurs, compositeurs, et editeurs de musique). However, the protection of authors' and composers' rights has never functioned in accordance with the formal legislation. Pirating and plagiarism have flourished for a long time within the music business; especially since the disappearance of vinyl records, cassette publishers have shown great ingenuity in avoiding paying composers' royalties or taxes. Several production houses have closed down because of problems with the tax authorities, only to open shortly afterward under a new name. In 1978, ONDA introduced stamps to be fixed to the cassette cartridge, resulting in new systems for avoiding taxes or copyright fees. For a long time, it was possible for buyers to take off the stamps and sell the cassettes to retail dealers for a lower price. When the glue was improved, many publishers simply declared a limited number of cassettes and sold the rest without stamps. Another method was to register fictitious songs under the name of a producing house which had no other function than this registration. Then the stamps would be resold to other publishers. A third way was to have "private" stamps printed or simply to buy them unofficially from ONDA.

Everything that happened in the publishing market depended on a network of personal contacts and alliances in a system of intense competition at all levels of production and distribution. This was a real-life mirror of the game of the *barrāḥ*. Importing raw material from abroad involved personal alliances with customs staff. Duplicating cassettes demanded personal ties involving not only credit but also trust that the duplicating plant would not pirate the product. Recording cassettes and printing cassette covers also demanded a relationship of trust for the same reasons. Thus publishers tended to cluster in closed circles around studios, duplicating plants, importers of raw materials, and in networks of distribution and cooperation, although these tended to break up into new networks.

Raï songs were known to have a short shelf life. In comparison with the more elaborate songs of the Egyptian stars, the Algerian *sh*ʿ*aabi,*[6] or the poems of the *malḥūn,* there were few evergreens. The success of a song was known within a few weeks and might not last long. In a system of rapid turnover such as this, information and an efficient system of distribution had immense value. Releasing and distributing a cassette at the right time demanded that the weaker publishers—those unable to control the whole cycle of production—enter into alliances with the stronger ones. Moreover, only alliances gave access to the secrets of the business. To some extent, alliances could prevent a similar product from being put on the market at the same time or prevent competing pirate versions from being released on the market within a few weeks of each other, but only to a certain degree. Thus one publisher was known to have pirated products of others for years without anyone being able to react. The story was that he had close relations with people in power in Algeria. This rumor was eventually confirmed after the fall of Chedli. Three months after Boudiaf's installation, he had to escape to Europe after being accused of importing stolen luxury goods into the Algerian black market.

When a cassette was ready for release, the publisher dealt with itinerant sellers unless he was powerful enough to have people working for him on a regular basis. The seller would take a certain number of cassettes from the publisher and usually earn one or two dinars for each one he managed to sell. How he did it was not the publisher's concern, and often the seller had his own network for buying, selling, and bartering with retail dealers based on his relations of reciprocity. Here again there might be tensions, since most retailers had a monitor with fast duplication and would rarely buy a large number of cassettes from their suppliers. Often, they offered the consumer six new songs on outdated cassettes for two thirds of the price.

All in all, the number of cassettes a publisher could sell was limited. In the press, the sales figures for major successes were said by the singers and some publishers to reach five hundred thousand. If these figures (which are impossible to verify) were accurate, they would not account for the number of publishers forced to quit the business each year; further, the number of publishers in the business would have been much higher than it actually was. The most reliable information I have came from an itinerant trader who claimed that he had personally distributed 120,000 copies of Cheb Mami's "Let me raï." This figure confirms what three publishers who had left the business told me: 150,000 was the maximum number you could sell for one of the rare top hits. Of course, with the systematic pirating and duplicating taking place in Algeria, the total number bought was almost certainly much higher, but this did not help the publishers. Several informants compared the business of music production with a game of poker, which is not far from Western fashion or popular cultural goods, with the difficulties in predicting which products will be "hits" (see Hennion 1983, Hirsh 1991).

In raï, many products did not "score." According to my estimate of the costs of production, between 7,500 and 10,000 cassettes had to be sold in order to reach the break-even point. Each cassette sold above the break-even point brought the publisher ten dinars a cassette—that is, if he succeeded in avoiding paying taxes and copyright fees. Basically, most publishers in the business worked as if they did not expect all their products to pass the break-even point, and most people in the raï business chose to ensure profit by taking minimal risks. This strategy led to a number of retakes, using similar tunes with different words, similar words with different tunes, and other sleights of hand.

Few publishers took the risk of a high investment in terms of capital or time in developing new products, since only the strongest were in fact able to defend their products against being pirated. The publishers chose low-budget recordings and saved money in as many ways they could. The recording process did not last more than a week. Playing errors were not corrected. If cassettes were left unsold, the tape and covers were reused for another recording. Of course, these practices had a great deal to do with the generally difficult conditions of production in Algeria, but they were also connected with the fact that raï cassettes were a transient commodity (see Thompson 1979) and were treated as such.

## The Singers

The publishers also treated the singers as transient commodities. Out of the fifty-three singers I counted, a large number seemed to originate from families whose conditions of life did not differ from those of so many Algerians: living in overcrowded houses, with parents having few opportunities to offer their sons. The information I have about thirty-three of the singers' fathers shows that the highest earners were a health technician, a baker, and the owner of a bar in France.[7]

Of the singers—most of them born between 1960 and 1970—only nine were employed in state-owned enterprises. Only twelve others seemed to have a steady income as unskilled workers or small traders. Only one had a high school certificate. The rest were living full or part time from their singing and had no school certificate, or only a middle school certificate or a certificate of apprenticeship which they rarely used. In fact, nineteen singers said that their education was that of school dropouts. Moreover, out of fifty-three singers I had knowledge of, only one was in the business of music publishing, and only two had any family relations with a publisher. A minority of singers who had invested money had done it in branches other than music—for example, a tea salon, a laundry, a bakery, a delivery van, a small restaurant, and a perfumery.

But they all had similar stories—beginning as youngsters playing music with friends in their local neighborhood, often imitating a favorite singer. It was a story of youngsters attending weddings, listening to records of their favorite singers, finding pleasure in singing, and subsequently being discovered by a publisher. However, the story says nothing about how many singers refused the publishers' offers to record or about the number of singers the publishers turned down because they made demands concerning payment or the sort of music they wanted to record.

Thus a raï recording singer was one who cooperated with a publisher in accordance with conditions laid down by the latter. This often meant working in a difficult atmosphere. One female singer, for example, was barred from the studios of Oran for more than a year after breaking her relationship with a powerful publisher. Since written contracts between singers and publishers were rare, most raï production took place through verbal agreements in which even the pay was often not decided in advance. Thus one singer was once forced to repay a publisher twenty thousand dinars because the latter claimed that he had not done his job properly. Another singer was forcibly deprived of his passport by a publisher at the airport when he was about to leave for France in order to keep him in the recording studio in Oran. Those singers who signed written contracts seldom found that it was to their advantage. One publisher offered a well-known singer a car in exchange for a ten-year contract to sing for him. The contract, which at the time of signing might well have appeared fine to the singer, clearly would have brought enormous profits to the publisher over the period in question. The singer later broke the contract and the publisher brought the case to court and won. The singer still has not fulfilled his contract; he stays abroad and is not particularly hopeful about going back to his hometown. Another singer signed a two-year contract with another publisher, who then chose not to use his voice while at the same time preventing him from being used by other publishers. Other cases basically like these differed depending on the position of the singers.

An implicit hierarchy could be said to exist among the singers. At the top were those who had gone to the West and whose cassettes sold in considerable quantities in Algeria. Then followed those who had recorded only a few records and who had to make their living in the cabarets or at weddings in the summer. Finally, there were those who had not recorded any cassettes, who rarely got jobs in the cabarets, and who had to make a year's income during the summer season. Only the top singers had some room to maneuver in their relations with the publishers. There were numerous examples of singers who had recorded their own songs, only to discover subsequently that these had been produced using another singer. Other singers who tried to finance master tapes without the assistance of a publisher later realized that the recording engineer had not mixed the tape properly—at least not the voice—but had kept the tape, later remixing it properly and selling it abroad.

The publisher was the person who had the connections with the studios, the distribution network, and so on. Some, however were known to treat their singers well, and a number of singers were linked with such publishers. Thus it happened that one of the central meeting places for the singers in the daytime was not the recording studio, but at the desk of one of the most powerful publishers or in the cafe next to his office.

Basically, then, it was the publishers who decided what to record and who would record it. Most singers made their first cassette without payment. The publicity that came from having recorded could increase payment at weddings, but only if the cassette was a hit could the singer try to bargain with several publishers for a better deal. However, none of the recording singers of raï I knew of had tried to make music in opposition to the ideas of the publisher. Thus their structurally weak position at live performances was reproduced in their relations with their publishers and was a constant feature in the production of recordings.

## "Writing" Songs

There were several ways of making recordings. First, the singers or publishers recycled songs already known to the public, recording them with new voices and new instruments. These might be early hits of the *wahrāni,* Moroccan tunes, or simply current tunes. Second, they used characteristic parts of well-known tunes, either as the sole motif or recombined with motifs from another song. An extreme example was a combination of "Lambada" with an old Oran favorite, "Ruḥī Wahrān" (Go Oran, originally of Spanish origin). A variation of this procedure was to take the vocal introduction, the *istikhbār,* from one song and add it to a range of other songs. This could be an opportunity for the singer to show the range of his voice and to introduce "real" words into the song, the words of the *malḥūn* poets and the *barrāḥ*. As such it revived the mixture of poetry, song, and music found in the live performance. Third, of course, a whole tune which had proved its success could be used with new words, or words from one song could be used in whole or part with another tune that again turned out to consist of combinations of earlier ones. The number of combinations was great.

An example will help to show further the kinds of songs that occurred in raï. Thus "Ma ḍannitsh natfārqu" (I didn't think we would separate; presented in Appendix 1) was a great hit in 1990 and there were innumerable versions. The first version is by Cheikh Naam, who was acknowledged by all singers as having written the song. The song (in fact a *chansonette*) was recognized by singers and listeners as being "one with words" (*kalmas*). Such songs are not those most representative of raï, but they still contain most of its characteristics. The song is interspersed with dedications, song lines are repeated, and there is no systematic alternation between the four-line chorus and the four-line verses.

The same holds true for Cheb Fethi's version. He starts the song with a poem, a spoken *istikhbār*. In the rest of the song, he has altered a few of Naam's words. Some verse lines have been omitted, the dedications are for other people, and the lines are not repeated in the same sequence. Finally, he has included fewer repetitions of the refrain, in which he has also made some slight changes. He does not need as many as Naam, since his *istikhbār* has already taken up some of the six minutes needed for a recorded song.

In the third version, Benchenet has added two new lines to Naam's song and has chosen to introduce the song with a sung *istikhbār,* which he repeats at the end. Otherwise, he is the only one to uphold a disciplined alternation between verse and chorus (to which he has also made some modifications).

In the fourth version, by Cheb Hamid, we find Naam's chorus used as an introduction with a slight change of words. The rest of the song consists of six song lines, two being repeated as pairs, followed by two lines of the initial chorus. Only a few of the original lines have been reproduced.

Thus, "Ma ḍannitsh natfārqu" shows how raï fluctuates between short songs of a Mediterranean type and a form in which the song lines seem to be treated as interchangeable units with an independence of their own. More specific examples of this idea are found in Benchenet's 1990 hit, "*Ṭilifūn ḥram*" (The telephone is forbidden [or out of order]), a song of separation in which the singer is calling a woman living in Oran, as well as Arzew, Marseilles, and Paris. Another example is Fethi's 1992 hit, "Laggi, laggi," (I implore, I implore [God for a meeting]), in which the singer praises a blonde, a redhead, and a brunette.

In fact, this form is nearly the same as that performed by female singers such as *shīkhas* and *maddāḥas*. Basically, they use a simple dance rhythm with a key phrase to which they continually return. The female singers—many of them illiterate—are steeped in an oral tradition, and their art primarily consists of formulas, that is, "a group of words which is regularly employed under the same metrical conditions to express a given essential idea" (Parry, quoted in Lord 1960:30). They thus create phrases on the spot by using phrases taken from other singers or by mixing words from two phrases they have remembered.

While the singers have their own formulas, there are also many formulas known to all singers, which give the songs a homogeneity in the sense that as soon as one has heard more than one song, one has the impression that all singers know the same formulas (Lord 1960:49), as if they are reusing, recombining, and reinventing song lines in a permanent "parataxic patchwork process" (Virolle-Souibès 1988b:198). The female singers not only make music, but they also play a role in the circulation of money and messages at the parties at which they entertain. In general, their improvisations are not only invested in keeping a song going, but are also directed toward the audience, simply touching people (and their purses) or raising money through dance competitions among the women (see Jansen 1987, Mebarki and Naceri 1983, Rosander 1991). The art of the singers is thus more than "a parataxic patchwork." Rather, the basic form can be described as a repetitive movement in time, embedded in a person-to-person social game, with sentences cast out to an audience in order to touch people, with a reliance on formulaic phrases to keep the movement going, and with a continual return to a key phrase.

In fact, male raï singers obtain a good deal of their material from female performances and recordings of raï. When it comes to the postcolonial history of raï, a main trend has been for men to change female songs into a masculine form. Bouteldja Belkacem's first two recordings, "Zizīya" and "Sīdi l-ḥakim," both from 1965, are examples of this. This tendency increased with the advent of the cassette. Thus a leading studio musician told me that in the late 1970s the publishers needed six songs to fill a cassette, whereas before they had needed only two for a single record. This problem was solved by exploiting the *maddāḥa* repertoire. Many male raï songs thus consisted of key phrases and formulas taken from female recordings. A famous example is "ʿAla zarga rāni nsāl" (I am looking for the brunette) which in the female version is "'*Ala l-azrag rāni nsāl*" (I am looking for the brown man; the brown man is synonymous with the well-known Muslim saint Sidi Abdelqader Jilali).

This inspiration, however, did not go in only one direction. Generally with raï, the clear boundaries which the researcher so eagerly looks for were difficult to find. Electric raï has taken and recorded *wahrāni* songs and given new words to *wahrāni* tunes, while composers of *wahrāni* have written songs for raï singers. Musicians playing *wahrāni* have played raï and vice versa. The fact that men have received inspiration from female performances has been mirrored by women exploiting male repertoires, men singing in the acoustic form in the same manner as women, and a few transvestites singing as women in the mode of the *maddāḥa*.[8]

In general, in the "official" histories of raï there has been a great deal of confusion with regard to the origins of the genre because investigation into the form of raï and the position of the singers has been neglected.[9] The Algerian press has typically described raï as a degeneration of the art of the *malḥūn*.[10] The connection between raï and the *malḥūn* lies in the fact that some raï singers have recorded some poems (or parts of the poems) from the *malḥūn* and some *shīkhs* of the *malḥūn* have occasionally sung in the raï style. In addition, the title of *shīkh* has not only been used by the interpreters of the *malḥūn*. Cheikh Hattab, Cheikh Boutaïba Saïdi, Cheikh Brahim, and Cheikh Sayah would all be called *shīkhs* even though they perform in the much more immediate art form described above.

All in all, one might conclude that raï recordings are close to oral performances if it were not for the problems of speaking about oral art in a country to which the recording industry arrived at the turn of the century (see Gronow 1981). Recording can fix songs so that they can be played again and again, with the regularities of written texts (Nettl 1985:61). Thus other singers can listen to recordings and learn songs by heart. Still, it seemed that the text should not be repeated or copied in its exact form. The poetics of the oral form was a cherished means of expression at the center of the raï aesthetics.

## Creating Raï

In 1990, at the first and only general assembly of the Association nationale des editeurs de musique (the music publishers' association), the meeting soon developed into an argument between the publishers and the general director of ONDA about copyright fees for raï songs. I was present at the meeting, as was a journalist from *Horizon,* who quoted a publisher from Oran: "Sometimes the raï songs have no words of their own. Everyone adds his contribution. The singer provides some lines, also the publisher and the studio technician. The whole, anyway, makes up a song and even a cassette. So I cannot see why we have to pay royalties for such products" (*Horizon,* November 13, 1990).

One central figure in the world of raï, an early *barrāḥ* of Cheikha Remitti and later of the top singer Benchenet, explained:

> The spontaneous song is typically raï. They are not texts. It is not poetry. It is not words; it comes out spontaneously. It is not *shiʿar* [making verses]; it is not *malḥūn.* You can sing whatever you like, and the proof, Marc, haven't you seen it on all these cassettes by the chebs. You find the same words in fifty titles. What you say in "Ṣḥab al bārūd" (People of the gunpowder) you can say in "Yā ma tabkīsh" (Oh don't cry). Because they are not texts, but that does not prevent it from being good music. It is valid, that's all.

A well-known accordionist who had accompanied and trained a number of singers within the raï and *wahrāni* styles explained: "Raï is not a piece of poetry. Why? It's because the words come like that. I could make a raï song right now for you: how I came here, how we met, what we said, what you like, what you have been drinking, what you have eaten, where you slept. Raï words, they come like that."

However, there does exist what might be called a conscious creative element in raï. At the center of a raï song is the refrain. I prefer to call it a key phrase to distinguish it from the types of refrains found in a number of Western pop songs functioning in "sectionally structured, goal-oriented discrete units with a clear sense of dramatic climax and closure" (Manuel 1988:23).

Among the singers and musicians of Oran, there was a clear awareness of the importance of the key phrase. They called it the *nakwa,* the identity card, while the rest of the text was termed *zirriʿaas,* grains to be dispersed. In raï, the most important thing when writing a new song was to find a *nakwa* which would touch people; a number of stories were told of how such new "songs" saw the light of day. A singer and songwriter from Sidi Bel Abbès told how he created the hit formula "Khallūni nabki ʿala rrāy" (Let me cry on my raï [my state of being]):

> One day I entered a bar. I drank three beers and didn't have any more money to carry on drinking. I started thinking. So much was

> I thinking that it caught me as a sadness. I started crying. When I left the bar, I said, why am I crying over some wine? A day will come when I can drink, but wait: I will invent a song about why I was crying. So I said, "*Khallūni nabki ʿala rrāy.*" I invented the music as well as the words.

Another singer told me about "Kadbu ʿaliyya gālu baddāla" (They lied to me, they said you were a woman of many men):

> I knew a girl, and I loved her so much. It was love at first sight, as they say. I went to people to ask about her. Is she all right, is she different from the others? They told me she was dating him and him and him. Well, I left the girl behind. Later, I came back and discovered she was a serious girl. That's why I say, "*Kadbu gālu baddāla.*"

According to its writer, "Ma ḍannitsh natfārqu" was created

> after I divorced my first wife. . . . I was sad. I left three children in need of love. . . . I started writing for this woman I had known, the first woman, my first wife. It was my first love, I started writing "Ma ḍannitsh natfārqu" for her.

The singer Boutaïba Sghir was in a bar with a friend. They were talking about a woman from whom he had recently separated. When leaving the bar, he said, "*Malgré tout, mazāl nabghīha,*" which became the hit, "*Malgré tout mazāl nabghik*" (In spite of all, I want you), which exploits a letter rhyme and the interchangeability of French and Algerian. Another singer was at a party and was waiting for his beloved who did not arrive, and he said, "*Tout le monde est là, maḥḥanti la*" (Everyone is here, my love is not), which became another hit. A third singer was married to a blonde while having a mistress who was a brunette. His wife was jealous and made a scene when he came home. He beat her up and the police had to interfere three times. Out of this came the song "*Bayḍa mon amour . . . samḥaliyya zarga*" (My blonde, my love . . . excuse me brunette).

Some of these stories occurred in several versions, and in fact many songs were not made by the singers themselves. In Oran, there was a whole business consisting of creating key phrases and songs. The singers could obtain verses, or buy material, from a number of professional song-line creators, some of whom had training as *barrāḥs*. Other singers were offered songs for which they paid five hundred dinars or more. A number of singers also received fan letters which included poetry; from these they selected sentences according to their professional intuitions. Finally, singers simply did what they were told by the publisher, who sometimes engaged a "*nakwa* writer" to make songs on the spot in the studio.

All these ways of making songs had several things in common. First, it was necessary to find a key phrase that would touch people. Second, what touched people might also touch the singers themselves. The song-line composers used experiences from their own lives, not only in order to find original combinations of formulas, but also with great awareness that the *nakwas* had to be taken from people's actual worlds. Several songwriters told me how they used scenes from daily life as motifs in their key phrases and how they frequently used expressions they had heard in the streets. The idea was to capture what was in the air socially as well as musically.

But at the same time the singers kept to the oral aesthetics of raï. Thus professional poets who sold songs to raï singers said, with some irritation, that singers would rarely sing the song as they had written it, altering some words or sometimes only using a few lines. One of the most obvious examples of this reworking is the song called "Yamīna," which was created by Mostfa Ben Brahim in the last century and which has been recorded in innumerable versions. The full-length version appears in Azza (1979) and tells the story of a lover coming to see his mistress after being absent for a long time. In it, the man excuses himself for having been away so long and the mistress replies, not believing the excuses. The whole is arranged as an elegant dialogue in seventy-five lines where the lines praising Yamīna are repeated only twice. However, in the hit version by Cheb Khaled, the publisher has taken lines 1 to 5, half of line 6, lines 11 to 13, 18, 27, 29, 30, and 33, making Yamīna's beauty the lead phrase, which is basically all that remains of the original poetic idea.

But the singers did more than that; they also allowed small amounts of their personality and style to appear in the song. For example, in one of the choruses of "Yamīna," Khaled substituted the name Yamina with *nagrita* or "black girl"—a girl of the people in a slightly erotic sense—thus altering the atmosphere of the song, changing it from the formalities of poetic expression into the lightness of a pleasurable play on seductive words.

More individuality is found in "Ma ḍannitsh natfārqu." Both Naam and Fethi have introduced the girls' names (line 8). These are not accidental. In some of the songs, the singers did add minor hints about their personal lives. For example, one singer often mentioned the name of his son growing up in France, and another once introduced the name of the street where his beloved was living. These messages could not be decoded by everyone, but otherwise they touched people through the stories they revealed. Thus a few singers have sung of their experiences in prison, and in September 1991 a singer released a song entitled "Gālu X māt" (They said X was dead). For a week or so, a story circulated in Oran that the singer had died. Spreading this rumor may have been an extremely malicious thing to do, but it also seems to have been quite remunerative.

## Recording the Song

While I was in the Oran area, there were six to eight studios working on a regular basis in Tlemcen, Sidi Bel Abbès, and Oran. The studios were furnished with equipment ranging from eight to thirty-two tracks. Those with the most sophisticated material charged the highest cassette recording price (up to forty thousand dinars). Those with small eight-track tables did not take more than twelve thousand dinars for a cassette. Publishers chose the studio on the basis of several criteria. First, they evaluated the sum of money to be invested in the product in relation to their expectations as to whether the singer and the songs would become a top hit. Second, they evaluated the abilities of the musicians, the recording engineer, the keyboard player, and the percussionist. Otherwise, publishers preferred to use the same studio in order to maintain a stable relationship with the studio owner.

A raï recording session could last several days, sometimes several weeks, since it often happened that the singer did not show up on schedule. If the same thing happened with the publisher, no recordings took place, even if the singer and musicians were ready to play.

However, the effective time used for recording six songs did not exceed more than a day. Sometimes the singer had rehearsed with the keyboard player in advance, depending on whether the singer or the publisher was to provide the songs for the cassette. Often the studio musicians were instructed on the spot. Either the publisher had a cassette of songs ready to be recorded in a new version, or the singer only needed to indicate the rhythm and a few lines of the song and the musician immediately knew its structure. The drum machine would be set to the right speed, a rhythm would be chosen, and the keyboard player would play the accompaniment a couple of times before the singer entered the recording room. Then the studio musician started playing a rudimentary accompaniment to support the singer. He knew the key in which the singer was most comfortable (often the same key for all songs) and the number of verses and interludes (or responses) he had to produce.

In fact, what the singer did while recording was not far from being a performance of acoustic raï. The singer kept to the tune and never went into an improvisation based on the harmonies provided by the keyboard player. When vocal improvisations did take place, it was in the phrasing at the end of a line or in the *istikhbār,* but even then the singer often sang one he had learned from another cassette. Everything happened as if the singer was singing with a *gaṣba* and *gallāl,* or an accordion and *darbūka,* and he often reproduced central elements from live performances.

The singers seemed to feel more comfortable maintaining person-to-person contact while singing. Thus every song began by introducing the publishing house and the singer. Then the singer offered dedications to people present in the studio, people outside the studio, local areas, towns, and so forth, and in the course of singing he sang sentences such as the following:

*Dalmonte ʿarīa walla 104 zādma*
Delmonte [a local area] is wide and the [Peugeot] 104 plunged in there

Cheb Khaled, "Gāltli hāk," (She told me, that's yours)

*Mālak w Ban ʿAli ana galūli ḥbab*
Malik and Ben Ali told me they were friends

Cheb Khaled, "Dallāli, dallāli" (My guide, my guide)

*Buʿalam, līla rgādi bināthum*
Boualem, this night I slept between them [two women]

Cheb Khaled, "Līla, līla" (This night, this night)

*Ya laman hbāla, ʿabdallah, ḥāsb l-birra sharrbat*
He's crazy, Abdallah, he thought beer was like sugared water

Cheb Khaled, "Rrāy shīn" (Evil raï)

*Rbāb l-aḥmar w yabghi ṣ-ṣahra w l-gmār*
The red *rbāb* [local bowed string instrument] likes a night in company and the moon

Cheb Khaled, "Testahel ya galbi" (You deserve it, oh my heart)

*Hadha St. Crépain w la ghaltīn*
Is this St. Crépain or are we mistaken?

Cheb Khaled, "Testahel ya galbi" (You deserve it, oh my heart)

*Ḥawsh Blaha ḍalma, l-maryūla zādma*
The house of Blaha is dark, the woman of pleasure goes in there.
Cheb Khaled, "Gultlak adieu" (I told you goodbye)

*R4 l-bahlūla, nurdīn ysugha*
The Renault 4 is crazy, Noureddine is driving her
Cheb Khaled, "Gultlak adieu" (I told you goodbye)

Connoisseurs of raï would know the publishers, musicians, brothers of publishers, instruments of studio musicians, cars of publishers, and so on, referred to in the lyrics.

Thus in a song, you not only found a voice, a number of formulas, and minor personal statements, but also improvisations emphasizing the direct social and communicative relation embedded in the raï performance. When recorded, the songs became a continuation on cassette of the live performance.

According to musicians and publishers, the atmosphere of recordings in the early 1980s was much less formal and tense, often with the character of a party, allowing for more improvisation to take place than in the early 1990s. But even then the person-to-person contact, dedications, and joking contributed to dissolving the tense atmosphere during the recording and made people smile and laugh, pleased, for example, at having their name called out in public.

Anyhow, the whole process of recording the singing was intended to last only six minutes, no less and no more for one song. There were few retakes. Even if the singer missed two bars, the recording was not repeated. The most important thing was that the rhythmic cycle not die. As soon as the singer had done his job, he hurried out of the studio, leaving behind the studio musicians, who would now adjust their skills to these transient songs. Adding music to the recorded song would be like adding another world.

## Recording the Music

Making raï music in the studio was a full-time job. The musicians played the whole day and sometimes at night. They did their job undisturbed by people coming and going or by television being on. They did not hide the fact that their job was often more tiring than rewarding in any but a pecuniary sense (except for a few talented newcomers who had not yet lost their enthusiasm). Most were paid on the basis of each cassette they filled up with their craft, and they maintained unstable relations with the studio owners. During the time I visited Oran, almost all had been circulating among several studios.

Most of the musicians were from the generation of musicians playing Western pop and rock in the 1970s and were taken into the studios because of their knowledge of and interest in the musical technology being used. Several told me that in many ways they had felt embarrassed in the early 1980s being involved with the musicians of the raï milieu, and many of them shared a characteristic with a later generation of musicians trained in the electric version of raï in tending to listen to Western music in their free time.

Although I did not succeed in establishing a representative sample of their social origins, the musicians I knew who played electric instruments seemed to originate from the upper levels of society in terms of education, occupational background, and bilingualism, in contrast to the singers and acoustic musicians. While a number of musicians and recording engineers had left school without a certificate, having invested their time in musical activities, several electric musicians had high school degrees. Some had studied in the regional conservatories, and others were sons of wealthy or middle-class entrepreneurs—something unheard of among the singers. Several of the leading names of the pop groups of the 1970s with whom the studio musicians had played and who now had stopped their musical careers were dentists, industrialists, and administrators.

From a musical point of view, the process of electrifying raï was a simple one. Without going into details here, the musical form of raï generally consists of a vocal or instrumental introduction to set the atmosphere of what is to come. This is followed by a popular rhythmic pattern[11] which is maintained throughout the whole of the song. The rhythm is to be associated to the sung phrase, which again is duplicated by the instruments.

When one is listening to the first raï recordings with electric instruments, it becomes clear that the acoustic form of raï was transformed in a process of analogy. The drum replicated the rhythms of the acoustic percussion, the electric bass filled in the low-pitched rhythm, and later the synthesizer took over the role of the earlier reed flutes, trumpets, *qanūn,* or accordion. However, the new instruments provided new technical possibilities. For example, the electric bass can play a harmonic figure, where before only drumbeats were heard, and the singer can sing higher and louder than before, and so on. In the earliest recordings, it was mainly the guitar that introduced something qualitatively new. Having no acoustic instrument to substitute, it was used to stress the upbeat, creating the outline of the sound of reggae.

Another possibility the newly introduced instruments offered was to create new preludes—that is, introductions to the atmosphere to come. Thus in the earliest recordings you might find songs introduced by drums or an electric bass figure taken from Western rock, whereas in later recordings the same would be introduced through a funk riff on a synthesizer.

Around 1982 to 1984, studios were rebuilt and the synthesizer and drum machine were introduced. These changes placed raï on a common digital, technical musical level with the pop music of the world, and the process of analogy was continued, leaving, however, the *drabki* (*darbūka* player and percussionist) as a representative of the acoustic style. The drum machine replaced the drum set, bongos, congas, and so forth, while the synthesizer substituted for the rest of the instruments.

In the early 1990s, the recording procedure varied only in the number of tracks available. Between four and six tracks were used for the drum machine (reflecting Western and Latin sounds, the latter already having been incorporated into the *wahrāni*). To this, the keyboard player added a background of harmonies, most often using the sound of violins and taking over the former role of the accordion while at the same time mirroring certain songs of Latin Europe or American disco. After this, he added upbeats (close to the idea of reggae) using the sound of piano, electric guitar, or organ. Then one track was used for working up the bass patterns, while on another track he added riffs, often with a brassy quality (reflecting both jazz and disco). Another track was used to create the response lines to the sung lines, where sounds as different as saxophone, *qanūn,* trumpet, guitar, piano, or flute might be employed (as in *wahrāni,* rock, Mediterranean pop, etc.). Sometimes an extra track was added in order to have two "voices" playing the same melody line in heterophony. Often the musician only made simple responses, but he might also improvise, using patterns or formulas he had heard in Western funk, rock, disco, and (sometimes) jazz records.

When the work of the keyboard player was finished, the percussionist added the acoustic hand drums, replicating and "filling the holes" left by the drum machine. Finally, one track was used to add electronic drum rolls, hand claps, and crossbeats.

Recording raï music thus followed a procedure similar to that in playback systems in calypso and reggae (see Hebdige 1987, Malm and Willis 1984), except that with raï, a song had to be made from scratch each time. The keyboard player and recording engineer saw to it that small variations were introduced into the songs. For example, the response lines were rarely repeated exactly the same way. Also, the job of filling in the last two tracks with additional rhythms and electronic sound patterns ensured that a raï song included enough variation to engage the attention of potential listeners.

Generally, it might be said that in the late 1970s, two sound worlds and two strata of Algerian society were being put together. Musically, a central feature of the recording studios was the retention of the acoustic beat of the local hand drums. Apart from the voice, they were the sole representative of the acoustic past. This is interesting because of the importance of the combination of voice and rhythm in general in Arabic and Algerian music: they cannot be dissociated from each other. This became clear to me when I took my guitar along to beach trips or drinking sessions outside Oran. When I played songs from the local repertoire, not many seconds would pass before I had someone in the group playing the rhythm on the wood of my guitar; we were two persons playing the same instrument.

This inseparability of what is ethnocentrically divided into melody and rhythm has been noted since the first Western descriptions of Algerian music (Hasnaoui 1990, Rouanet 1920, Salvador-Daniel 1986, Vigreux 1985). Thus the acoustic elements—the voice and percussion—are representatives of the basic rules of raï music. They might be called elements that *sum up* the historical continuity of raï within its rhythmical and tonal universe. It might also be said that these elements have been *elaborated*. In the course of time the newly added instruments, harmonies, and rhythmic patterns have explained the basics of raï to their time (see Berkaak 1993, Ortner 1970). It might be said that the acoustic raï of the late 1970s (in which was embedded the story of earlier rural raï, the *shīkha,* the city of the 1950s, Egyptian film movies, etc.) was re-elaborated with electric instruments representing a Western Other.

Furthermore, in Western rock or within World Music it is well known that Western youth—in a quest for "freedom to consume"—use musical references from groups with a history of oppression or music with metonymic references to imagined liminal spheres in the Third World (see Berkaak 1993). It is possible that the upbeats of the guitar, the electric sound, and certain riffs and musical formulas in raï might refer to what are perceived as specific spheres in the West—parties, discos, and so forth—featuring groups possessing or having gained access to consumptive power. It might even be said that in its re-elaboration, raï succeeded in relocating sounds from the outside world into a local bodily practice in specific performative settings (see Stokes 1994:5).

## Visualizing Raï

The songs were, of course, the central element in this process of relocation. But recorded raï was not only a question of sound; it also involved images before reaching the consumers. Once the recorded song had been duplicated on cassette, it was presented to the consumer with covers. The photos on these were often fuzzy, and there were frequent printing errors which the publishers had not bothered to correct. However, several motifs could be found; I will describe only the most common ones.

Very few of these covers had any thematic connection with any of the songs—as, for example, the large stairway leading to the main station in Marseilles, which referred to Chaba Zohra's hit, "Saknat Marseilles" (She lived in Marseilles). A style was presented rather than the content. One motif did represent the name of the singer alone. This category, however, was in the tradition of Islamic non-figurative art, the covers being bordered by ornaments of stylized flowers like those found in the stucco work of large villas in Oran or in North African mosques. Most others had in common a photograph of the singer dressed in jeans, Terylene trousers, a jacket, a leather blouse, T-shirts, or summer shirts. The latter were sometimes opened to the chest to reveal a gold chain, while a sweater was casually worn around the shoulders. Other photographs depicted the singer in clothes often used for performances at concerts and weddings.

All in all, the singers were dressed like most young men in the large towns of Algeria who wished to appear well dressed. There was no long hair (only short hair or hair cut in the Afro-American style, for example, like Lionel Ritchie). There was no special dress for the singers. They seemed to want to be well dressed but not dressed up, and some had chosen to emphasize an aspect of their personality that they shared with a number of Algerian men, such as their love for small children. Thus a number of covers presented the singer with "a child" or "his child."

Three visual motifs seem to have been modeled after the photographs young people typically kept in their family albums from holidays, souvenirs of friends, and so on. Sometimes the singers were pictured in a photographic shop, often with a "beautiful" background: palm trees, a beach with palms or pine trees, exotic landscapes such as lakes with a forest of fir trees, a lake with a background of snow-clad mountains, or the painting of a woman in traditional dress in front of a wedding procession. Other photographs were taken in the open air, with a mountain or a public park in the background, or with indications of the origin of the singer and the song, for example, the tower blocks of the Front de Mèr, the waterfront of Oran.

If these motifs resembled those found in the private photograph albums of youngsters, three others, by contrast, indicated that the man portrayed was specifically *not* like all youngsters. One motif presented the singer in a music shop; another depicted him at the place of production (the studio) interacting with the technology he employed (e.g., microphone, earphones, multi-track table, etc.). Finally, many covers presented the singer in live performances: "singer with a microphone," "singer with synthesizer," "singer with electric guitar."

A last motif differed radically from those described above: Some cassette covers featured female raï singers. It was rare for women raï singers to be photographed "live" (Chaba Fadela, Cheikha Djenia, and later Chaba Zahouania were among the exceptions). Instead they were "veiled" behind photographs of models from European magazines, some lightly dressed, others presenting the latest European fashion.

Covers where a layout had been created to single the product out from the great majority of cassettes were rare. Instead, the publishers added slogans such as "the king of raï" (Khaled), "the prince of raï" (Mami), "the princess of raï" (Zahouania), "the king of sentimental raï" (Hasnī), "the Brel of raï" (Naam), and "the regretted" (Zargui). In addition, small slogans were printed such as "guaranteed duplication," "mono-stereo," "dolby," or "100% raï," "novelty 87," "success 90," and "the Best of Raï Story." The latter cliche was written in English, but otherwise all front-cover texts were in French. As with the song lines and street names, the covers were therefore far from the Algerian national policy of arabization (and far from the inside cover of Barclay's Khaled record). This also holds true for the back cover. The titles were written in Latin characters using homemade systems for writing the spoken dialect. They did not always follow the order of succession of the songs on the tape. Sometimes the titles did not even correspond to the content of the tapes, a title was found to be not on the tape, or a song turned out to be a retake of another title.

The cassette "hardware" was similar to its contents, an element in a domain of mass-produced, uniform goods of transient value to which had been added small inventive details: the photograph of a singer surrounded by minor slogans, key phrases surrounded by "verbal grains," and a tune and rhythm with entertaining musical variations.

The songs were sung by young men willing to put their voices into music they had been performing for a long time and who were specialists in adapting to audiences as well as to the demands of *barrāḥ*'s and publishers. They were also polite enough to adapt to press inquiries, although with an unease that made it obvious that they were hard to get hold of.

In the press they had been confronted with a discourse that placed them in the "univocal" romantic tradition of the inspired individual, which, on a worldwide level today, seems to be nurtured by the music industry in its packaging of "geniuses" (Frith 1991:285) on the basis of copyrights. In this sense, one person comes to stand as the creator of one product, as if there were a unilinear correlation between the two.

Musical activity is more complex than that; it is much more open-ended. This must be taken into account with all popular, commercial music if we are not to end in the complete aestheticization (or rejection) of these products. Furthermore, the specific characteristics of raï must be captured. Several of the elements described in the preceding pages could apply to other musical genres in other parts of the world. However, the making of songs was nevertheless related to a specific musical form and a specific musical game in a specific society.

Raï was a cultural product embedded in socioeconomic relations, which meant for the consumers that Oran, the center of raï production, was the last place that anything new would be released, simply because it was also the town where pirating could most easily and effectively be carried out.

Once a cassette had been released, the consumers could not be sure of going into a cassette shop and obtaining it, even if it had become the latest hit, since the retailers stocked it only if they had relations of reciprocity with the publisher. Thus looking for a cassette inevitably led consumers to a certain understanding of the socioeconomic processes of music making.

While looking for a song with a given title, one could never be sure about its content, except that the lead phrase or title would be included. Thus, when one bought a song, one had to listen to it in the retailer's presence to be sure what was on the cassette; that is, buying involved personal, face-to-face contact.

Most songs disappeared as rapidly as they were released, while some became hits for a couple of months. Most then had to be exchanged for new ones, not only because people got tired of them, but also because tapes did not last long because of their inferior quality.

In Oran, raï could be heard constantly. One way for listeners to follow news of the latest releases was Channel 3 of the Algerian radio or Médi 1 in Tangier. While I was in Oran, the television started a weekly video hit parade, "Bled Music" (Hometown music), which made a great impact and included some of the established raï stars. However, loudspeakers roaring from local cassette dealers' shops, music heard at friends' places, and tapes recommended by the dealer when consumers came in and asked, "*Kayn jdīda*" (Is there anything new?) or, "*ʿAṭini le dernier succes ntaʿa . . .* " (Give me the latest success [i.e., song] by . . . ) were equally important in the dissemination of raï. From there the songs were liberated from their places of production and entered the social life of consumption. Raï was not only to be heard in the city of Oran; it was also captured and given meaning in social life. The chapters that follow will gradually venture into the main aspects of this problematic.

# 4

•

# Young Men in the City

The process that took place in the passage of raï from producers to consumers was not a simple one. "Bayḍa mon amour," for example (See chapter 3), was in many instances simply understood as a love song featuring blondes (and it was actually recorded by other singers as "Zarga mon amour" (My brunette, my love); but just as frequently the blonde was interpreted as the image of an ideal life in the West and the brunette as the symbol of a lousy life in Algeria (I will deal more thoroughly with these images in chapter 7).

As such there was as much concord as discord between producers and listeners, which rested on the fact that on one hand the songs contained "objective" features such as the text and the melody and were conceived in an environment of considerable social similarities between producers and consumers. On the other hand, these features were understood from each listener's specific background, his interest in and knowledge of the songs. This again opened a debate through which raï entered the wider society.

The question, for me, became one of specifying more precisely what took place in transferring songs from producers to consumers, from playing to listening. In the initial stages of my fieldwork, I carried out a number of structured interviews of raï listeners with the idea of reaching a certain statistical overview of the consumers of raï, their social backgrounds, and their motives for listening. I asked them about their family backgrounds, their favorite songs, their opinions of different songs, and so forth. But this gradually appeared to be a none-too-rewarding approach, at least within the time I had at my disposal.

Since raï turned out to be closely linked with men's private lives, their perceptions of morality at large, and their relations with women, I opted to relate to people with whom in the course of time I could build a relationship of confidence and trust. For me this meant people with whom I sympathized and with whom I myself felt confident.

In the pages to come, I will share the information and observations that these seven people related to me.[1] They came from different social environments: some were not keen on raï, but most were. They all enriched my understanding of the social significance of raï and my discussions with them are the point of departure for the remaining chapters. By focusing on them, I use the literary device of describing social life in Oran in terms of individuals. I also use this device to illuminate the background for the generalizations I am making about social life among youth in Algeria. "The distance is often enormous between the brute material of information . . . and the final authoritative presentation of the results" (Malinowski, quoted in Clifford 1988:29). In my case, my more or less intimate experiences with a relatively few people helped me systematize the less detailed observations I had made in the numerous encounters I otherwise had. I start by describing the seven men one by one and build to general statements about the social milieu that is responsive to raï songs. The stories and interpretations of raï in this study represent a field of possibilities for how raï was perceived and used and how it influenced social life in an Algerian town such as Oran.

## Nasser

When I met Nasser, he was twenty-two years old, the oldest of five brothers, and was studying computer science at the University of Oran. I met him one day when he came to collect some books he had lent to one of the sons in the family I was living with. He had played guitar in his teens, and that interest brought us together. He many times invited me to the outskirts of the city, where he lived with his family, his grandparents, and his two uncles and their wives and children. Together they owned a villa in a huge garden with a small annex where Nasser had his quarters.

Nasser was one of a large family originating from one of the old cities of Algeria, Nedroma. Three generations had ventured into professions such as law and high school teaching. Nasser's parents (who were cousins), both of whom had university degrees, had returned to Nedroma, his father having opened a law office. His grandfather had arrived in Oran in the 1950s, working at a menial white-collar job in a French enterprise. At that time he had two small rooms in the overcrowded El Hamri (one of the popular areas of Oran), where he and his wife raised eight children. After 1962, they moved out of the area and subsequently succeeded in getting hold of the house where they now lived.

The old couple had made the pilgrimage to Mecca and were shown great respect, but this did not prevent an open attitude on the part of his uncles and aunts toward Nasser, who could invite friends to his house and maintain privacy in the annex. The family was firmly anchored in Nedroma social life, while being open to liberal and intellectual values emanating from France. Nasser's uncles and cousins fasted during the month of Ramadan, but most were closer to the left wing than to the Koran, except for an uncle who had turned Islamist while studying in the United States.

Nasser spent most of his time studying. He played tennis twice a week and otherwise spent his spare time with friends, most of them cousins, plus the girlfriends he attracted. He had spent several holidays abroad in Spain and France with his parents and had once gone on his own to visit an uncle (a pharmacist) in Paris. Most summers he rented a house with his cousins near the sea outside Oran, where they spent their days playing volleyball on the beach and sometimes going to a local disco in the evening.

Nasser was brought up with *andalus* music, Nedroma being one of the centers of this genre. However, it did not turn out to be his greatest musical interest. He went to the major *andalus* performances, but this was, he said, mainly to meet his friends and to enjoy looking at the beautiful women present.

Nasser mostly listened to French pop or American funk and disco. The annex allowed his home to become a central meeting place for a group of young men and their girlfriends. Sometimes he arranged disco parties at his place, with cake and lemonade. Most boys—from the university—would attend the party with their girlfriends, who stuck close to their men and did not dance with others without their boyfriends' explicit permission. Several girls would put on makeup when they arrived at the house, and some changed in order to look more risqué. At six o'clock in the afternoon—by which time the teenage girls had to be home—they changed back to a "public" outfit.

Nasser seldom bought or listened to raï, but it was played at the parties I attended, mostly in instrumental versions. He explained why:

> Raï can be good at parties because the rhythm makes you feel like dancing. It is not the same with disco music. When you play raï, people really get into the dancing. When you play Western music, there are fashions to follow. There are new dances coming up, where you have to learn the steps. You are not free. With raï you lift the arms. You make the hips move and you go for it. It's natural, we've been raised with it.

But most of the time funk and disco were played, and the youngsters would dance as couples. When raï (or Moroccan music) was played, they would dance more individually or in a circle.

Nasser did not listen to raï when he was on his own:

> The sound is important. I like to hear classical music with a good sound system, and raï at a party. But to listen to raï, no. I listen to Western music, something relaxing, but with a nice sound. I like to listen to something that evokes memories, and since I do not listen to raï, it does not make me recall anything. I am used to hearing Western music, but at parties the most important thing is to have a good sound so that we can have fun. When you say that a party was nice, you think first of all of the sound, the loudspeakers, and after that you think of the music.

## Mustapha

The first time I met Mustapha was in a cafe in the center of town, where he was sharing a table with Kader, whom I already knew. Like so many times before, sharing a table with a newcomer meant engaging in conversation. When people realized that I was European, the discussion often ventured into matters such as the conditions in Algeria—the beauty of the country, its natural riches, and the corruption of the elite which had ruined it all.

Mustapha was twenty years old at the time and had for the third time sat the examination for the General Certificate of Education without success. He had spent one year unemployed with no illusions of finding anything reasonable to do except by means of personal relations. Actually, at the end of the year, an acquaintance of his father helped him get into a technical school.

Mustapha lived in the center of the city. In the early 1970s his father and mother had arrived in Oran from Tlemcen, their hometown. His father, a civil servant, had been transferred from one division to another of a state company and had installed his family in a six-room flat. The family had no economic problems at that time even though it was not as well off materially and educationally as Nasser's family. The family's biggest problem was to find housing and jobs for the grown children.

Mustapha was the youngest of the children, all of whom lived with their parents. The oldest brother, who did not have a diploma but nevertheless had a white-collar job in a state-owned company, was married and had one son. Their oldest sister was also living there, following her divorce. Another brother, twenty-nine years old, was establishing himself as an independent electronic engineer. A third was employed in the gas complex of Arzew, where he had been trained for two and a half years. Finally, a fourth brother, who had passed his General Certificate of Education, was unemployed and had not been accepted into further education.

During his period of unemployment, Mustapha gradually lost the energy for bodybuilding, the sport he had been following for four years. He started doing bodybuilding, he told me, after reading in a magazine that muscles make men. Otherwise, he spent his time with his male friends, most of them school acquaintances, who would come into the city center in the evening.

Mustapha had never been abroad. He spent his summers at the seaside with his parents and uncles in a house owned by his extended family, close to the Moroccan border. Mustapha did once have a girlfriend, but no sexual experiences, a fact he did not hide. At the end of my stay in Oran, he fell in love with a cousin on a summer visit from Belgium, with whom he intended to discuss whether they could agree a common future. Otherwise, he prayed five times a day with his father in the local mosque. Even though he was critical of the regime, as everybody was at the time, he was not politically involved, but rather a firm believer. We spent many hours together during which he would explain the beauties of his faith, but first and foremost (like many Algerians) the scientific validity and rationality of Islam.

Like Nasser, Mustapha was not interested in *andalus,* the music of his town of origin, which he mainly heard at family weddings. Mustapha liked Western music: Sandra, ABBA, Boney M., but also raï, although it was mainly his elder brother who brought raï cassettes home. However, it was not all kinds of raï music he listened to:

> Most of the time I listen to Western music. I don't understand what they sing, but I always follow the music. When I find some beautiful music, I listen to it even though I don't understand it. For ex-

> ample, I don't listen to Khaled, but nevertheless I listened to his latest cassette when my brother brought it home. This was because he had used modern instruments, and there is the rap style, disco and all; but I am not fond of Khaled himself.

The record he referred to was Khaled's Barclay record. Otherwise, he listened to recordings from raï's synthesizer period, and mostly to singers of his own age such as Hasni and Nasrou.

Mustapha made another important distinction in his musical tastes. There was clean (*nqī*) raï, and another raï, which was not clean. He rejected the latter, and he certainly would not listen to it in the presence of his family. For Nasser, such considerations were not important at all, since he did not have any interest in raï. But for Mustapha, the difference made a difference.

## Hasni

I met Hasni one of the first days I was in Oran. I had chosen a certain restaurant because it was cheap and clean. Hasni was working there part time to help his uncle. Hasni was crazy about raï and could sing most of the latest hits.

When I met him, he was twenty-six years old and working as a clerk in a state company. In the evenings he was studying for a School of Commerce exam. His father was from a village between Oran and Mostaghanem and had caused his son many problems. The father had been in "the milieu"—that is, he had spent a good deal of money on drinking and women, and the family had had to move a number of times due to their poor economic situation. When Hasni was twenty, the situation of the family improved. His father stopped drinking and started praying, and a brother-in-law found him a menial job in a high school. A sister of his father offered the family one room in her house in the village, and little by little the family managed to save enough money to obtain a three-room flat. Here Hasni, the oldest child in the family, had a home base with his brother and three sisters (none of them had high school certificates).

Hasni's situation was, however, less critical than it might seem to be thanks to his mother's relatives. His maternal grandfather, who came from Mostaghanem, managed the restaurant he had worked in as a waiter during the colonial period. He had found a huge apartment for his family in the center of town. At his death, the eldest son became the leader of the family and ran the restaurant with a brother. Both lived in the apartment with their families, while their three sisters, who had all gone to school, were married, one of them being Hasni's mother. Two others were in France.

Hasni had to a large extent been raised by his uncles. When I knew him, he would stay at their place during the week, going home to his parents on weekends. He was a firm believer in the qualities of Islam, but he had not succeeded in praying regularly for more than a month at a time, and he was opposed to the politics of the FIS. Otherwise, he spent the evening in front of the television (the family had a satellite dish, as did Nasser's and Mustapha's families) or with a group of young men from his local area, talking and smoking hashish. On the weekends, he would smoke, drink, and play cards with locals in the village. Although he had a wide network of acquaintances, he often said that it was impossible to trust anyone and that he had no friends, a fact he would express in the short poems he wrote.

He had twice been to Toulouse to visit his family, but otherwise one of his great pleasures was to spend the summer with a "French" cousin who brought him clothes and who also had a car. Hasni was a great seducer. During rush hour, he would go for a walk in the streets and often succeeded in making contacts. Sometimes this led him to take a room in a hotel—managed by an acquaintance of his—to spend the night in private company. When I met him, he had no positive things to say about women's moral or intellectual qualities. Later he met a woman with whom he fell deeply in love, an experience which changed his attitude. Little by little he succeeded in getting the consent of his parents to marry her (at first his mother's). But when I left Oran, he had a big problem. His father was in charge of the family's bank account, in which Hasni's monthly salary was deposited. The father, although he had abandoned his drinking habits, had not lost his taste for luxury, foreign cigarettes, and good food, which he bought for himself. Thus Hasni did not know how to obtain enough money to buy the furniture for the bedroom and jewels for his wife, and to pay for the wedding party.

Hasni would listen to Western music such as Whitney Houston, Phil Collins, and Rock Voisine, but mostly he listened to raï. He was keen on all the raï singers and most of the songs, but he listened mainly to new releases. At family weddings there would be raï or Moroccan music. Hasni explained that it was all right to listen to raï in the company of his family at a wedding, but not in other settings:

> In front of my father, no, I'll tell you right away, I cannot listen to music in front of my father, except for Ahmed Wahby, Blawi el

Houari, and Abdelhalim, Umm Kulthoum, Warda [stars of the Egyptian song tradition]. But the raï people, Boutaïba Sghir, no, because of the words. . . . It is not considered very appropriate unless there is a wedding. In a wedding you can hear it with the family, the father, the mother sitting there. They don't care because it is a wedding for all. OK, the mother supports her children, either the daughter or the son—she stands by them, but the father, what does he want? He wants to see a boy, a young man, he wants to see his son a real man. . . . So being a man himself, he considers raï to involve debauchery, alcohol, beer. It is used for drinking, to get drunk, to smoke hashish, to get a woman, to forget the future. The idea of the father is that as long as his son listens to raï he will waste his youth. Yet he knows I do it. He knows I listen to raï. He knows I love raï. He knows I write raï, but sometimes you are serious and sometimes you are not: *shwiyya rabbi, shwiyya galbi,* a little for my God, a little for my heart. . . . You do like this and you do like that, you don't say your prayers and you believe in God, you believe in God and you don't pray. That's how it is, raï. It is all I like. . . . When I listen to raï it does something to me. It reminds me of things. It reminds me of old memories. It is as if I talk to myself.

## Djillali

I met Djillali one day I when went to meet Ali. Ali took him along because he knew Djillali wanted to go to Europe and was interested in meeting a European so he could find out how to get a visa and learn more about what Europe was like. For his age (twenty-four years), Djillali had several big problems. He had lived all his life in a flat in one of the popular parts of Oran that surrounded the city center. The area consisted mainly of small houses in narrow streets (two or three rooms opening on a courtyard, a *ḥawsh*), or two- to three-story houses with one- or two-room flats opening on to a common courtyard in between large houses built before independence. It was in such a house that Djillali lived until it one day started to fall in. Such cases were becoming more and more frequent in Algeria while I was there. Djillali and his family consequently lived in a tent for nine months before they succeeded in obtaining a three-room flat on the outskirts of Oran in an area of newly constructed prefabricated houses.

Djillali was the oldest of four children (one brother and two sisters were still in school). His father came from Annaba; he had worked in

France for thirty years and had married there. He went back to Algeria in the mid-1960s and married Djillali's mother, who was half the age of her husband. Djillali had no contact with his half-sisters in France or with his uncles on his father's side. Apparently, they were rather well off, living in Annaba. On his mother's side, there were two unmarried uncles working in menial jobs and three aunts, two of whom were widows.

Djillali left school at sixteen and received training as a warehouseman, but he did not obtain a job and remained unemployed. He spent most of his time thinking of how to get to Europe. He had once worked in a Spanish vineyard, but in May 1991 Spain started demanding entry visas. While I was in Oran, Djillali succeeded in getting into France illegally through Spain. However, he was caught in Lyon and put in prison for three months before being deported to Spain. There he was caught again during police raids preceding the Barcelona Olympics and was escorted by the police to the boat.

His days were now spent in the same way as a number of young men I met. In the morning, he went down to the city center by foot (which took him half an hour), where he spent some time with former neighbors and did some shopping for his mother at the market. He would then return home by foot. In the afternoon he would sleep and then do some physical training. He had earlier liked judo but had lost his enthusiasm. After that he would go back to town to have coffee in a cafe known as "the unemployeds' cafe" because the coffee cost half a dinar less than elsewhere. In the evening he spent time in front of the television or smoking a joint outside. Sometimes he saved money to buy a bottle of wine for Thursday night, "to forget his problems for a while."

Like Hasni, he had many acquaintances or comrades, but he only counted one as his friend. Unlike Hasni, he had not had any girlfriends on a regular basis. His first sexual experience had been in a brothel. Sometimes he would date girls he met casually, but while I was there without any great success. Most of the time he did not actively seek contact with the opposite sex.

Djillali often talked about politics and what he read in the newspaper or saw on television (his family had not yet acquired a satellite dish). He voted for the FIS so that they could "settle" accounts with the regime. He wanted to pray but did not because, he said, he was drinking and had too many problems, and he did not want to be a hypocrite.

Djillali was knowledgeable about raï, which he listened to (as well as to Western music) at friends' places, at weddings, and on cassettes he sometimes bought. He explained how raï told "about the circulation of our society." But at home he was even more strict than Hasni: "I don't listen to raï at home. Some people can. There are some songs you can listen to, where they have cleaned up the words, but in others they haven't."

## Kader

Kader (twenty-three) knew Djillali and Ali. He lived in the local area where Djillali and Ali had grown up. I met him one evening when Ali, at my request, had invited raï fans to discuss their points of view with me over a glass of tea outside Kader's house. The latter lived in a *ḥawsh* with three rooms, a small kitchen, and a courtyard his family shared with another house. His father, who was seventy, had retired. He had done a number of unspecialized jobs, first in his hometown, Tiaret, then for five years in France. In 1954 he returned to Tiaret and married Kader's mother, and then moved to Oran, where he worked in a garage.

In Kader's house lived an older brother (who worked as a ticket inspector for the bus company), his wife, and their three small children. Another older brother was unmarried and unemployed, doing some occasional jobs as a house painter. A younger brother had left school at the age of fifteen, like Kader. Both of them did some trading on the black market. Otherwise, Kader had four sisters, all of them married. One of them turned out to be the only one in the family to obtain a General Certificate of Education. She later succeeded in obtaining employment with Air Algeria and married a doctor.

However, Kader's situation was more problematic. He had left school early, done minor jobs, and ended up preferring the freer conditions on the black market, doing what was called *trabendo*. This activity could be at least as remunerative as the minimum wages offered in town, and for a long period Kader went regularly to Morocco to buy children's clothes. However, he was not a skilled salesman. He stopped traveling to Morocco, disgusted by the bribery needed to cross the border. When I met him, he was satisfied with selling goods that were provided to him by people traveling abroad or simply selling minor goods offered to him "on commission."

Like Djillali, Kader could not envisage how to create a future of his own. He was not earning enough to make any significant savings. His only hope was to get to Europe and join the large number of other young men from his local area. Kader was also persuaded that he would find true love in Europe. He had had several experiences with women in his teens, but when I knew him, he mostly expressed disgust for women.

He often returned to the story of how his first great love had betrayed him, and even though a good many women showed an interest in him, to which he was sensitive, he did not, except once, respond to any invitations.

Kader's everyday routine consisted in going to "work" in the morning, taking his goods to one end of rue de la Bastille (in the center of town), close to the food market. In the afternoon he would sleep and then do some physical training. Like Djillali, he had lost the energy for more organized training, in his case, karate. Around five or six o'clock he would go down to the city center for coffee. Like many of his acquaintances, he did not like to stay in his local area because of all the problems, as he said, and of too many people being there. Kader never seemed to have any particularly close friends, although he had many acquaintances. Once a week he would go out of Oran with neighbors his own age, to the beach or to a small park, as he said, "to cheer himself up" and find some peace. Otherwise, he did nothing. He had never been abroad, but once he had played the *mizān* in a raï group in the cabarets and at weddings, an experience which had also "disgusted" him because of quarrels in the group over money.

Kader had a good knowledge of raï music and a weakness for the songs of Farid el Atrache (the great Egyptian singer and movie star). Otherwise, he had followed in the footsteps of his father and eldest brother, who five years before had started to go regularly to a mosque known to be close to the FIS. Kader went there every Friday. He was generally in favor of the FIS and their criticisms of what he thought was a corrupt regime, but this did not prevent him from being up to date with raï music.

> Sometimes my father listens to raï, but my older brother doesn't like it. Sometimes my father leaves the room when my younger brothers listen to it. Sometimes he says nothing. He's like that. Like me he prefers Khaled, the voice. He says he's superior. There are people praying who listen to raï and there are people who listen to raï in front of their parents and there are those who don't. People are not alike. I don't listen to raï every day, only when a new cassette comes out.

## Ali

Ali (twenty-eight years old) lived in the same area as Djillali and Kader. I met him one day in a taxi on my way home. The lack of public transport meant that people competed for and shared taxis. We made small talk until Ali discovered that we were being followed by another car. Twice we stopped in an attempt to lose it, but without success. The second time Ali went out to ask the three men in the other car who they were, but they turned around without answering. This led to a discussion of my nationality, the secret police, and the purpose of my stay, from which it emerged that for a number of years Ali had worked for a raï publisher.

Ali's father came from a village near Aïn Temouchent and had arrived in Oran in the late 1950s to work in the local brewery. He had since stopped working, and Ali was now the one in charge of the family. An elder brother, living in northern France, was unemployed but nevertheless managed to send valuable contributions to the family in foreign currency. In Ali's *ḥawsh* lived his parents, two brothers, both unemployed, and a divorced sister and her child.

Ali had started his working life in the SNTF, the state railways, and had been a frequent guest in the bars of Oran. Here, he met a publisher who at that time was making his first efforts in the raï circuit. One year before my arrival, however, Ali had dropped the raï business, and a noticeable change was taking place in his life. He had started working on the black market, but on a much larger scale than Kader, importing Italian clothes and shoes on regular trips to Naples and reselling them to drapers' shops in Oran or using his connections to sell them on commission to Kader, among others.

After quitting his former occupation, Ali also started praying. "Before I was constantly drunk, and I was never at home," he explained. "Now that I am praying, I don't drink, and therefore I do nothing." When I met him Ali was not interested in politics, but he gradually drew closer to the ideas of the FIS. Finally he spent most of his time with the organized FIS group in his local area. He frequently criticized people for not practicing their religion 100 percent—that is, for not praying regularly, and doing things like going to the beach to look for women, while professing their faith in Islam and their support of the FIS.

Ali had been to France on several occasions for short pleasure trips. Now he spent most of his time providing for his family, accompanying them on medical visits, and so forth. He would often say that he trusted nobody but the people of the FIS. When he was on his own, like Kader he would leave the local area. Most often he would fetch his girlfriend, who worked at the hospital. He had met her after starting to pray, but he did not know what the future would bring. She was from a rich Kabyle family, so Ali did not think he would be able to marry her.

Ali was a great connoisseur of raï, the music he had listened to most in his life. He said with regret that he had even listened to raï in the presence of his father. But now he rarely listened to music at all. One day he told me: "They [the FIS] sent a delegation to Saudi Arabia to consult the real learned men [*ʿulama*], and they said that it is not only raï that is forbidden. All music is *ḥrām*, Marc, there is nothing to discuss."

## Houari

Houari (twenty-nine years old) had also been in raï circles. In fact, shortly before I met him he had been interviewed in the local press about the way raï had attracted so many youngsters at the time of its appearance. One day a journalist I had known since my time in Paris pointed him out to me in a cafe.

Houari was, as he said, a true Oranian, that is, a true city dweller, a fact that for many youngsters in Oran was emphasized as important. His father was born in Medina Jdida in the heart of Oran, and his mother arrived with her parents from a village close to Maghnia in the 1940s. His father had worked in the mines of northern France for three years and had married in the mid-1950s. Little by little, he had succeeded in establishing a prosperous grocery store. In the mid 1980s, Houari's parents (now with nine children) moved to a four-room flat in a new development on the outskirts of Oran.

Houari worked in the National Water Supply Company as a technician, but four months before I left Oran, he was dismissed along with several of his colleagues. Although he never had been abroad, he was now trying to find a way to leave Algeria by any means. Houari was the second child in the family. One older and one younger brother worked with their father. A younger brother, the only member of the family who followed the FIS, was an engineering student. Three sisters and two brothers were still at school.

Like Ali, Houari had spent most of his free time in the bars and cabarets of Oran, coming home only to sleep. He had stopped that kind of living now: "I had to choose which path in life to take," but he did not, like Ali, start praying for that reason. He spent most of his free time with a group of old friends from Medina Jdida, including two cousins and a brother. They had shared many experiences in their lives, he explained to me. Now they had involved themselves in the left-wing circles of the town. Not only did they frequently go to the cafes, where local intellectuals held forth, but Houari's dream was to write a book on raï. He had a poetic sensitivity. Already in school he had earned pocket money by writing love letters for his classmates, and he continued developing the art of writing love poetry in French.

Houari listened to some Western music, but mostly to raï and *wahrāni*. At home he did not listen to raï in the presence of his father, whom he described as a strict Muslim. Like the others, he seems to have had a close relationship with his mother. Nevertheless, when friends visited him at home and the music was playing, the door was closed to the female members of the family.

## The City and Styles

Djillali, Kader, and Ali knew one another and sometimes had coffee together downtown; but while I was in Oran their relations did not appear to be intimate friendships so much as the consequence of having spent a long time in the same neighborhood. The three did not know Nasser, Mustapha, Hasni, or Houari, except for Kader, who sometimes went to the same cafe as Mustapha. Otherwise they were all strangers to one another, each having his own networks, in which I became involved. Sometimes they saw me in company with some of the others, on which occasions they chose not to greet me. It was often only afterward, when they told me, "Yesterday I saw you with someone here and there," that I knew about it. At other times they chose to greet me and the person I was with, but later expressed "wonder" at the kind of people I went around with or warnings not to trust anyone.

What they all had in common, however, was that their teens had been accompanied by the growth of raï. Also, they all lived in a city which fifteen years after independence had seen a tremendous turnover of inhabitants and demographic growth (See Benkheira 1982; Brabrant 1975, 1977).

Before independence Oran had a predominantly European population. In fact, when the French took over the city in 1831 the local inhabitants were expelled. Only in 1845 was a city planned for the native population and surrounding tribes in what the French would call Village Nègre (Tinthoin 1953), while the Algerian population called it Medina Jdida. During the colonial period the local area was an important part of Oran, with a high concentration of Algerians. Its *taḥtaha,* or central square, was famous for its cafes and entertainment, and still in the early 1990s Medina Jdida was a bustling marketplace in the city.

By 1930 Oran had grown from its original 4,300 inhabitants (Lespes 1938) to a town of approximately 130,000, including a Muslim population of 30,000. In the course of time, the city attracted a number of immigrants, in particular from Spain, and it also included an important naturalized Jewish population. It was only in the 1930s that the impact of the Muslim population began to be felt as a consequence of the world depression, which forced a pauperized rural population into the town. Between 1926 and 1936 the Muslim population rose from 20,000 to 46,177. In 1948 there were 82,247, and in 1953 there were 100,000 (Tinthoin 1953:11). At the end of the war of liberation, which uprooted even more Algerians from the uplands, there were 220,000.

Algerian independence marked a new era for Oran. Within the first two years, two hundred thousand Europeans left the city and one hundred thousand Algerians entered it (Brabrant 1975:321). Thirty-nine thousand lodgings were redistributed (Semmoud 1986:130), which led to a profound recomposition of the social tissue of the town. From Les Planteurs, a shanty town around the ravine of Ras el Aïn, and from the overcrowded areas of Medina Jdida and El Hamri, the Algerians moved to the historic early center of the town, Sid el Houari and the Jewish Derb (both of them today close to a state of ruin). Others went to the Franco-Spanish working-class belt surrounding the town center—Eckmühl, Plateau, St. Pierre, St. Eugène, and Bel Air. The city center itself became dominated by a bourgeoisie of military officers, government employees, and a population originating from Tlemcen, one of the few cities in Algeria historically to have had an established entrepreneurial and educated elite.

Later, a further class differentiation of the local areas tended to appear, in the 1970s through state management of the housing estate, and in the 1980s through the privatization of housing and state-financed apartments for government officials, university employees, and entrepreneurs. But still the local areas of Oran did not have a uniform class structure. In the 1990s, within the same housing block people could be found from a variety of origins, with different socioeconomic possibilities. Even in the center of the town, newcomers of lower class origins had established themselves in rue de la Bastille, actually one of the first places, together with Medina Jdida, where raï cassettes appeared on the market in the late 1970s.

The whole population of Oran experienced the general disintegration of housing conditions. In 1966 there were 340,000 inhabitants in Oran, and in 1987 there were 930,000 (ONS 1988). In 1984 it was estimated that 60 percent of people in Oran lived in nuclear families and 40 percent lived in extended families (Fodil 1987:231), and that the number of persons per lodging was between seven and nine. At the time of my fieldwork an acute need was felt for housing construction and renovation.

Oran also went from being a city with a European majority to being a thoroughly Algerian–Muslim city. This was not so much in terms of state policies, which had changed street names in Oran, but in terms of spatial segregation of the sexes and the duality of inside and outside, family life versus public life. For Mustapha, Hasni, Djillali, Kader, and Ali, this meant that most of their meetings with men of their age took place outside the home. This was less the case for Nasser, due to his better accommodation, and for Houari, whose family agreed that a room should be at his disposal in the daytime for meetings with his friends.

In general, a man from outside the home seldom entered it directly, whether a *ḥawsh* in the popular area of El Hamri or a tenth-floor apartment in St. Eugène. A member of the family would enter before him to prepare the way. If the "stranger" wanted to contact a friend on his own, he would shout or whistle from the street or send in a young (and therefore innocent) child with a message in order to make his presence known. Dwellings in Oran are visually closed to the outside, though I was often amazed at how open they were in terms of their inhabitants' awareness of sounds on the outside.

Once inside, the stranger entered directly into a room reserved for the sons of the family. If there was no such room, there were few visits by nonfamily members. In most cases, the son's acquaintances just met the father for a polite greeting; otherwise the latter would stay out of his son's affairs. In many families, the visitor would be presented to the mother and indulge in small talk with her. In several families, brothers or cousins near in age shared their free time together. But in others (as was the case for Hasni and Kader), the brothers lived separate lives, the younger following the orders of the elder.

Sisters or sisters-in-law kept to themselves, occasionally knocking on the door to give the brother a message in the doorway or venturing in to serve the tea. Frequently they would hide themselves away completely, as when a musician's wife hid in the cupboard while I was being shown around his new apartment, or when I stayed with a local journalist for a week on my first trip to Algeria. He was known as the only one in his local area to wear his beard "Quartier Latin style," while his brothers, members of the FIS, had beards in the "style of the Prophet." For the whole week everything was arranged so that I would not encounter his brothers' wives. This worked except for one morning, when a woman suddenly stood in front of me while I was washing in the courtyard. We were both equally surprised and confused until she jumped behind a sheet that was hanging out to dry and waited until I had finished my ablutions.

There were, of course, a number of families who did not take things to such extremes. In Nasser's family there was a free mixing of guests of both genders. In several families with few rooms at their disposal, little notice would be taken of one's presence once one had been introduced because of a common understanding that males and females belonged each to their separate spheres.

Nevertheless, things did happen in varying degrees indicating that the presence of a male stranger might endanger the peace of the family, or more precisely its females. Outside, in restaurants and at some public events, certain spaces were prohibited for single males and reserved "for families," that is, for men with wives or women without male company. Even in the recording studios the notion of separation was upheld when female singers recorded. Although regarded as transgressors of such norms by the simple fact that they sang in public, they did not—contrary to the male singers—leave the recording room at all during the session. Their men (managers or lovers) moved freely among the male musicians in the recording engineer's booth.

But although the Muslim city had taken over the European town, this did not mean that the West was absent, and not only because Western music could frequently be heard. As with raï music, Western motifs were inscribed in persons and in the tissue of the city. A friend of Houari "looked like Humphrey Bogart"; a singer was called "Johny" [Halliday] in the 1970s because he played the guitar; the area where Nasser lived was called "Hollywood"; and Kader called his area "Chinatown." One day, while waiting for an overcrowded bus, Houari laughed at all the "Indians" climbing up into it. Djillali likened his tented camp to Brazil, and when the army Islamists started their killings in the spring of 1992, Oran was for a long time called "Switzerland," a neutral area.

The West was also present in the sense that one of the most frequent introductory statements made to me was that in Algeria there was nothing, *wālu*. Nothing to do, nowhere to go, no way to have fun—implying that there was plenty of those things somewhere else, that is, in the West. These statements would be further elaborated by massive declarations that Algeria had no future, that there was no way to make a living or develop individual capacities, whether as a sportsman, a musician, or a student in whatever subject you might imagine.

In fact, few amusements were offered in Oran. Of four youth centers, only two were open to the general public. Of the twenty-two officially functioning cinemas, most were in a rather shabby state and showed a limited repertoire of videos. Sports seemed to be the most common way of spending free time. In summer there were the beaches, of which one was called "La Cinque," after the French television channel, because it was there that lots of girls and wealthy youths could be found displaying the latest fashion in bathing suits.

During Ramadan some discos were open. At other times, there were also the cabarets and dancing restaurants (which Djillali and Hasni also visited), but they were expensive and, when I was there, were considered dangerous. There were also bars, often "stages" for a performance of generosity—rounds being offered to acquaintances or newcomers at other tables and leading to heavy consumption of wine or beer. These were too expensive for most people, who chose instead to buy a bottle of wine now and then or, more often, to smoke hashish, which had become increasingly available since the opening of the Moroccan border in 1988.

Despite the lack of opportunities in terms of leisure activities, there was in Oran a keen awareness of fashion and an interest in clothes and perfume. If money was available, men went out together to buy clothes, commenting on and flattering each other's choices. In the summer of 1991, loads of baseball caps and pirated copies of Ray Ban sunglasses were being offered on the black market.

However, in Oran it was difficult to find styles of dress that signaled the existence of any sub- or counterculture in the manner described in literature on Western youth (see Fornäs et al. 1984, Frith 1983, Hebdige 1979, Willis 1978). It was not the style of clothes that differentiated the seven young men, but rather that men like Kader, for example, possessed only a few clothes and had to share them with his elder brother.

However, there were differences in appearances between young men in Oran. The most significant were the Islamists, who wore *qamīṣ* (a long day shirt) and grew beards (in honor of the Prophet). This style of dress was not specific to any youth or street culture but was characteristic of all age groups within the Islamist movement. Moreover, there were many young men in Oran (such as Djillali, Kader, and Ali, and to a certain extent Mustapha and Hasni), who, although they were not pro-FIS, did not consider themselves to be opposed to the Islamists. They talked of them as "real Muslims," and they knew that their style signaled among other things that the wearer had forsaken women, music, and alcohol for the benefit of "a pure, sacred life." The *imām* (leader of the congregational prayer) in the part of town where Kader, Djillali, and Ali lived in was called a saint precisely because he had never done anything, not even looked at a woman.

Young men like Houari, Ali, Kader, Djillali, and Hasni, however, did think of themselves as being in opposition to other categories of youth, especially people originating from Tlemcen or the Kabylie. They were known not for any different style of dress, but for having a dialect or language which differed from the Oran dialect, plus a musical tradition of their own. According to the stereotypes, the Kabyles, because they were industrialists and hotel owners, and the Tlemcenians, because they were highly educated, possessed an advantageous social position in Oran, keeping to themselves and not marrying their women off to non-Kabyles or non-Tlemcenians.

On the other hand, there were the the *tshi-tshis,* in opposition to whom Mustapha also defined himself, and to whom Nasser (laughingly) said he belonged. The expression was synonymous with rich, spoiled youngsters who were snobbish, drove their fathers' cars, went abroad on holidays, and imitated Western lifestyles. According to the stereotype, they avoided military service, were physically weak, and obtained women only because of the money and cars they possessed. Once they got hold of a woman, they let her go around as she pleased. All in all, they had become effeminate through their imitation of the West and their possession of Western consumer goods.

In this sense, they resembled a fourth category in opposition to whom Nasser also defined himself—young men, many of whom had visited Europe, who wore earrings, long hair, or ponytails. Young men I knew tended to dislike this fashion. They said that every man was free to do as he liked, but that they did not know the context in which Western men dressed like that, and that it was not good for a man to imitate a woman. Michael Jackson was not a favorite in Oran.

Nor were homosexuals. They were not to be associated with; they were feared or despised. One explanation was that since God had not created men like that, they were deliberate perverts. According to another explanation, they were said to have been corrupted by watching too many X-rated films showing intercourse "against nature." In a third and milder version, they were said to be people who had had too much contact with women, for example, being raised in families without a male authority figure.

Fundamentally, most of these categories were established according to notions of access to material power and of gender; thus a link was made between consumption and sexuality. These categories also incorporated some features of raï listeners themselves. A man should be strong, in good shape physically, and open and generous toward others rather than keeping to himself or excluding others from his life. Mention of the expression *mrubla* made people laugh with pleasure, for it implied gangs of youths, staying awake at night, chasing women, fighting other groups, and drinking out of the same small glass in good company.

A man was supposed to be active and prepared to defend his rights and not to let other people criticize him without reason. One way of introducing newcomers into the group was precisely by inverting this ideal, by saying for example, "Look, this man is a thief," "this man only loves money," "never trust this man," whereupon people would laugh and recognize this as a game that explored forbidden territory.

Another value was showing restraint. Young men dressed like the singers on cassette covers, wearing clothes in a "simple" but "nice" style, which in Algeria meant non-Algerian clothes from Spain, France, Italy, or Morocco purchased on the black market. But such an ideal did not prevent the *maryūl,* a man who enjoyed the pleasures of life, from being valued. When men "confessed" how they loved going to Morocco for drink and prostitutes or witnessed others showing off their latest mistress in public, this would lead to a discussion among others whether this made them look like fools. Frequently people concluded that they were simply men enjoying themselves and that they were free to do as they liked.

In this respect, the young men were agreeing with the widespread feeling in Oran that men should respect the autonomy of others, that they should not interfere in others' affairs. It was said that the advantage of living in Algeria was that everyone treated everyone else as equals. In public life, the notion of equality did seem to be respected, especially in encounters between people from different social strata who were unknown to one another. It also meant that people cherished and defended their sense of autonomy. A man, for example, often thought nothing of breaking an appointment if something more important came up; nor would he find it strange that a last resort in a case of insult would be a physical fight.

In many ways life in Oran was carried on like the games of the *barrāḥ* at weddings in that there was the same professed belief that no social distinction should appear. However, the opposite trend towards differentiation was real enough. In Algeria's economic crisis, this differentiation was translated into uneasiness given the difficulty in disregarding the purely economic interests that were embedded in the appearances of respect, autonomy, and the generosity of gifts (see Bourdieu 1980:200). In Oran, there was the frequent suspicion that if a stranger treated you with respect, it was because he had some ulterior motive in mind.

With regard to consumption, what all seven men and their networks had in common was their description of life in Algeria having become a jungle, with everyone protecting his own interests. They could all show you a villa in a popular local area and ask, "How do you think he got the money to pay for it?" They could show you the numbers of Mercedes driving along the sea promenade and ask, "How do you think they can afford it?" They could all tell stories, sotto voce, of how army officers used public money for private purposes. More loudly, they told about the employee of the local state-owned supermarket who kept a stock of saucepans for himself and only sold them to people from whom he expected something. And there was the official responsible for distributing places to the summer camps in the commune, who kept a number of places for himself as a strategy for finding an apartment of his own. The basic question when one was in need of something was not "Where can I get it?" but "Who do I know who has access to information about where I can get it?" or "Who owes me a favor?" There was a resemblance between everyday life and the more commercial circle of raï publishers.

For people like Kader, Djillali, and Ali, this meant a daily life that was difficult to handle. They belonged to the at least one-fifth of the active population which was unemployed of which four fifths were under thirty years of age, and 82 percent of whom had a level of education below the Middle Course (*Le Matin,* April 28, 1992). They did not have sufficiently powerful networks to create a future for themselves in the Algeria of the 1990s. While waiting, maybe to go to Europe, they involved themselves in petty commerce on the black market, which had become a central field for the redistribution of and competition for the flow of decreasing surplus value in Algeria. If men ought mostly to exchange gifts rather than look for egoistic pecuniary interests, if they ought to show respect and generosity, having coffee in the cafes remained one of the few occasions for displaying this value. In this case there was always a giver, and no accounts were kept.

While I was in Oran, a main pastime was to stay at home and watch French television, afterward discussing what had been shown. Secondhand magazines from France, drugs, sports, and fashion were also subjects of discussion. Other interests were studies (for Nasser and Mustapha), how to get to Europe (mainly for Djillali and Kader, but also for Ali and Houari), politics and religion, and, importantly, where to buy things at a good price. Finally, there were women. They were a main resource and topic of conversation in the young men's lives. There should be no mercy if someone tried to take your woman. There was a general understanding among men that they possessed such values as generosity, autonomy, and respect in their relations with the female part of town. Finally, if male strangers seemed to endanger the peace of social life in Oran with regard to women, the mere presence of the opposite sex did bring certain disturbances into male life as well. Raï songs dealt with these disturbances, which took their own form in the Algerian crisis. As such, men's notion of raï and of women were closely intertwined, as will be clear in the next chapters.

# 5

•

# Listening to Raï

In this chapter I will go into detail about how Nasser, Mustapha, Hasni, Djillali, Kader, Ali, and Houari perceived the raï songs I played for them (see Appendix 2 for the words to the songs). These interviews were conducted at the end of my stay, in the month of Ramadan and the month that followed. Nasser was interviewed at his home, Kader, Djillali, and Ali were interviewed in one of the few public parks in Oran. Mustapha was interviewed on the roof of his house, and Houari in a back room of the restaurant while he was smoking a joint. Finally, Houari was interviewed in my hotel room after Ramadan, before we set out for a joyful time in a restaurant which had a live nighttime band. The interview procedure consisted in playing a number of songs, each representing an important genre within the raï of the 1980s. Then I would ask them for their immediate thoughts about the text and music. Most of the time, they started by explaining the significance of the key phrase of the song or the ending of the song. Afterward, I questioned them more about the music, for example, if it was danceable. Then we heard the song again or went through the text I had brought along with me.

The result is that the lines have been overinterpreted and endowed with meanings that would normally pass unremarked, accredited a much greater significance than that of background music, which is often their function. An intermediate sphere was established between the daily listening of the Oranian's and the anthropologist's quest for translations of "the meaning of raï" into academic language: it is neither here nor there, but is rather some combination of both spaces.

While replaying the songs I did not seek to standardize the questions I addressed to my informants. If the temptation to create the illusion of a quantitatively representative inquiry ever existed, I nevertheless went for as open a discussion as possible in order to provoke significant insights into the social meaning of raï. Thus, where the comments of some listeners on certain subjects are missing, this is because the discussion took another direction.

In this chapter, I quote their comments on the songs at length. In this sense, the text is imbued with a quality which might resemble what has been called "polyvocal" or "dialogical" modes of authority over the text (see Clifford 1986, 1988; Dwyer 1982; Tyler 1986). However, my text is not written with these ideas in mind, nor with the idea of exposing the vulnerability of this project or the vulnerability of Western civilization (see also Marcus and Fischer 1986). My informants formulated themselves in ways my literary capacities cannot convey, and still I seek to give a glimpse of the creativity of young Algerian men. I also seek to explicate parts of my own experience of wondering and "discovery" regarding what took place in the transfer of raï songs to social life.

## **"Dīri dār"** (Make a home)[1]

The first time I heard of "Dīri dār" was in Paris at the start of my fieldwork. I had read in the press that some raï songs were considered "raw" and vulgar, and I asked the owner of a bar in the twelfth arrondissement, who at the time specialized in playing raï music, to give me the names of the hardest hitting songs. The first he mentioned was "Dīri dār," which belonged to the early repertoire of electrified raï: "words that hit people, a song that hits hard."

The song is one of the longest recordings in raï and contains many of the lines often found within the raï repertoire. It also contains a paradox for the uninitiated listener. The melody has a progressive form leading to a refrain, but the text does not take the same direction as the tune.

When I played the song to Nasser, he did not at all like what he heard:

> This goes way back in time. The sound is not at all perfect, and it has a rhythm that moves like a snail. Moreover, the use of the instruments is bad, no playing technique. They play anything, the accordion, the organ, anything. I am not well versed in music. I don't have a musical ear, but there are many errors. At times, it's a disgrace. Sometimes they use the wrong instrument or one that isn't in tune with the others.

Nasser was thus in agreement with a number of comments made in the press and elsewhere criticizing the producers severely and characterizing the sound of raï recordings as sometimes "cutting through your bones." In fact, I was told by the producer of the song that the recording took place under difficult conditions and was made in one "take." Imagine a small room with two microphones and a two-track tape recorder. The drum set and the amplifier have been placed at the back of the room, as far away from the microphones as possible. Close to a microphone is Khaled, his hands busy playing the accordion while the producer whispers the words into his ear. He has not been told to learn them by heart, and he does not understand all the sentences that are being whispered, as one can hear in line 10.

Nasser rejected all the songs I played him, as did a number of people with similar social and educational backgrounds, although from time to time they admitted that they might be moved by a song or two. Nasser did not like the sound system of raï in the broadest sense. He described the singers he had seen in Oran as "dirty" and "vulgar," and the producers as a real "mafia" in the town.

Nasser's comments support the suggestion that a history of art might be one of things valued, or if not, a history of taste (Passeron 1991 : 265). Nasser's comments brought forth imagined spaces and social settings that differed from those of the young men who were more positive toward raï. The same applied to some of the comments of Mustapha, who did not like the song either:

> Though this song is Khaled's, the first time I heard it was by [Cheb] Hamid. It was with Rachid and Fethi. They made the first modern songs with sophisticated instruments with synthesizer and all. . . . You can't dance to this song. That's because it's heavy [*tqīl*], and the instruments following the song are ancient ones, that's all; I don't like it. When I heard it the first time, it was with Hamid. I liked it very much. It was only later that I realized it was Khaled's.

Here, Mustapha was repeating what he had said about the difference he perceived between the sound of the older recordings of the 1980s and the later ones using digital synthesizer and drum machine. Although Mustapha rejected the sound of "Dīri dār"—as did Nasser, who was used to and could afford another sound—he did not reject all the songs I played for him.

As for the remaining five listeners, it turned out that "Dīri dār" had indeed once been a hit, though it never became a long-term favorite. The song did not have at all the same effect on them as it did on Nasser and

Mustapha. They were acquainted with raï's conditions of production and distribution. They seemed used to the scratches on the cassettes and seemed to approve of the informal mode of performance.

HASNI: The song is a little sad . . . it's not too good for dancing. It has a very, very slow rhythm. There are those who dance to it, but you will only find one or two on the dance floor. Those who know how to dance, they dance, but . . . it is made for listening to among friends, among colleagues, at weddings, because Khaled started playing at weddings.

DJILLALI: You can dance to this music without any problem. It's dance music, good music, pop raï. You find the drum set blending with the *darbūka,* the keyboard, and the guitar, varied instrumentation.

KADER: I like this song and everybody liked it. The style is raï reggae. You can also call it a "slow" [from French *un slow*].

ALI: I still have the music in my head. When I hear it, I feel like drinking again.

HOUARI: I don't like this song [laughing], not to put too fine a point on it. But how we danced to it. That was the time we wanted to write songs and form groups. The music is good, a little bit heavy [*tqīl*], but not very much. You can dance very, very well to it. All the numbers on this cassette were good. Benchenet recorded it too.

It is obvious that the five listeners did not agree completely in their appreciation of this song, as was the case with all the songs I discussed with them. On the other hand, none of them had any problem with the instruments or the sound. Furthermore, they contributed to Nasser's and Mustapha's verbal categorization of the music. Nasser and Hasni called it "slow"; Mustapha used the expressions "modern," "old," and "heavy"; Djillali and Kader, respectively, used the expressions "pop raï," and "raï reggae," and Houari used the term "heavy," as did Hasni. Thus we have physical expressions characterizing the music (heavy : light; slow : fast), expressions associating raï with other musical genres (pop, reggae, a "*slow*") and expressions dealing with diachrony (old : modern).

Altogether in Oran, besides the expressions raï, pop raï, and raï reggae, there was also "disco raï." These labels were often used in opposition to the acoustic urban form of raï, which was termed "old raï," or the rural form, "raï of *gaṣba*" (raï of the reed flute), "raï of the *shīkhs,*" or "raï of the *shīkha*" (raï of the old/wise men or women). These could be opposed further to the "raï of the chebs" (youngsters). Another expression was "clean raï," which, as we shall see, implied songs that did not deal overtly with the topics of alcohol and sexuality. This expression was mainly used for songs that appeared during the second half of the 1980s and was opposed to the expression "raï," which then referred mainly to cabaret songs in the early 1980s. A number of these songs could be termed *rrāy shīn* (evil/bad raï) or *rrāy tālef* (raï that leads astray). These numerous expressions indicate that music can be associated not only with sounds and instruments, but also with a wide variety of discourses such as other styles of music, categories of people, ages, social spheres, and moral conduct. Thus their description of the *musical* part of raï provides a first step in bringing raï out of its "pure" musical structure into the social world.

## Now the Words

The distance between Nasser, Mustapha, and the rest of the young men becomes obvious through their comments on the words. Again, Nasser had no sympathy for the song:

> You can understand some words, but to put them together, it's not possible . . . Maybe it talks about the social environment, of the principles of society. Maybe there is a lot of prostitution, of this and that, which jeopardizes the principles of society . . . "May the house of your mother be empty." That's an insult, it's vulgar. . . . He assigns the girl a certain position, which means describing her as a prostitute. That's what the Ricard, the alcohol, the partying is about . . . Moreover he sends out a challenge in the sense that he says to people, let her do what she wants. It's none of your business. Probably he's talking about the social surroundings. . . .

From disapproval, he suddenly relates to the challenge made by the singer. He identified the song with the singer, as Mustapha had done in his comments on the music. Thus Mustapha's rejection of the song was directed against the singer as much as the words.

> In this song he sings about a girl who had neither a house of her own nor a child. She stayed that way, a street girl. She drinks Ricard. She walks in the boulevards and all, and Cheb Khaled is giving her the advice to make a home. I cannot listen to the words in front of my father. It is because of *khla dār muk* and Ricard. You cannot listen to it with the family. You must have a little respect [*qdar*]. "*Khla dār muk*" is vulgar. It's like wishing a disaster on

someone, or on an enemy. You say "*Khla dār muk*" and you wish that his house might become empty, that he will have nothing left in his house. He will be on the streets, a vagabond. You do it with bad intention. I don't like Cheb Khaled, because he mixes everything up and there are vulgar words in most of his songs. The proof is that they never show him on television. When he is on, it's when he sings something by someone else, for example, the songs of Ahmed Wahby and all. That's it.

The other five commented on the song in a much more positive way:

DJILLALI: In this song, he's telling about the world of cabarets and parties. It's a fine song that is aimed at women who do not think about their future. You hear that he says she enjoys Ricard and she walks the boulevards. This means that she hasn't got time, she is always being invited to places, she goes to clubs, to bars, and all the time she spends the evening in men's company, with alcohol, smoking. "You were caught up by your beauty" means that when you were really beautiful, you didn't take advantage of it to get a husband and marry. "*Khla dār muk*" is a curse; someone wishes that another's house will become empty, that he has no children, nothing at all, only the walls and the roof. He curses the woman because she has spent her youth drinking, smoking, and dancing in the cabarets. While she was pretty, she used it to make eyes to the men in the clubs, and instead of marrying she ruined her health. So it's all over for her, according to what he says.

It is worth noticing that Djillali did not consider "*khla dār muk*" to be a vulgar expression, but a curse, as did Hasni, Kader, Ali and Houari. Hasni and Kader even understood *tsawwag* differently from Nasser:

HASNI: It's a very old song, where he asks the person to have a family. You have not made a home, you wanted the Ricard and to walk the boulevards. You don't have any little children. Let her strike me [*ḥrubni*]. Mind your own business. OK, he hasn't said it directly, but you can guess that it's she who hits him. "*Khla dār muk*" is a phrase you use all the time. It means that you nearly beg someone for something. The song is quite moving. He gives her advice. It's the story of a woman who hasn't been able to raise a family because she's too busy sleeping in men's arms and he finds her walking the boulevards. She works in the cabarets or she's trying to get rich industrialists. She's kind of messed up.

KADER: I like this song and everybody liked it. It talked about a woman, of her situation."You haven't made a home; you don't have any little children; you liked the Ricard and the ballads on the boulevards. Let my love strike me; it is none of your business . . . "By this he means that the woman is hitting Khaled. But he also gives her advice in making a home, to marry instead of dragging herself around the streets. I cannot hear "Ricard" and "red wine" at home.

It is therefore obvious that there were many different ways of understanding the song, not only in terms of appreciation, but also in terms of language use. Finally, there was a difference in the meaning attributed to the song depending on the individual life experiences of the listeners:

ALI: When I first heard it I liked the words and the music very much. "You didn't have a home, you didn't have little kids. You like Ricard and walking the boulevards"—on the boulevards you see a lot of things, and that hurts.

HOUARI: It's because of this and some other songs that raï became hated, because the song speaks directly. She likes the ballads on the boulevards. People always say "Look, oh, all those girls that are prostitutes." When you listen to this song you're shocked, but the real meaning is to try and warn the many young girls to take a proper path and not abuse their freedom. When he speaks about prostitution, people reject the song completely, but the song is really politically critical, and at the same time it contains advice to take the proper path—because "Ricard" and "boulevard" mean the opposite of what a young girl should do. Her road is to know how to have a home, a family, a husband, kids and all that. "*Khla dār muk*" is an expression calling someone to order. It isn't vulgar, it's an insult frequently used in order to moralize, to warn someone. It was with this song that we started to see our problems.

However, in spite of their different attitudes, there was a noticeable similarity among the seven men in the way they treated "Dīri dār" as a kind of narrative. Several times they offered a description of the song as being on the same discursive level as speech: "He sends out a challenge," "he asks the person," "it talks about . . . ," "he gives her advice," "he curses the woman." Thus they all focused on the singer, but more than that, they discussed "Dīri dār" as if it were speech.

Obviously, one reason for this peculiarity was the situation they were in, with me asking them to explain and elaborate on what they heard. But it is worth noting that there is an expressive continuity with the artistic message—words taken from the song could be used to speak about it (see Passeron 1991:259).

Nevertheless, this way of giving meaning to raï songs was repeated for all the songs I played, and it resembled the most frequent ways of describing the significance of raï in the media. Just as Djillali explained that "raï tells about the circulation of our society," an extremely frequent comment on raï (among both its supporters and opponents, as well as in the press) was that it "says something about the problems of society," "about the problems of the young," or "about social life." Other frequent comments were: "When I hear this or that singer, it is as if I hear my own story," or "when I hear that song it makes me remember a time when . . ." Thus people tended to represent raï songs in the way that Willis has criticized as a vulgar approach to pop music, that is, "treating the songs as ciphers arbitrarily signifying social events" (1978:40). But as we shall see, the seven listeners did not succeed in creating a complete narrative out of the song.

"Dīri dār" mainly deals with women, or rather with men's relations with women, and here the notion of *maḥna* is central. Nasser wondered:

> What is *maḥna?* I thought *maḥna* was a woman; maybe it was his lover; maybe it was a pain; maybe it was a joy. I never succeeded in understanding it . . . Some say it's a person, a woman; some say it's his love. . . . Sometimes, when you say *maḥna,* you mean effort. He makes an effort in order to achieve something. It's the sweat, that's *maḥna.* Others say no, it's happiness, you see?

According to Djillali: "*Maḥna,* that's adventure . . . The real meaning of the word is 'desire,' but the Algerians use this phrase to express the idea of an adventure full of problems." Thus they both came quite close to more lexicographic descriptions of the word as referring to a "carousel" or "drinking bout," but also "[hard] trials," "the beloved person," "the object of desire" or "the object of the lover's torments" (see Beaussier [1887] 1958, Virolle-Souibès 1988b:205). Houari followed the same line of thought: "*Maḥna* is the body itself, with its sufferings, its problems and worries, the peace of the body. You might also say it's a woman." Here, he was linking up with Hasni, Kader, Ali, and Mustapha who—to use Ali's words—said: "*Maḥna,* that's the woman."

The *maḥna* is the key topic in raï. "Dīri dār" and the *maḥna* concept deal with a number of men's attitudes about and relations with women.

KADER: She must not believe that her beauty will last forever. What she has is not eternal, she will not live in eternity.

DJILLALI: She was caught up by her beauty. She has sold her jewelry. You know, the jewelry, that's her beauty; she hasn't kept it. She gave herself away to others, and she didn't stay respectable like a real woman. She can be in company with any tradesman or industrialist, drink with him, spend evenings with him, and because of all that she is tired out.

ALI: *Ḥdāydak,* that's the jewelry . . . *saḥḥit,* that's the man's strength. It's a woman who thinks she's somebody but who'll then regret it.

However, in other verses, the description of the woman changes.

MUSTAPHA: The great eye is fatal, but he doesn't die. It means that she's fascinating, her gaze at him is fascinating, and she's so beautiful. "'*Aynīk naymīn*" and "'*aynik na'asīn*" means the same. It's about sleepy eyes. It's erotic.

HASNI: The big eyes, they kill . . . not in a literal sense, in another way.

KADER: He speaks about women who have beautiful eyes. They kill you . . . and the meaning of "your eyes are like mine" is that they are weary. It's sexual. The eyes are like those that Farid el Atrache sings about.

DJILLALI: The great eye is something really beautiful. It stands for a very beautiful woman. The man who falls in love with her will die [he laughs]. It means that people admire her so much that they fall ill. Each time they look at her, they fall ever more in love.

ALI: The great eye certainly stands for a beautiful woman, and "*shuft shufa,*" for sure that means he's seen a woman who looks like his girlfriend. "*Na'asīn*" and "*naymīn*" are similar expressions. Her eyelids are a little lowered, as when someone smokes *kif* [hashish]. He's like that. . . . There are women who have eyes like that; they are very beautiful.

In other parts of the song, the physical and mental state of mind of the person involved really gets worse.

MUSTAPHA: He won't have a girlfriend in order not to suffer. This means that if he gets a girlfriend there will be trouble. He will have problems. "*Gwāymi*" expresses the fact that the woman has the power to make him weak, to demonstrate his physical state of being.

HASNI: He says he won't take another girlfriend in order not to have problems with his woman. She won't scold him with "Why did you do this and that," if he doesn't have another. "*Tfashshli l-ʿAḍam*" is really an ancient way of speaking. "ʿ*Aḍam*," that's the bone. It means that he is thinking so much about her that he has cracked his bones. But he will not take another "love." Otherwise, he will think too much. He'll become really crazy. *L-ʿawda* is a vulgar word.[2]

KADER: He says that she will not succeed in changing him. *L-ʿawda* is a whore.

DJILLALI: I won't have a woman and she won't be able to weaken my arm. On the one hand, he might be talking about sorcery here. On the other hand, it might be that he doesn't want to go with a chick who is beautiful and who hangs around clubs. He won't lose his strength, his bones. . . . The singers always talk about their physical state of being.

ALI: He says something like, "I prefer to be alone instead of having a woman dominate me, to break my neck," if you like. I think it has to do with sorcery. *Lʿawda* is a *maryūla* [a free girl; see chapter 6].

This seems to be linked to the mental state of being:

MUSTAPHA: *Ḥrig,* that's sorcery, *sḥūr*. . . . They made him burn so much that he hasn't been able to sleep. When they make sorcery, the other will feel warm, even if they are separated by a long distance when you bewitch someone, as far as I know. I've never tried it and I've never seen it done.

KADER: He didn't feel sleepy, and he thinks he's been bewitched. It hurts him. He is never at ease. . . .There are things that are written. There are things to be eaten. There are things they make you swallow. There are things, I don't know, that they hang on a branch, a piece of paper with some writings on that they hang on a tree.

DJILLALI: They [women] have done something to him, and he wasn't able to fall asleep. He turns on his right side, on his left, on his back. He's disturbed by sorcery. Sorcery's always done by a *ṭālab* and it's always girls who go to him. They say to him, "You see, my love isn't with me anymore; he loves another." So the *ṭālab* prepares something to facilitate the whole business with a button from a shirt belonging to the man, and the man doesn't feel normal. He gets burnings. Each one has his methods. The man starts feeling he is missing something. He sees the girl in his dreams. He has nightmares and everything.

In general therefore, "Dīri dār" refers to a variety of expressions describing men's relations with women. In Oran, some said that "raï is always about women," and it was frequently stated that men started listening to raï after breaking up with a woman. Other statements were that "this and that singer is good to listen to, when you are in love" or "I don't listen to raï because I don't have a girlfriend at the moment."

I believe that focusing on raï can lead to an understanding of the complex relationships young men have with women in Algeria and of the sociopolitical importance of this dialectic. But before the discussion of this in the following chapters, it is necessary to proceed with the analysis of how raï songs were given meaning "outside" their musico-poetic structure.

First, it is necessary to see how the listeners related to the *poetic form* of raï because the more or less linear logic applied to the song lines up to now cannot be maintained for the whole song. The lyrics are full of inexplicable statements. What was in the letter the postman brought (lines 13, 14, and 15)? Why were Oran, Marseilles, and Normandy mentioned (25, 33)? Who were the people from Algiers (line 15)? And finally, who was Mohammed (28, 36)?

## The Poetic Form of Raï

I began with the question of what was in the letter. According to Mustapha, "His girlfriend is from Algiers; she sent him a letter and it is she who is calling him. She is so aggressive that the man who reads the letter becomes sad." And Hasni: "It's the woman who wrote the letter." But for Ali it was clear: "It doesn't make sense." For Djillali, too: "It doesn't mean anything. It's a gift to the inhabitants of Algiers." And Kader smiled: "He's crazy, Khaled. He says the postman brought the girl folded." Finally, Houari explained:

> It has nothing to do with what he wanted to say. I tell you, with Khaled you often find contradictions. He sings a song and suddenly the postman brings him a letter summoning him to Algiers. It has nothing to do with the rest. It is an arrow. He shoots off a line like that.

I can add to these statements the fact that in music sheets dating from the start of the century (Yafil n.d.) we find a song entitled "Jātni briyya." The same title is found on Khaled's Barclay record. In another song,[3] Khaled sings the line "*ḍārba séchoir w fayta ʿala bulvār*" (She did her hair with a hair dryer and went to the boulevards), which is not far from the idea expressed in line 2 of "Dīri dār." Lines 12 and 34 of "Dīri dār" can be found in the song "Dablat galbi" (see below), as well as in a range of other raï songs. Elsewhere, Virolle-Souibès (1988b:211) mentions a song recorded with Cheikha Hab Lahmeur entitled "*Khla dār muk.*"

However, this still does not help clarify what the letter says. I therefore propose to stop at the word *ndab,* a verb (also found in line 21) which describes the way women express their grief, tearing their cheeks with their nails when a person close to them dies. Mathéa Gaudry (1961: 194) described this way of mourning as characteristic of the south of Algeria in the 1930s. She explained how she heard a poet sing, "I will lacerate my face with cards, because of the girls of Bou Alam," and she said that even though it was a female gesture, the singer used the expression to show the depth of his sorrow.

It is thus possible to conclude, in the first instance, that the poetic expressions are often not recent ones and that they are used to express situations in which deep emotions are involved. It is thus reasonable to imagine that the letter must include news of a particularly horrible event—not an everyday event, but nonetheless something that someone might witness in the course of a lifetime.

I think this is the case for most of the poetic lines I have brought forward for interpretation so far. They deal with matters that are not part of the daily routine, but which may be relevant for a number of listeners in the course of their lives. Not everyone has a great love affair every day. Not everyone is bewitched, and not every woman drinks Ricard. The songs of raï are thus intended to touch people in general, but to do so by venturing into theoretically conceivable, nonmundane events which might move people when expressed in words (see Hoggart 1971 for an early analysis in this vein).

This provides a key to the understanding of line 25, which obviously deals with a person who has left Oran to go to Marseilles. This was also an event that was out of the ordinary. Although a good many listeners had made this journey, nevertheless not everyone had taken the boat to France. However, the logical problem is that the sentence clearly has nothing to do with either the preceding or the succeeding lines.

I had the opportunity to put this question to the person responsible for recording the song in the early 1980s. He told me that when they were recording it, they needed lines to complete it and simply added this one. The listeners seemed to have understood this procedure perfectly well.

MUSTAPHA: I don't know, he has mixed it up, it is one too many, it has nothing to do with the rest.

KADER: It's about travel or something like that. He talks about something else. It has nothing to do with the story. It's just to fill out the song, because I think he comes back to the theme.

DJILLALI: He talks about a traveler. You may say it's about someone who makes the journey over the sea. It's a bit commercial, because there are many Algerians in Marseilles and they listen a lot to raï. In this way, it pleases people in Marseilles and they buy raï cassettes.

ALI: It's commercial. With raï you have to sing like that to complete the song.

HOUARI: It's like that with raï. You find lines included which have nothing to do with the text. When the singer recalls the line, he sings it.

Thus among consumers of raï—and contrary to the official, media version—there seemed to be an awareness of the lines' embeddedness in a socioeconomic cycle. It was a realism that seemed to come from the experience listeners had gained from participating in live performances. Thus all seven listeners knew that Mohammed was someone present in the studio at the time of the recording, and Kader knew that Normandy was the name of an Oran side street.

Most of them did not mind lines like that. The one with whom I discussed the song in greatest detail was Houari, who on several occasions proved himself the keenest in arguing for a certain coherence in raï songs:

MARC: But doesn't it bother you that he starts singing about a postman in the middle of the story?

HOUARI: No, not me, because when you are alone in your room, you might start thinking about a girl you once knew, what she is doing now: "OK, she has become a whore, but at the bottom of my heart I still love her. I would like her to send me a letter, because it was my first love."

MARC: But then you are the one to make the connection.

HOUARI: OK, I'll start all over again. When I'm alone, I ask myself what has become of her. She was mine and all that. Then she did some foolish thing with someone else, but nevertheless I ask her to make a home instead of coming and going everywhere all the time.

Despite myself, I would really like her to be my wife, so I wait for the postman to bring me a letter from her.

MARC: OK, that's the connection you made. But Khaled did not make one like that. Can you also make a connection with "the mountains of Oran?"

HOUARI: OK, I say, if there is another *maḥna,* what he says is, that the boat sailed away. You do not see the mountains of Oran anymore, but the mountains of Marseilles, you see them. Logically he has gone somewhere else, in this case to Marseilles, maybe to sing, maybe for some other business. He has forgotten her.

MARC: But you really think that's the idea?

HOUARI: If it's not me, if it's not Khaled, it will affect another, because that [third] person is not concerned by this song, but this particular phrase concerns him, because he left his chick in Marseilles and now he's in Oran. That's why I tell you that raï touches everybody. You cannot tell who listens and who does not listen to raï. Me, for example, sometimes I like a song because of a single phrase. I think a person is capable of liking this song because of one phrase.

Houari's last statements were repeated by Mustapha in a manner which also reflected how he considered that men's independence and autonomy ought to be respected.

> Each listener interprets it as he wants. If someone has a problem with a girl, he can use this phrase for his own problem, even if his problem is not the same as the singer's. The problems are not the same. I have a problem. The other has got a problem. When listening to this song, each will adapt his own problem to it.

Thus among the listeners, raï songs did more than index social events in daily life. Hennion's (1983, 1989) approach is relevant here. Working from the idea that music as a nondiscursive medium cannot be captured by discourse, he "encircled" it by following it from production to consumption. He thus focused on the social labor carried out to create a relationship between performers and their audiences. In this endeavor, Hennion made an analytical distinction between two kinds of live performances: the European classical music concert and the European rock concert. In the classical music concert, everything seems to function as if the music were the sole object of devotion, as if the artist and the audience did not count but were actors in a drama greater than themselves (Hennion 1989:51). The fact that the solo pianist may turn away from the audience, that the orchestra is uniformly dressed, and so forth, all function to subordinate the actors to the music. In the rock concert you find the opposite. The music becomes subordinated to a relationship between performer and audience. While the classical musician's body is trained to serve the music, the music of the rock musician serves his body (ibid.: 52) in order to form a relationship between the performer and the audience (ibid.:46). When the rock concert "takes off," the crowd becomes mobilized in successive undulations and follows the body of the performers as if in a common trance (some actually get up on the stage, but once there they no longer know what they are doing there (ibid.:44).

But Hennion's (1989: 50) idea is, of course, that the relationship between performer and audience is a created one:

> Why else would we find . . . the stage fright of the stars, the complex rituals of getting things going, the necessity of warming up the audience, to respect the "timing" of its excitation minutely . . . if it were not because this difficult work represents a job of equalization [between artist and audience]? Either it takes off or it does not.

Even though official institutions for the education, performance, and dissemination of classical music operate as if music were the sole object of attention, a pure relationship with music does not exist.This is shown, for example, by the practice of "dressing up" for a concert (Mariet 1978: 60) as well as by the fact that distinguished artists do not deny themselves the pleasure of being acclaimed superstars or of performing well-known musical works. On the other hand, the commercial and material interests of the market cannot completely rule out the importance of music per se for the rock or pop concert.

A good deal of the work involved in putting on a concert resembles that involved in producing records and cassettes. It even seems as if what I will call a "primary point of reference" is found in the records in the meeting between the audience and the artist, a point of reference which can be a "primary scene" as a live performance. The live recording is the obvious example of this. Another example is folk music recordings of the 1960s, which had as their model the folk club, where there in theory was no separation between performer and listener: "The aesthetic emphasis was less on technique than on truth, and the musical 'honesty' of performers was measured by what they didn't do" (Frith 1983:29).

The primary point of reference need not be a live performance. Many songs have films as their reference. An obvious example is Mozart's twenty-first piano concerto, which today (at least in the Nordic countries) is associated with *Elvira Madigan,* rather than the concert hall. Other examples are American, Indian, Egyptian, or Turkish musicals. For example, from what Stokes says, the structure of Arabesk songs is quite similar to that of raï songs in the sense that they are "of an oblique and indirect nature, lacking any clear narrative structure" (1992:142). But, he continues, "In the context of arabesk it is easy to see why this should be the case, since the narrative structure is present in the films of which the song is only a part. . . .The text does not have the function of imparting a story because the story is already known" (ibid.:142–143).

In raï, it is only recently that videos have started to be produced. The dedications and song forms mark the simultaneous presence of giver and receivers (see Miliani and Belkadem 1981:11). Ben Naoum (1986:10) has written that the "raï of the 1970s and 1980s existed only in the stream of the masses in vibration, at the wedding being celebrated or the cabaret being invaded . . . invaded as a function of the rules of the party."

I would not formulate it so directly. As indicated on cassette covers, the primary point of reference in raï is also the recording studio and its technology. Nevertheless, the comments of several listeners did show a mastery of the form of raï that led back to the logic of the party, and at least of a situation of exchange and competition in words, music, and emotions, as is found at weddings and in cabarets.

The existence of a primary scene in raï can be emphasized by two further examples. When I took part in raï concerts in Paris and Copenhagen, it was obvious that many in the Maghrebin audience behaved differently from the Westerners there, mastering the dance rhythms and calling to the singer while he was singing. They requested songs and dedications from him and some of them jumped onto the stage to have a photograph taken with the singer or to dance with him. It seems that the spotlight on the stage and the darkness of the concert room were not apprehended as devices meant to create an asymmetrical meeting between the audience and the star. For them, we were at a wedding party as well as a concert. The second example is provided by the producers of "cross-over" records in raï. Consciously or unconsciously they have all acknowledged the existence of a specific primary point of reference in raï: the informal, improvised quality of the music and the dedications have all disappeared on the records.

Generally, therefore, it seems that even if the unity of space and time is broken between performer and audience (Stockmann 1991:332) in a mass-produced product like raï, social relations are still embedded in the product—a primary point of reference, in other words. This will become even clearer when we come to the song entitled "Dablat galbi."

However, there is more embedded than a primary reference to the party, the recording studio, and the social game of exchange. In what follows, I will focus on the fuzzy quality of raï before dealing with the music, the voice, and the persona of the singer. Clearly, once it is recognized that the performative form of raï is embedded in the tape recordings, and once it is realized that raï consumers are aware of this, it becomes difficult to maintain from the texts the thesis that raï is fuzzy or to deduce any fuzziness in the state of mind of the consumers, as was done in the press story (see chapter 2). The fuzziness lies elsewhere. The main comments about the next song, "Sʿaīda bʿaīda," were as follows:

NASSER: I have understood nothing except for "*mani mhanni,*" that's all, "*ya l-mwīma māni mhanni.*"

MUSTAPHA: It's difficult because the singing has been reproduced in a gentle manner . . .

HASNI: I have some difficulties in understanding it. . . .

DJILLALI: It's a difficult song, I don't understand everything.

KADER: It's a very difficult song.

ALI: Sometimes Khaled drinks when he is recording in the studio. He is not pronouncing the words correctly, he's slurring them. If he sang fluently I could explain it to you.

## **"Sʿaīda bʿaīda"**: (Saïda is far away)

There are several reasons why I chose this song. First, I was often told that it is emblematic of the style known as raï *trāb,* the literal meaning of which is "soil raï." This expression conveys associations with the Algerian countryside, and songs in *trāb* often express painful experiences.

A second reason for selecting "Sʿaīda bʿaīda" was that I did not grasp several central parts of the song.[4] However, it seemed to me that the song might be touching directly on the theme of sexuality and expressing the vulgarity I had so often read about in the press. I was thus interested in playing the song to my friends both to obtain a proper translation and to discuss any hidden meanings that could be found. But as already indicated, I did not find the answers I was looking for, even though I did come closer during my stay in Oran. It was only back in Denmark—after intensive listening with my friend Salah Tariq—that the final version was established.

In Oran, Nasser said:

> He plays the accordion while he sings, but it should be playing when he is silent. All the instruments are playing while he is talk-

> ing, and you really have difficulties in understanding. I would say it's worthless. In the beginning he says: "*rabbi, rabbi khallīt n-nās. . . .*" Certainly someone has returned home and then he asks himself, "What am I going to tell them. I left her. I came here and I didn't bring her along." Well, that is what I understood, and after that he says: "*Ya dhrāri:* my children." Finally: "*Bnāt l-yūm* . . . those who hold on to those girls, they fall," which means that maybe you cannot count on women today.

The other listeners did not understand much more than Nasser, except for Houari, who had heard the song in a different version (and except for *ḍrari,* which Nasser had understood as "children" [*dhrāri*], not as "pain"). All the way through the discussion, the song seemed to mean something neither of us knew anything precise about. Nevertheless, it did not prevent the discussion from being meaningful, as, for example, when Houari situated the song in a broader context:

> It's a very old song, a song which has marked all eras, because it is a broad song. It's timeless. There's no well-defined site. It's the same type as "*Hizīya.*" You find the tent, the horse and everything. The ancestors, in other words, those who had a horse, were someone fine. Those who didn't have a horse at home were nothing. He's in front of the tent. He tells the horse not to make any noise, because, I think, he's going to enter the tent. Later on, it talks about a *bujādi,* and this is the first time he goes up into the forest. He's a *bujādi* in the sense of a *baṣṭa.* There were women in the forest, and she says: "*Gāltlu sallam w ma bghāshi*ʿ*ainu fi l-ḥāzam y ḥall*"—"Kiss me"—but he doesn't want to kiss her. He has his eyes on her belt; he wants to open it. And since he didn't want to kiss her, the woman thought that he had a heavy problem or his heart set on another woman. But for him it wasn't that, he had his eyes on the belt, he wanted more. Then she wanted to bite his tongue, either at the wedding or at the *wa*ʿ*ada.* It's crazy love, and that's why I think "Sʿaīda bʿaīda" is so long and they have left out parts of it.

This is an interesting interpretation, first, because Houari introduced a line from another version of "Sʿaīda bʿaīda," and second, because he describes the song as an extract from a longer poem which could be pieced together on the basis of a sufficient number of versions. As such, he thought it similar to "*Hizīya,*" a love epic (see Sonneck 1902:136) which tells the story of a couple like Romeo and Juliet set in precolonial Algeria.

Ali, however, interpreted the song in a more profane manner:

> Before, Saïda was the town where you found the greatest number of prostitutes, a lot of liquor and all that. That's all. Saïda is a town where you can have fun. When someone is not able to go to Saïda, he sings this song. It's very vulgar, as for example "*l-ʿawd.*" He speaks about his sexual organ, you see, "Do not scare the *maghbūna.*" The forest is equal to the *baṣṭa.* In the night there are women, guys, and alcohol. They all have their woman, roasted meat. There are the words of the *shīkhs,* of before, it's an old song, and not everybody understands it.

In his interpretation, Ali was thus confirming that the song might be touching on subjects of a sexual nature. His interpretation of "*taḥwās l-ghāba* was also supported by Djillali, Kader, and Hasni:

> DJILLALI: "*Taḥwās l-ghāba*" has a double meaning. Before, the people spent evenings in the forest with wine, women, raï music, and everything until the morning.
>
> KADER: "*Taḥwās l-ghābaba*" means walking in the forest. People call it a "*baṣṭa.*" They go there and bring women along. They take wine with them. They get pissed and make love there. But here he doesn't say that. There are words you cannot say. Otherwise, it won't sell on cassettes. They say it in a different way.
>
> HASNI: "*Taḥwās l-ghābaba*" means walking in the forest, but in reality he doesn't talk about the real forest. He talks about "the milieu." He compares the two and says that the milieu of girls and women is like the forest.

Elsewhere, in "*Faṭma, Faṭma,*" Cheikha Remitti sang "*Taḥwās l-ghābaba w r-rgād w l-xashshāb, wa ʿaallmūva l-mujahīdīn*" (Walking in the forest and sleeping behind the bushes, it is the freedom fighters who taught us this; Virolle-Souibès 1989 : 53). Virolle-Souibès notes that in the 1950s the line referred to Algerian freedom fighters and symbolized the hardships of the Algerian people, whereas after independence it became associated with social marginality (ibid.). In the Khaled version, the freedom fighters are gone, replaced by a *bujādi,* an inexperienced man.

There are thus several possible directions to take in reaching an understanding of the song. I actually had the opportunity to talk with its publisher. Like Houari, he explained that it was an old song he had heard on a record by Cheikha Rahma el Abbasiya dating from the 1950s. It told the story of a man who had a problem with a woman and therefore sought refuge alone in the forest, where he was hunting and learning how to survive. But the publisher also said that line 8 was out of place. He explained that the idea behind recording the song was to prove that Khaled was capable of singing in *trāb*. They therefore chose lines they remembered from earlier versions of the song, without necessarily placing them in the correct order. Khaled later recorded three more versions of the song, one of which was the one Houari referred to. The producer also told me that they whispered the text in Khaled's ear during the recording. Sometimes Khaled would not understand what they whispered, and sometimes they could make him sing anything.

Thus, again, the basically "oral" model of raï reappears. We find a number of independent lines, some of which may move the listener through the tension established between what is stated and the "eroticism" of what is meant, and it becomes obvious that it is not on that level that the fuzziness of raï is to be situated. Rather, it lies in the technological and economic conditions of production, which for "Sʿaīda bʿaīda" means that the music disappears at times and the words become unclear. On another level, the fuzziness lies in a social context similar to the one found in the production of raï. Unless one has the appropriate network of alliances to establish face-to-face contact, one cannot know the secrets of the song (and maybe there are none). There is no other site from which to obtain an overview.

As noted, however, even if "Sʿaīda bʿaīda" was fuzzy in this sense, commentary on it was meaningful. To start with Nasser:

> I don't like the rhythm. We tend to live in an era where speed is a factor, and raï, for us, is characterized by its rhythm. When you say raï, you refer to its rhythm, which is a bit similar to the reggae sound. But here it is totally a mess, what shall I say, two sombreros, 90 percent spirit . . . The song makes me imagine the kind of group listening to it, lying around a low table. There is wine. There are girls of certain habits. There are drugs. . . . The room is full of smoke. . . . I could not imagine myself in that context. . . . It is not even a song which would make me relax. . . . When the violin plays something, it hits your nerves more than relaxes you.

His rejection again showed how music enables people to determine a period in time, to associate with other musical genres, to use physical expressions, and to relate the music to particular moods and emotions. It also shows how images can be created without the need for any explanatory text. Some of these points were also made by my other interviewees. Mustapha:

He has used too much violin, accordion, and tomtom, and besides I am sure that the origin of this song is a *shīkh* of *gaṣba*. It's in the style of *gaṣba*. . . . Quite honestly, I don't like it. If I had a cassette with this song on it, I would pass over it. It's not my style, neither the music, nor the words. Especially when I don't understand it . . . above all the *shīkhs,* because they are very difficult, very strong in words. Their meaning, their purpose—I can't grasp what they are about, never.

The idea of the song being old was also a recurring theme in Hasni's, Kader's, and Djillali's comments, but they were much more positive.

HASNI: This is raï; this is the real raï. It's from the time when Khaled started singing. He started with songs like this at weddings and so on. It makes you want to cry, because when he sings, he sings from the depths. It breaks your heart. It makes you think; it makes you thoughtful, but you really have to concentrate when listening to it. They are ancient words, really hard . . . a long time ago they let words fall. They were about vulgar matters, like Cheikha Djenia, before her, Cheikha Remitti. Raï was like that, but not in a direct way. Young people today almost never listen to that, because there is modern music, the "*slow,*" Hasni, and so on. It's for grown-ups, those who have known raï. Khaled's fans listen to it, those who really like raï. Some have stayed with the early raï and there are those who follow the raï of today, my generation. There are those who listen to all of it. Those you might say are real raï men. They listen to raï. They love raï.

DJILLALI: The singer says that he's not at peace, and even the music fits what he is saying. When you hear the music, you are listening to a drama. He's searching for something he hasn't been able to get hold of. The music and the words are heavy. There's no happiness, because the song is not made for someone to express his happiness. When someone dances he expresses his happiness, and in this song there is none. Judging by the voice, someone is suffering. He uses a voice of suffering. He has problems. It's an old song which tells about the old ways of people, how they lived, how they spent the evenings. The songs of the *shīkhas* are not easy to understand. They speak by means of examples. They won't give you a direct sentence you can understand. You can't open them immediately. The raï singers, they have shed some light on the words, they made them easier.

KADER: I don't understand anything except for the music. I like the

> music, but I don't understand the words. I can't explain it properly because it is *gaṣba,* that's the way of the *shīkhs.* . . . The *ʿarūbis* [peasants] speak like that. It takes time to work out the double meanings in raï. Older people [adults] can explain the song for you. . . . It is not for dancing, but there are people who dance to it. There are those who prefer the reggae style. It's a beautiful song. It touches you. . . . Even if I don't understand the words, I've understood it very well, because there's a sense of pain [he starts singing an *istikhbār* by Farid l-Atrache].

It is therefore clear that although the listeners did not agree on whether it was a song of the *shīkha* or of the *shīkh,* it took them back in time or to another place. It is hard to say whether this was due more to the text fragments or to the instrumentation. But it is obvious that even when it was not understood, the song did convey meaning. In songs an important interplay takes place between the nonverbal and verbal elements, in which the former play a main role.

## Music and Voice

One singer, twenty-four years of age and extremely popular because of his soft voice and sentimental songs, told me the following anecdote to explain how he tried to put all his emotions into his songs:

> I have seen girls cry in front of me when listening to my cassettes. For example. "Līlat ʿars bkīt" ['The night of (your) wedding I cried'], many girls have wept in front of me. I touched them. They felt I suffered, even though I stood there in the shop and smiled. But the cassette told another story—it showed something else. It showed what was here [in his heart]. Even though they saw me there laughing, playing, having fun, they knew that inside I was hurt. I was deeply wounded.

There was no doubt about the singer's honesty in telling about the feelings he put into his songs. At the same time, his anecdote also demonstrated one of the central aspects of mass-produced songs. What he actually described was two encounters at one and the same time between audience and artist—the first, an imagined space of sorrow created through music and singing, and the second, one of physical presence, the singer smiling to the girls.

The basic medium for the creation of an imagined space within songs seems to be music. Music can be described as moving forms of sound in realms of duration, which is something radically different from the time in which practical life proceeds. They are not ten minutes or some fraction of a day. "Musical duration," as Langer wrote (1953:109), "is an image of what might be termed 'lived' or 'experienced' time—the passage of life that we feel as expectations become 'now,' and 'now' turns into unalterable fact." Music thus enables the listener to evoke memories and scenes and in particular to be in temporal synchrony with the singer in order to use or reject the images suggested by his performance.

Music can even alter the significance of a text or create tension within the song itself. In raï, it is common to use light music with a sad text (as in the case of the next song, "Dablat galbi"). Taken as a total expression, a song in raï can have more than its textual value. One famous song,[5] revived in 1984–1985 to become a hit, told how the husband of today was asleep while his wife went out, how people did as they pleased, and so on. Overall, it could be said to deplore the disintegration of Algerian family values. At the same time, the song had a good dance rhythm with a call-and-response character. When heard live, one of the pleasures it gave the audience was to sing along to the reply. Later on, in the recorded song, the singer went on offering dedications to women present in the studio, indicating that his world did not conform to the family idea. Thus while on the level of discourse the song could be said to deal with a rather serious matter, on the level of musical expression it became a song of pleasure, of singing along and making fun of a world turned upside down.[6]

But most often, I have noticed how listeners of raï credit the songs with the power to move them to remember another time or place. In the case of "Sʿaīda bʿaīda," Houari and Kader made the connection through associations with other songs, but the clearest example was Nasser's evocation of a setting with sombreros and 90 percent alcohol. The same was evident in Mustapha's approach to raï and his comments on the kind of raï he listened to (see chapter 4). "I always follow the music," he said. "When I find some beautiful music, I listen to it, even though I don't understand it." He did not like Khaled, but nevertheless enjoyed Khaled's Barclay record "because he has employed the instruments, and there is rap style, disco, and everything."

If raï has the potential to make people move their bodies or experience emotion—the power to invite people into created spaces—it can also move people to think about aspects of their own era. I found that the most common characterizations of raï in the early 1990s were that "raï is original music"; "raï is original music which touches an obscure part of the Algerian being"; "the music makes you want to release yourself"; "raï is rhythmical"; "the music is fine"; "raï makes you wanna dance"; "raï makes young people dance"; "raï is light (*khaffīf*); "it is the only Algerian music which makes you wanna dance"; and "raï is fast music."

But, equally frequent were comments like "raï is modern music"; "raï has been civilized with electric guitar, drum set, and all"; "raï is universal music because it is rhythmic"; "raï has been developed 100 percent because of the instruments"; "raï is music of our time with instruments such as electric bass and synthesizer"; and "raï uses the technology of the third millennium." These expressions indicate how raï can be considered a model for the creation of an imagined space in the present. Together with the frequent use of labels such as "pop raï," "disco raï," or "raï reggae," these comments show how raï can be seen as contributing to the relocation of space from the outside world into an Algerian scheme. However, the comments about "Sʿaīda bʿaīda" also show how listeners—when in time with the singer—can relate to his voice. Djillali spoke of "someone suffering according to the voice." Hasni felt that "when he sings, he sings from the depths. It breaks the heart." And according to Kader, "There was a sense of pain."

Several writers have dealt with the importance of the voice in music, noting how the response to music is, to a large degree, physical (Frith 1983:15). We often speak with our lips to explain and with our throats to convince (Burrows 1989:394), and we relate to "the grain of the voice," defined as "the body in the voice as it sings" (Barthes 1987:188). In raï, people do relate to the singer through his voice. The *istikhbārs,* demonstrations of the singer's abilities, tend to be favored. Several times friends of mine made me stop outside the shop of a cassette dealer in order to listen to an *istikhbār* being played out into the street. I also heard people being moved by the "grain of the voice of singers" in more joyous songs with comments like, "Let's go to the beach, be beautiful, be brown."

Publishers in Oran were aware of the importance of the voice. This was one of the reasons for the number of remakes in raï. Each voice would "give a new person" to the song, and each voice would have its fans. Publishers were constantly in search of new voices—particularly young voices—to replace the older ones in order to attract new generations of listeners.

In a broad sense, the most important site of distinction between different productions of raï was the singers' voices. This is suggested by the facts that the musical accompaniments were always done by the same musicians, there were many remakes, and the same formulas were used over and over. Presenting a voice that was worth listening to was a basic part of the aesthetics of raï. When I participated in the first festival to take place after the military takeover in October 1991, a number of second-rank singers performed. To the great irritation of the press which had gathered to cover the event, most of them sang the same four or five latest hits. In fact, what most of the singers had tried to do was precisely to compete in differentiating themselves from the others using not the music or the text, but the voice. However, this alone is not enough to explain how raï reached its audience through cassette tapes. People also attributed personalities to voices. Comments about second-rank singers' voices might be that they had a voice like Hasni, or like Khaled, or others. One raï singer was known as a *maryūl,* a man who enjoyed the good life (women, food, drink). Another was known for his sentimentality and was good to listen to when you were in love. A third was known as a serious man who always sang proper words.

Thus, on the one hand it is perfectly possible to agree with Frith's (1983:164–165) idea that

> we enjoy hearing someone sing because they are expressing something else, not because the voice represents the "person" behind it, but because the voice, as a sound in itself, has an immediate voluptuous appeal . . . what is involved in musical pleasure is not significance but signifiance—the work of signification; our joyous response to music is a response not to meanings but to the making of meanings, and jouissance, like sexual pleasure, involves self-abandonment, as the terms we usually use to construct and hold ourselves together suddenly seem to float free. . . . Think of Elvis Presley—in the end this is the only way we can explain his appeal: not in terms of what he "stood for," socially or personally, but by reference to the grain of his voice.

On the other hand, however, in raï the grain of the voice can be separated only with difficulty from an imagined sociocultural body that produces images through songs. This became evident as the discussion of "Dalbat galbi" proceeded.

### **"Dalbat galbi"** (Ruin of my heart)

I chose to play "Dalbat galbi" for my interviewees, first because I knew it was rather well known, and second because it represented a style that differed musically as well as textually from the older repertoire of electrified raï—the music was digital and the words were "clean." Here again I encountered a difference of view between Nasser and the others.

NASSER: I don't like the music. It has the same chorus, the same thing being repeated all the time. . . . It's trivial, very trivial. I am attracted by specific rhythms. This one is good for nothing else but for background noise when you are cleaning your house.

HASNI: The music's splendid. It's good. It makes you wanna move. It's raï. It has the raï rhythm. It's a bit sad, but sometimes a sorrowful person feels like dancing to release what's inside him. He might have a secret that he can't tell anyone. In order to get relief he drinks, he quarrels, or he dances. Like myself, I write when I want to release what's inside me. Because I have secrets I cannot tell to everybody. Every man has secrets. Some may have four secrets, and they only speak about two of them, and keep two for themselves. I talk about my secrets and I write them down. Then, when I read them, I know I'm talking to someone. And to whom? To myself, I am talking to myself. In this way I try to see myself, to recover, to manage, all that.

DJILLALI: It's a beautiful song. The music is great. It makes the listeners dance, the admirers of this song. Even if it is a song of suffering, the music hits you on the other side. It's happy. You can move your body.

KADER: I like the music and the text.

ALI: At the time I saw the song as being very good. The rhythm and the words.

HOUARI: The music is beautiful. Rachid's music is always nice.

But this time Mustapha did not agree with Nasser.

MUSTAPHA: This song with X,[7] I heard already in 1985, I think. They released an album with all the raï singers on it, Khaled, Hamid, Sahraoui, and Fadela, even Rachid and Fethi. Each singer had a song, and among the ones I liked, there was this one. It's a beautiful song with a nice atmosphere. It's by Rachid and Fethi's group. It creates a party atmosphere, even if he talks about problems like all the other singers. When you dance, you do not pay any attention to the words. You follow the rhythm and leave your problems behind. Myself, I danced to it [he laughs timidly] at home. I had a cassette.

Like Djillali, Mustapha noted an opposition between the moods of the music and the text. He also elaborated on what made the difference between this song and the preceding ones. He situated himself in the group of Algerian youth who listened to raï because of its musical capacity to actualize the world in an Algerian context: "The music is by Rachid and Fethi; they have sophisticated material, and I think that attracts everyone who likes this kind of music. I liked this song because they used synthesizers, drums, and all that. I liked the song because of the music."

The text was again rejected by Nasser:

> You have "*dablat galbi,*" I don't understand what "*dablat galbi*" is . . . there is also "*dartu fiyya rrāykum*" . . . it means that they say, I don't know to whom, "You did to me as you wanted. You did something bad to me," something like that. Some people have God helping them, but I don't get the story. Surely he must be telling a story. There are certain words coming up constantly, but to put this together. . . .

The other listeners thought that there was nothing difficult to interpret, that it was a "direct" song. Line 4 did not pose any problems since the obvious meaning was that the woman had said something more painful to the man in love than a wound from a knife. They agreed that the bird's nest was nothing but an expression of love. Nor did line 5 pose any difficulties, since "the hunter" stood for men chasing women and "the pigeon" was the girlfriend of the man in love. There also turned out to be general agreement that the song was about a man who was in torment because of the absence of his lover and that the song had a good deal to do with enemies.

MUSTAPHA: In raï they always sing about jealousy, because they sing about sadness, that he and she split up because of jealousy or maybe sorcery . . . and it exists, because when someone separates it is often because of misunderstandings, *l-qīl w l-qāl* [gossip]. I had a friend who had a girlfriend, but he got trouble from other people. They told the girl not to date him, "He's mean and everything," even if it was a friend. I know him very well. She believed them, of course. They had problems and they split up.

HASNI: "They added to my heart" means that they told things about her which were untrue. That she goes out with someone else, that she walks the streets, for example. So he starts feeling that she's a burden, which means that they did all they could to separate her from him. He starts suffering. They say that she's no good, and they might give him proof, visual proof. They have seen her here and there. He loved her so much that he didn't believe them, but still they've broken his heart.

DJILLALI: In raï, there are always enemies, there are always problems.

KADER: Everybody has enemies. There are people smiling at you, but they think they are superior and I can't stand them. They're haughty and arrogant and they always want you to be down. If they see you are a little bit well off, they don't want you to marry. They don't want you to buy a car. They become jealous.

ALI: Enemies are always people from the local area, members of the family. You don't know who exactly. They can interfere in a couple's relationship. In your neighborhood, for example, someone is dating someone else. I can go to their parents and say that their daughter is doing this and that. Or an old girlfriend might do it, if you are dating someone else.

HOUARI: You see, in our lives, they always argue because of women. Families break up, so there is always jealousy . . . and when you are dating someone, you always get a lot of questions: "So you are dating this and that girl?" There are people who are always there without anything else to do. They hear everything.

In general, while raï deals with men's relations with women, it is certainly also about others' attitudes toward men and women dealing with one another. In fact, "Dalbat galbi" turned out to be one about a particular man's sociocultural situation. Here the borders between the listener's own persona and the image of the singer become unclear.

I found that there was an even more pragmatic attitude to "Dablat galbi" than to the song lines that seemed out of place in "Dīri dār." Mustapha's comment on line 6 was: "Maybe he hasn't got any enemies. He uses it only to embellish the words and so on. To make the situation more critical, more moving . . . but this does not necessarily mean that he [the singer] has problems." And Kader's comment on line 5 was: "He says it just to get some money. You can sing raï also. You go on stage. You say words like that and you become a singer." While Ali was swaying between two interpretations of line 6: "Sometimes, to make the song longer they sing anything, sometimes they sing words that are true. This can be true, Marc, because maybe you have enemies and you've got a girlfriend and she is very sweet and her mother is mean. What do you do? You sing this phrase." These comments were close to the comments most frequently put forward by raï opponents or skeptics—that "the singers sing whatever enters their heads." They are also related to changes that took place during my fieldwork, particularly in 1992. At that time, a number of singers had left Algeria to sing in France, which meant that two singers, Cheikh Naam and Fethi, who until then had had only minor successes, were in great demand among the producers. The response of raï listeners was to treat them with respect, *ʿandhum klām*. Unlike other raï singers, they had "words" and were thus placed "above" the rest of the singers—that is, not as chebs but in the line of inheritance of the *shīkhs* of the *malḥūn*. They were placed in the category of grown-ups, of the ancients who possessed the proper words at the proper time. In fact, both singers had deeper and also less glamorous voices than most raï singers. Their singing style was declamatory. They were closer than the chebs to the performative ideal of the *shīkhs* of the *malḥūn*. As noted, raï provoked much criticism about having "no texts," "no poetry," "no words." However, although due respect was given to singers with words, this did not mean that those without words were rejected. This was evident in the interviewees' comments on line 10.

MUSTAPHA: He just added this sentence to make some publicity for the pianist. He says that Cheb Khaled and Rachid are there and Cheb Hamid is in the middle.

HASNI: There he is, in the studio of Rachid and Fethi, maybe Hamid is with them. He talks about him, not of evil, since they are friends. So he *barrāḥs* for them. The meaning is good. There are no problems because Rachid is present.

DJILLALI: It's a little bit like showbiz: Khaled, that's the singer, Hamid, that's Cheb Hamid, and Rachid, that's the producer. This means that it's a sort of an advertisement because advertising is a bit different with Algerian raï. In the song he says the name of his friend, and that's show business, because they do it for money. Not everyone, sometimes they do it for nothing, without money, but there is always something. They've always got something in mind. There's always an interest. Even if he doesn't ask for money, it's a friend of his and so on, he does it because next time his friend will return the favor that he's mentioned in the song. People like it. The proof of that is that the people mentioned are often important tradesmen, producers, industrialists. This means that they always have something in mind—it's not for pleasure, doing favors. The next time Khaled will mention X's name in a song. Nothing for nothing.

ALI: It has no meaning. We talk like that here: Mohammed is there, Bouabdellah is here, and Marc is in the middle.

HOUARI: Khaled and Rachid: he *barrāḥs* like a *barrāḥ*. You see, Marc and Salim and Mohammed *wāsṭa,* he is in between the two of us. It's a group. It's a *tabrīḥa.*

We are back with the recording studio and the live performance, where we found the *barrāḥ,* with power over words, knowing how to use them in order to unite and separate. When the *barrāḥ* was absent, the singer took his place, though without his proficiency. Most often, the singer was in a weak position and served people for the money they offered him. The singers also found themselves in situations of negotiating purposeful exchanges in order to turn what appeared to be gifts into exchange values.

In fact, it seemed as if this position of being exchangers of "money for emotion" accounted for the degree of contempt for musicians in Algeria among more well established parts of the population.[8] "We like what they do, but not who they are," a fifty year-old family man told me. I knew two men in their thirties, who had been playing *andalus* and *wahrāni,* respectively, at weddings; they stopped playing in public after finding jobs in a bank and an insurance company. Both argued that "no one would take me seriously if I were seen at a wedding one day and in the office the next."

But for a number of raï listeners, the position and role of the singer elicited not condemnation, but empathy. The position of the singer was not far from that in which a great number of listeners found themselves. The singers were not only voices with names which had become known in the course of the 1980s in Algeria and in the West; they were also endowed with a personality. The most remarkable result of the discussions concerning "Dalbat galbi" was that it was not the key phrase which provoked the greatest interest, but line 8:

HASNI: X is singing. He is opposed to Khaled in the song because there was a time when Khaled sang a certain song, and X sang another one and answered him. Because of Y. Both loved Y. And X sang to say that he loved Y and that people did everything to separate her from him. So once Khaled sang to X. He couldn't talk to him face-to-face, so he sings him a song. And what does X do? Instead of going over to see him, he sings him another song, which said that in spite of everything, I want her. I do what I want with her. She's my love. That's what he's singing about.

Here we see the didactic game of the *barrāḥ* again, changing a real contest into a game so that the conflict will not break out into the open. Gossip surfaces:

> KADER: He is married to Y and that gives him pleasure. He loves her very much. There are people who say that Y bewitched him, but it's not true. It was love that came from God. He loved her, because he could have gone to a *ṭālab*. He makes things, but this came from God.
>
> ALI: He had a thing with a woman who was a singer, and people started criticizing him. You know his story. People said he had married a streetwalker because she was a girl from "the milieu." That's why he always sings about those things. He talks about himself in some songs.
>
> HOUARI: X always complains. When he married Y, many people blamed him. That's why, in many of his songs, you feel that there are many enemies. Like here, I think he even talks about her parents. The line "*ana bghīt maḥḥanti,*" he sang it all the time: "I loved this person, no one has the right . . ." Every evening, when he started singing, he sang "I don't give a damn," and so on. In Oran many people were talking. And when he married Y, he left home. Now he lives with her and has offered her father a car.

As we shall see in chapter 7, these stories reflect the preoccupations of many young Algerian men. They also show that people relate to the singers and their doings in either a positive or a negative way. Nasser considered the singers dirty and vulgar, and Mustapha stated that he did not like Khaled because he mixed everything up. Kader said that he listened to Sahraoui and Khaled and that he preferred Khaled "because he is sincere when he speaks. He speaks of what we live, of the reality we live." Khaled was also Houari's favorite singer, but for different reasons. "Many youngsters listen to Hasni. Many girls listen to him. They recognize themselves in Hasni, the generation that is growing up. But me, for example, I do not listen to Hasni. I lived with Khaled, if you like, which is why I recognize myself in many songs—he's a great *maryūl*." Ali, however, took a different view. One day I asked him and his friends in the FIS how they could be against a song like "Dīri dār," since in many ways it seemed to have a moralizing content. They reacted in unison: "Yes, it may be a song of advice, but to take advice from Khaled—never!"

In raï, people often established an imaginary relationship with the singer, but rarely with another musician. Some musicians, such as Bellemou, Mohammed Maghni, and Rachid and Fethi, were known because of their instrumental, musical, or technological innovations. Naturally, the closer people came to actual musical production, the more they knew about the instrumentalists. But when people spoke of their preferences, they inevitably gave the names of singers. People tended to attribute the whole of a song to the singer, and they looked in the song lines for examples of the singer's individual expression.

As mentioned above, the Algerian media seldom ventured into the personal lives of the singers. If they did, they followed the custom of presenting a public person as acting according to the dominant family norms of respect. This way of presenting people in public was approved of by raï listeners, but it did not prevent them from creating unofficial images of the singers through stories told elsewhere. A number of rumors and stories circulated in Oran. Every local area had its more or less well known raï singers about whom people told stories.

In Kader and Ali's area, there were two cabaret singers. People knew that the first was married, that a big fight had broken out at his wedding, and that he had had an affair with a woman living in Perpignan. They also knew that he did not make any recordings because his father did not want him to be known to a wider audience. Of the second singer, it was said that both his parents had died, that he lived with two divorced sisters and a brother who had been a musician, and that he had turned to praying. A second brother had left town for good to travel around the country. A third had a job, but had broken off relations with his brother, who survived by singing at weddings and doing business on the black market.

In another local area, people could tell where a famous singer lived, where he took his morning coffee and joint. They knew that he had been a promising football player and that he had given it up after his first successful recording. They knew that his mother had been divorced and worked as a cleaner, and that he himself had been married to a woman living in Marseilles and had had a child with her. In a third area, it was said of one singer that he had divorced his wife because of problems between the two families. They had witnessed his increasing consumption of alcohol and knew he suffered from diabetes, many of them visiting him as soon as they knew he had been sent to the hospital.

Stories like these spread to other local areas. Thus, in one version another singer was said to have left Oran because of problems with the police. A woman working in a club, with whom he had had an affair, had falsely accused him of being a pimp. In another version, he had been married to a woman working in a club, but had met a French woman with whom he went to France even though she was older than he was. Since then, he had stopped singing. In yet a third version, the singer did not have any problems at all.

Of course, the better known the singer, the more stories there were. The largest number of stories circulated about Khaled, and together these stories created a multifaceted image. Some said that he was surrounded by *shikūrs*[9] who took money from him for protection when he stayed in Oran. Other stories told how he was sent to prison after driving into a man while escaping from a crowd which did not want him to leave a wedding (a story that a journalist in *Actuel* also seemed to have heard; see chapter 2). Others told about the amount of alcohol he consumed before going on stage or about his relations with numerous women from the cabarets. Many of these stories were mixed with descriptions of how he was a simple, friendly man who participated and sang for nothing at the weddings of the poor.

While I was in Oran, people closely followed his appearances in Central Park in New York on French television. They were uneasy when Khaled was presented with a bag from Tati (the low-budget Parisian warehouse), a big bleach-blonde, and a bottle of red wine on a "smart" music program on Canal Plus. Others worried about the earring he was wearing and disapproved of the fact that he agreed to perform in Israel. However, most of the stories were local stories that, although they included some unusual elements, but also featured problems that a number of listeners could identify with. They were mostly told without any condemnation or moralizing. If men did relate to one another in public life through categorizations of the *nisba* kind (see chapter 3), they certainly also oriented themselves in the social landscape through unofficial stories of a more personal and emotional kind. Although they related to the public style of the singers, the listeners focused on the singers' problems as if the latter were in a position of weakness, like themselves.

Thus it was clearly difficult to separate the body of the voice as it sang from the sociocultural constitution of that same body singing about social events. On the other hand, it was evident that the folk model of raï—treating the songs as ciphers arbitrarily signifying social events—was insufficient. It seemed rather that the primary point of reference to the party, the music, and the worlds the music actualized, as well as the jouissance of the voices and the sociocultural story of the singers in a situation of fuzzy socioeconomic conditions of production, seduced listeners into identifying with the singer and his words. In any case, the songs did not have univocal relations to their audience. They were open for discussion reaching from and into society. This should become clearer in the discussion of the last song, "Jibuhālu," sung by a woman.

### **"Jibuhālu"** (Bring him to her)

I chose "Jibuhālu" because several cassette dealers told me that it was particularly popular at the time of my trip to Algeria in 1990. Later, I heard it in different versions on cassette, video, and at a public party for women in Oran. But when I played it for my seven male informants, none of them had heard it before or knew who the singer was, except for Mustapha:

> This is a song by Chaba Zahiya. I know it because I was at the beach last year with the family and they listened to it often, especially the women, because it's in the style of the *maddāḥas*. At weddings, they invite the *maddāḥas* with traditional instruments, so Chaba Zahiya has got the style of the *maddāḥas* with the voice and all. My sister has got a cassette of Chaba Zahiya's. She prefers this style since the music is modern; the style creates a good atmosphere. You can even dance to it. Even at weddings, they play the style of this song on cassettes, Chaba Zahouania, Zahiya, Amina. I like the music and also the voice [he laughs], but only if it is with modern music. I don't listen to the *maddāḥas* playing traditional instruments. The real *maddāḥas,* I don't like them, but this music, I like it.

When it came to details about the content of the song, the men were unanimous that the meaning of the key phrase was quite clear. The singer implores the members of her family to bring the bride to the groom, even if enemies try to prevent the wedding. The remaining lines center around the problem of which woman to marry. Again, I found differences in the interpretations of some of the lines and difficulties in understanding some of the words. And again there was a pragmatic attitude toward the fact that the song did not systematically develop a story. Nasser showed a slightly more positive attitude than previously:

> It's the good beginning that started the movement; otherwise it's very monotonous. I liked the rhythm at the beginning very much. Most raï songs start like that, but the words are really jerky. You might think she's intoxicated, the way she sings, so it was difficult

> to understand what she sang. She sings maybe to get rid of her dependence, to break with conformity. The song talks a bit about the state of society. Ten years ago it was not the same. Now, there is a certain liberty. But otherwise, it is the style of the *maddāḥas,* you see [he sings the rhythm]. . . . It was the same for I don't know how many minutes, "*jibuhālu bni ʿammu,*" so it becomes rather boring, except for the beginning, which was really nice.

As noted, Mustapha experienced a good deal of pleasure with regard to the music, but otherwise he was ambivalent, especially about the words: "No, I don't like these words. It's womanish. Usually I don't listen to women's songs because they sing about men. What can I do with that?" Houari was also ambivalent about how the song might be used: "The style is mixed, half *maddāḥa,* half raï. The men do not dance to this song, they dance to a heavier rhythm. This one is more *maddāḥa* than raï. But it's OK, the song. It is about an *ʿazab* like us, a bachelor." But when it came to Hasni, Djillali, and Ali, there was complete rejection:

HASNI: You told me it was Chaba Zahiya. She sings a song I haven't heard, because most young people in Algeria do not listen to that. It's for women, like the *maddāḥas*. It's got the *maddāḥa* rhythm [he sings it]. I have no taste for this song. I don't like it. It doesn't make me wanna dance. The women, yes, but not me.

DJILLALI: I don't like it. It doesn't concern me. It only concerns the singer. It doesn't concern people in general. That's why she's not very well known, this singer. You see, it's a bit personal, not general. I prefer songs that touch everybody. And when she sings that her enemies will pay, she knows very well it's not true. Through whom will they pay? Through God? No, there's no communication between her and God, so they'll pay with their own means. Maybe she's going to make sorcery against them.

ALI: It's mellow. It's *maddāḥa.* The women can dance to it, and men too. But I don't like it. It's stupid and that's all.

Only Kader did not have a negative attitude toward it: "The music is fine and the words too. It's a little bit sad because she says "*jibuhālu kūntra ʿalli saluhālu.*" She wants the boy to be happy. There are people who do not like the *maddāḥa*. It's for women and there are songs that are fine. But I listen to the raï of Khaled and Sahraoui."

Clearly these comments indicate that great care is needed when one is generalizing about men's attitudes toward music (and toward women, a subject I will explore in the following chapters). There is no unanimous rejection of the song or the singer. There is no unanimous emphasis on one particular element to be disapproved in the song. However, the comments tend—in the negative—to confirm that several important elements need to be considered to understand raï. The men disapprove of Zahiya's song because it contains another primary point of reference (the women's party), including another "body" (the women's dance). They disapprove of it because it contains expressions of another kind of social event (through women's gaze on men), and because another sociocultural persona is singing (a woman).

The men's approach to this other, female, world is at the center of male raï; it is also at the center of the last part of this analysis, which ventures into a consideration of the wider significance of raï in the 1980s. I start with the early 1980s—the period of the raï boom—and trace how the themes of raï mainly evoked spheres of pleasure in Algerian society. Afterward, I will continue with a discussion of raï songs dealing with love, which became the dominant trend after the breakthrough of raï in the mid-1980s.[10]

In the following chapters, the reader should remember that while the song lines at the level of discourse can be said to deal with rather serious matters, at the level of musical expression they can become elements of pleasure, of singing along and making fun of a world turned upside down. Sometimes, they were only elements of singing along, and many, when not taking hold of their listeners, were merely like wallpaper, coloring the city with sound.

# 6

# Transgressions in Raï: The Weak Side of the Strong[1]

The spaces into which the raï songs of the early 1980s took their audience were actually the ones from which they originated, the cabarets. In this chapter, I will highlight the importance of male spheres of pleasure such as these. I will describe how, through references to the clubs, raï songs defied notions of authority and regulation in Algerian society, how, especially with regard to the family, they could become emblematic of a society in which Islamism was on the rise.

The cabarets were male spheres of pleasure, consisting of alcohol and women, that is, "women without men" (Jansen 1987). Jansen has described how, in Algeria, women without male financial support and control tend to be found in occupations generally considered impure or as transgressing public morality. Included in these professions are jobs such as bath scrubbers, peddlers, sorceresses, singers, and courtesans.

Jansen used the term *qaḥba* for the latter category, including in it prostitutes working in recognized and licensed brothels that are subject to police and medical control. Such women are often placed there as a punitive measure after being caught streetwalking a number of times. There are also independent prostitutes, "free women" working clandestinely as well-to-do courtesans. Then there are the less well-to-do who make contacts in the street, use the telephone in the post office, or work in clandestine brothels. Finally, at the bottom of the scale, there are physically or mentally handicapped prostitutes, who often live and sell themselves under extremely poor conditions (ibid.: 161–163).

In Oran in the early 1990s, the importance of the controlled areas of prostitution was diminishing. Rather, prostitution in the form of brothels was scattered all around the town in private apartments. In addition, a number of large hotels functioned as meeting and working places for "professional" women. Some cafes and parks were also known to be places of contact, and on the main streets, one could find women actively engaged in contacting men. There were also women working from home or from bars, tearooms, or restaurants, where they dated men, making arrangements for the evening, which would often start in a restaurant and continue in a cabaret.

The categories of women described by Jansen were recognized in Oran, but men also made the distinction between *qaḥba* and *maryūla,* which is central to the context of raï. One man in his early thirties who had been immersed in the nightlife of Oran described the difference between *qaḥba* and *maryūla* as follows: "When you see a beautiful woman and you know she can be laid, she is a *maryūla.* But a *qaḥba* is one who walks, who makes her living like that." A young *barrāḥ* who also had knowledge in such affairs emphasized that "a *maryūla* is not a *qaḥba.* The former is an old expression, a woman who smokes, drinks, dances, gads about, but for pleasure, not for money. She is *zahwāniya*" (an expression having the sense of being merry, joyous, fond of good living, a lighthearted person [actually the artistic name of both a male raï singer and a female raï singer, Cheb Zahouani and Chaba Zahouania]).

In Oran, the distinction between *qaḥba* and *maryūla* was in fact less demarcated than it would appear from these two statements. If in certain situations the *maryūla* had more positive connotations,[2] it often tended to be used synonymously with *qaḥba.* Nonetheless, the distinction still had relevance, for it perpetuated the idea of an age-old practice where—despite official efforts to discipline prostitution and concentrate it in exclusive areas—"professional women" were not only traders of sexual services, but were also addicted to enjoying wine, music, singing, and hashish with chosen partners in nighttime entertainment (Bertherand 1857, Kerrou and M'Halla 1993, Lepoil 1947, Poitiers 1955). For example, until recently brothels had programs of entertainment featuring *shīkhas* in the company of *barrāḥs,* which men could attend. The *maryūla* was therefore not associated with women offering five minutes for a hundred dinars in "reserved areas." She was much closer to being a lover than a *qaḥba.*[3] It took some time for me to realize this, but as I became more immersed in the world of raï it became obvious that a number of love songs from the early raï repertoire in fact were songs of love for the *maryūla.*

Some raï lyrics did invoke controlled prostitutes, such as

*Min kabrat hiyya, daf'aat bintha consigne*
When she grew up, she pushed her daughter into prostitution

Cheb Khaled, "Ḥasdūni fik" (They were jealous of me because of you)

*Maha tushrab r-rūj w hiyya l-birra, dda ṣūghri*
Her mother drinks red wine and she drinks beer. I lost my youth

Cheb Khaled, "Dallāli, dallālli" (My guide, my guide)

But the raï of the early 1980s mainly brought its audience into a relationship with the "free women."

*Matḍablat sh-shfār w tji 'andi l d-dār, nsharrabha w r-rikār, khuya 'aīnāni*
The woman with the drooping eyelashes will come to my house. I will make her drink Ricard, believe me, brother, openly.

Cheb Mami, "Ghīr l-bayḍa w ana" (Only the blonde and I)

In fact, this lyric is also found in at least one female version, "ghīr ḥbibi w ana" (Only my friend and I) with Chaba Zahouania, in which she sings "*Nsharrbuh r-rikār ya khūya 'aīnanī*" (I will make him drink Ricard, believe me, brother, openly; see Virolle-Souibès 1988b:211). It is not certain whether the female version came before the male one, and the line may have originated in older songs. But there is no doubt that the male raï songs of the early 1980s take a good deal of their inspiration from the *shīkhas* entertaining men at *baṣṭas* or pleasure parties.

*Haya nṣaddu ya l-maryūla*
Let's go, oh girl of pleasure

Cheb Khaled, "Haya nṣaddu" (Let's go)

*Ḍ yāf rabbi Yamina, ḍ yāf rabbi Hafiḍa, ḍyāf rabbi Faṭima*
We are the invited of God, Yamina, Hafida, Fatima

Zargui, "yāf rabbi" (The invited of God)

Thus many lines deal with the idea of having a party, and even more, with the pleasurable things that were brought along in order to create a suitable atmosphere:

*Baytīn fi zabūj w ḥshān w r-rūj*
We spend the night under the wild olives, with a meal and red wine

Cheb Khaled, "Ma natzawwaj ma nrabbi kabda"
(I won't marry, I won't tie up my feelings)

*Ana njīb l-wiskī w l-kuka ʿalik*
I'll bring the whiskey and you the Coca Cola

Zargui, "Ḍyāf rabbi" (The invited of God)

*Nwajadlak l-mashwi w mʿaah l-wiskī*
I'll prepare the grilled meat together with whiskey

Cheb Khaled, "Ḥalli l-bāb" (Open the door)

*L-mizān w l-ʿaqliya w nṣabihu l-ḥāl*
The hand drum, and hashish, and we'll have a good time

Cheb Khaled, "Shkūn addāk" (Who took you)

And some lines even included practical advice:

*L-birra min l-ḥassi takhruj bārda*
The beer which has been in the well is [nice and] cold

Cheb Khaled, "Līla nakhbaṭha" (Tonight I'll get drunk)

These lines might, of course, be descriptive of parties without women, but many indicate that men's consumption of alcohol, food, and so on, was given heightened pleasure by the presence of females:

*Nssakru, ndaffgu, kubbu, zīdu, mazāl l-ḥal*
Let's drink, pour the glass, one more. We have the time

Cheb Khaled and Miloud, "Kubbu, kubbu" (Pour out, pour out)

*Dhik ṭ-ṭwila ya dhik l-ʿarīḍa, dhik l-gṣīra tahdar fi l-hwa*
The tall one, the thick one, the small one, she is intoxicated and talks wildly

Cheb Khaled and Miloud, "Kubbu, kubbu" (Pour out, pour out)

And a number of lines certainly deal with the possible culmination of the good time spent in the company of women:

*Nabghi s-slām l-rāgba w yhawwad z-zdār*
I love kisses in the neck that go down to the breasts

Cheb Khaled, "ʿAlāsh ḥbībak tansih" (Why do you forget your friend?)

*Farshat s-sādra w ghaṭṭaha ḥbibha*
She made a bed out of jujube and he was her cover

Cheb Khaled, "Rrāy shīn" (Evil raï)

*Dītha lil l-ghāba w khlaʿaha l-dhib*
I took her to the woods and the wolf [male sex] scared her

Cheb Khaled, "Ya Ṣ-Ṣayāda" (The huntress)

*Tʿaanagna fi r-rūshi w kasset kulshi*
We embraced on the rocks [cliffs] and she took everything off

Cheb Khaled, "Rrāy shīn" (Evil raï)

The places where pleasure parties were held were most often described as taking place outside public view. Thus the railway tracks, the beach, and the woods (remember "Sʿaīda bʿaīda") are synonyms for *baṣṭas* in raï songs, unless the scene depicted took place in much poorer circumstances:

*Baytīn baṣāṭa ʿala ḍāw kamyūn*
We spend the night doing a *baṣṭa* in the light of a truck

Cheb Khaled, "Hay waddi" (Oh, my luck)

*Farshat l-karṭūn yana w ḥlalha n-nūm*
She made a bed out of millboard and sleep suited her well

Cheb Khaled, "Yali, yali" (Here, here)

However, the lines need not depict a setting at all, but might contain joking:

*Ntiyya ḥamāma, ana gūrille, talgi encore ʿala kull*
You are a pigeon, I am a gorilla. Let everything loose

Cheb Khaled, "Mānish minna" (I am not from here)

Or they might evoke the sexual act for the listeners in an indirect way by giving the audience the pleasure of envisaging what was really going on:

*Smʿaat l-gallāl, jāt bla ḥzam*
She heard the *gallāl* and she came without her belt

Cheb Khaled, "Ghīr ddūni lil dārna" (Just bring me to our house)
[A publisher told me: "You've got to be a fool if you don't understand that a woman without a belt is a naked woman."]

*Bin l-ḥūt s-sagiyya w l-mā ifūt*
In between the fishes [woman's breasts] there is a river where water flows

Cheb Khaled, "Ma natzawwaj ma nrabbi kabda" (I won't marry, I won't tie up my feelings)

*L kabūs w l mukaḥla w l-barnūs l-ūbār*
The pistol [male sex], the gun [musket, i.e., the female sex], and the burnoose of camel hair

Cheb Khaled, "Līla nakhbatha" (Tonight I'll get drunk)

## The Cabarets

In the early 1980s, a main location for pleasure parties in the city of Oran were the cabarets. It was here that song lyrics, like those presented above, accompanied by new instrumentation, proved their success. It was here that a publisher claimed to have noted on a piece of paper that beer was for Arabs and whiskey for foreigners, and it was here that publishers and singers tried out new songs to see whether they might be a commercial success on cassette (it was also from here that Western journalists wrote fascinating accounts of "liberal Algeria").

In the early 1990s, few *gawris* or foreigners came to the cabarets and the competition among publishers meant that new inventions would be jealously hidden. According to most witnesses, the atmosphere in the cabarets had become more violent than ten years earlier. I myself was impressed in the first days after my arrival in Oran to learn that men often protected themselves when going to cabarets with razor blades or knives. The first time I toured the cabarets with a singer, the dancing was interrupted by a huge fight. The doorman suddenly stood on the dance floor waving wildly with a sword while the customers hurried out of the door or jumped through the windows.

Nonetheless, there one could find women smoking, drinking, and dancing with men in close union. Here, men took "free women" out, talked with them, had fun with them. Here, couples publicly fondled each other, kissing and displaying public behavior which was very rarely witnessed outside such places. This was underlined by a common saying that if you wanted to take your wife out, you should divorce her first.

Raï music in itself was a central medium for contact between men and women. The men tended to dance individually, but would at the same time use dance movements as part of a dialogue with the women present. Working with the pelvis and establishing the same movement confirmed contact between a couple, which could subsequently lead to an exchange of telephone numbers outside the sight of male competitors. Another method of contact was to use the game of dedications surrounding the singing. A man would address a woman by paying for a song that had a title referring to the girl's personality. If this manoeuvre was carried out cleverly, it could result in a private appointment with the woman. If not, fierce fights could break out.

Basically, the relationship between men and cabaret women was more than sexual. A thirty-two-year-old grocer who was married with three children cried one night because the mother of the woman he loved had started asking him for money to take her daughter out on the weekends.

A thirty-five-year-old dentist who was married with two children had for a long time been supporting a woman from the cabarets in an extra flat he owned in town until his mother showed up and in order to prevent a divorce asked him to stop. One well-to-do trader, although married, would take his mistress with him away from home and allow her to fondle him in public, joke with him, and declare her love for him. An acquaintance who lived in very bad economic, family, and housing conditions said that some nights he went to a certain restaurant to pick up a woman when his wife was at her family's place. He then bought some bottles of wine to share with her, but the best thing, he said, was to talk and relax with her the whole night.

The relationship with the "free women" sometimes led to serious love affairs and couples deciding to stay together, but it was known to be a delicate situation and that marriage would be difficult. Parents would rarely agree to such a relationship, and it was commonly thought that once the woman had tasted the "free life," going out when she wanted, she would have difficulties in settling down as a housewife. It also required capital to enter a relationship with a *maryūla,* either to provide her with an apartment or to entertain her in public in the restaurants of "*le milieu.*" It was also commonly acknowledged that the women often played on "several horses." Thus having a relationship with a "free girl" required a man to be able to defend his position with money and his prowess in the physical fights that broke out in the cabarets.

A number of raï songs from the early 1980s took their listeners into these problems of nightlife, dealing with the frustrations of maintaining relationships with "free women":

*Galbak qasi w hbībak, lāsh tansih*
Your heart is tough; why do you forget him?

Cheb Khaled, "Ashḥāl bqatni nuṣbur" (How much can I endure?)

*La sakkrūni bāsh ndīr kulshi*
They made me drunk, to treat me as they wished

Cheb Khaled, "Shaḥfiyya ana lli bghīt" (It serves me right, I was looking for it)

*Ṣahr l-lyāli wʿaar w nti mʿaamda*
Nights out are tough and you accepted it

Cheb Khaled, "Nsālfīk" (You do concern me)

*Ma ndīrha l-amān, lqītha mbaṣṭa fi l-jnān*
I don't trust her; I found her in good company in the garden

Cheb Khaled, "ʿAlash twalfīni nabghīk" (Why do you make me want you?)

And often the road to crime was not far away:

> *Khāfi ʿaliyya l-vula ṣʿaība, yak l-barāj fi kull ṭrīg ki ndīr*
> Have fear for myself, the wheel is difficult to handle, there are barriers all over the road, what shall I do?
>
> Cheb Khaled and Miloud, "Kubbu, kubbu" (Pour out, pour out)

> *Ṭabu jnābi ʿala s-sīma l-bārda*
> My ribs hurt because of the cold cement
>
> Cheb Khaled, "Shaḥfiyya ana lli bghīt" (It serves me right, I looked for it)

> *La fāt fiyya sinyīt, taskhu kwāghti*
> It is too late; I signed; I soiled my personal papers
>
> Cheb Khaled, "Ma ḥlāli n-nūm" (Sleep doesn't suit me)

It was often a world of little romance, as the songs themselves recognized:

> *R-ragba w l-maryūl ana ma yabghīh ḥadd*
> No one wants the tough guy and the flirting woman
>
> Cheb Khaled, "Ṣṣubri, ṣṣubri," (Have patience, have patience)

> *Mulāt zūj wulidāt fi l-ghāba tbāt*
> Mother of two children and she sleeps in the woods at night
>
> Cheb Khaled, "Liyya, liyya" (For me, for me)

> *Tabʿaat r-rikār, samhat ṣ-ṣghāri*
> She followed the Ricard; she forgot her small [children]
>
> Cheb Khaled, "Shkūn addāk" (Who took you?)

> *Nṣawwaṭha w nbakkiha shaffuni wlādha*
> I'll beat her and make her cry; I pitied her because of her children
>
> Cheb Khaled, "Dallāli, dallāli" (My guide, my guide)

Some lines present "solemn" and "moving" expressions such as

> *La ilaha il allāh w kānat katba*
> There is no God but God, and there is destiny
>
> Cheb Khaled, "Tastahel ya galbi" (You deserve it, oh my heart)

which evokes the first part of the *shāhada* (the credo of Islam).

Last but not least, the lyrics express a world that cannot be reconciled with the ideal life of the family.

> *Fḍāt ʿala mwa, kull yūm njīha ʿama*
> I did many bad things toward my mother; every day I come home blinded [from drinking]
>
> Cheb Khaled, "Nti, nti" (You, you)

*Rrāy l-ghaddār talaftli rrāy w khalītli d-dār*
Treacherous raï, you made me change my ways; you made me lose my home

Cheb Khaled, "Nti, nti" (You, you)

This was the world of raï, in which the hard life of "the milieu" was expressed in terms of raï:

*Ṣaḥḥa rabbi nastahel, yana rrāy darli*
Thank you my God, I deserve it; raï did it to me

Cheb Khaled, "Tastahel ya galbi" (You deserve it, oh my heart)

*Rrāy shīn, win mṭalʿani, rrāy d-dūni wīn dayni*
Evil raï, where do you lead me? Hard raï, where do you take me?

Cheb Khaled, "Rrāy shīn" (Evil raï)

In the early 1980s, a whole range of lyric sentiments in raï grew out of, and evoked, spheres of lust and pleasure in Algerian society. They emphasized a particular way of altering the boundaries between gender roles which predominated in everyday life. For the locations were not only places for women to move in male spheres, displaying male features through body posture, smoking, and drinking alcohol in public (Danielson 1991, Jansen 1987, van Nieuwkerk 1992, Rafik 1980), but also locations for men to play down conventional modes of manly behavior and to display indeterminate markers of sexual identity (Stokes 1992, Wikan 1977).

This indeterminacy is evident in raï songs. There is not only an interchangeability between male and female expressions. Male singers tend to sing in a high tessitura, while the most favored female singers sing in a low register. When listening to duets, the untrained ear can have difficulty discriminating between the male and female voices. These indeterminacies in raï can also be exemplified by the frequent successes of male child singers. Thus two singers who started their careers as boys explained that they had success because "I sang like a woman" or "I had the voice of a woman." At live performances in Oran in the early 1990s, one could find not only masculine women, but also a group of effeminate men playing with great success as *maddāḥas* at women's wedding parties.

Transgressions of gender roles were acknowledged as a fact in the spheres of lust and leisure in the Oran area, where the singers themselves profited from their nights spent in a milieu with easy access to women. For example, one singer well known for his effeminate expression while dancing was thought to be a homosexual. He actually got married (for three months) to a female singer in 1991. Subsequently, the couple recorded a cassette showing the wedding picture on the cover, while declaring themselves "the second legitimate couple in raï." By this they evidently implied that other duets were mostly sung by men and women who did not have legitimate relationships. However, even though the transgressions were acknowledged, the transsexual singers and the effeminate male dancer still had difficulty being admitted to the cabarets. It was impossible for the latter to perform there, and the former had to stop an otherwise successful performance while singing in a restaurant during the Ramadan of 1992 because some of the audience threw *tebrīḥas* to stop the performance. Generally, the indeterminacy of gender boundaries in the cabarets was accompanied by the exaggeration of other aspects of male behavior,[4] to which fights leading to fatalities were a testimony. The cabarets were places of intense male competition for women; the men were constantly on their guard concerning their competitors' moves. I knew some for whom the excitement of the competition—in an "unregulated market"—was as great a pleasure as contact with the opposite sex, and some for whom the fight was sought in itself. Naturally, this made the profession of the cabaret singer a difficult one.

Many lyrics in raï were thus born in an arena of transgression and a competitive form of conspicuous consumption. The lines were meant to touch people, either amusing or arousing them. Others played on the supposed emotional tension between "normal" and "marginal" life, or on the possible emotions of outsiders in witnessing people who had "surrendered" to the spheres of pleasure.

The interesting fact, however, is that it was also these lyrics—sung by young voices in a socioculturally weak position and amplified by Western electric instruments using sounds and formulas with references to parties and discos in the West, which achieved such success outside the spheres for which they were primarily intended. The "mobile" cassettes brought the voices out of the cabarets and lent evidence to the hypothesis that a change in gender roles and in the notion of leisure time was becoming of acute concern in Algeria in the 1980s.

It seems as if a potent relationship between music and sexuality was established in raï that could be compared to similar phenomena in the West. But the early 1980s was also a period when the Islamist movement was on the rise among Algerian youth. This movement shared with raï a preoccupation with relations between men and women since its main idea was their public segregation. This indicates that establishing any direct parallel between youth cultures in the West and youth conditions in Algeria would be a futile enterprise.

## Raï and the Family

Thus, for many Algerian families, listening to early raï posed problems, as raï in general has done. People I met during my fieldwork in Algeria rarely commented on raï without mentioning the problems of listening to it in the family. It was not the musical part as such that was problematized, but mostly words such as *slām* (kisses), *rūj* (red wine), *birra* (beer), *sākra* (drinking alcohol), *mkhabbat* (getting drunk), or *taḥwās l būlevar* (walking the streets) and the whole range of associations they evoked. Even the simple evocation of the woods, the beach, and raï music itself could create embarrassment in many family circles.

The interesting thing about these problems was not so much that it could be awkward to listen to rather crude expressions in the company of the family, but rather that the listening seemed to take place in differentiated contexts according to a certain hierarchy within the family, in which the roles of father, mother, sister, and brother were constantly at stake. Frequently, young men would not listen to raï in front of their father, but would do so in front of their mother, brothers, and sisters. Sisters rarely listened to raï in front of their fathers and brothers, and sometimes brothers would not listen to raï in each other's presence.

The values at stake with regard to listening to music varied with the family (as in the case of my seven informants). In a few families, music was not listened to at all when the family was gathered together. In some families, raï could not be heard at all, while in others only some categories of raï could not be heard. Basically, listening was organized on the basis of different age and gender groups. Early raï, in particular, could not be listened to in the family when other members were present. Most of the young men I visited at home turned on raï only when a door could be closed to other members of the family. Otherwise they listened to it outside the family—in the streets, in cassette shops, in cars (those few who had access to one), on the beach, in the woods, on vacant lots in the cities, in bars. Before the rise of the Islamist party, they listened to it at concerts or at rare disco parties in rented halls on weekends. However, there was one important exception to these practices. At weddings, raï could be enjoyed by all members of the family in each other's presence.

This practice—that you do something in one situation that you do not do in another—has been called by some a "supreme hypocrisy within the Algerian family" (Ben Naoum 1986:11). When I asked about the reasons for the listening patterns, most answers were brief, such as, "I don't know," or not very elaborated ones such as, "The words are vulgar," "it is shameful" (*'ayb*). Most often the explanation was that it was a matter of respect (*qdar*), that it was simply not good to listen to subjects like drinking and women in front of your family. With regard to the wedding, the most common answers went like this: "I don't know, when we party we forget about the words," "at weddings we blow off steam," "at weddings we lose our heads."

However, the contextual or differentiated practice of listening did appear in a number of other situations as well. For example, an accordionist who had played in the local radio orchestra and had also participated in numerous raï recordings was living in extremely poor circumstances (one room for himself, his wife, and his five children). He did not sing at home in front of his family because he *ḥashāmt,* as he said (he felt uneasy, shy, ashamed, embarrassed), even if his family knew his voice and songs from the radio. On another occasion, I was discussing raï with left-wing people from Oran who in many respects were extremely liberal, for example, in lending rooms for their friends' trysts. When discussing details of early raï, they automatically lowered their voices in order not to be heard by the women in the adjacent room.

This contextualization also appeared in many families who had linked their televisions to a satellite dish to receive French television programs. In the families I knew, the television would be on the whole day, as if it were another (constantly) communicating family member. Some films, however, showed love scenes and couples kissing, and a number of advertisements used sex and eroticism to keep the attention of the viewer. In some families the advertisements were passed over as if they had gone unnoticed. In other families, they "zapped" the controls when they expected an immodest advertisement to appear. In yet others the head of the family removed the connection to the satellite dish when he was not at home, leaving only the "kiss-censured" and therefore "kiss-free" Algerian television for the rest of the family. In families where they had space and money for two televisions, there were divisions in who saw different kinds of programs together. In one, the head of the family retired to watch movies alone while the rest of the family stayed together. In another, which had no male head, women watched television together, while in an adjacent room men of the same age watched the same program.

Cigarette smoking followed a similar pattern. Women were not supposed to smoke at all, while men smoked according to the context in which they found themselves. Nasser, for example, who lived in a liberal family, never smoked in the presence of his father and grandfather. Everybody knew that he smoked, and his grandfather actually told me that he knew, and he knew that Nasser refrained when in his presence to show him respect.

Hasni was also a great smoker. When we played cards in the back room of the restaurant, he hid his cigarettes every time his uncle approached, though there was no doubt that the uncle knew. I asked several people about this smoking "system" because it also relates to drinking habits as well as to listening to raï and watching television. The explanations were again brief, most often being: "I don't know why," frequently followed by "out of respect." When I pressed Hasni, Nasser, Djillali, and Houari, I received answers like, "Not to seem old or grown up in front of your father"; "you don't talk about sex in front of your father"; "you don't drink either."

Finally, this "situated" practice with regard to the family was also reproduced in raï songs themselves. I gradually realized during my stay in Oran that despite raï's incessant interest in exploiting extraordinary events from daily life, it never had lyrics dealing with problems within the family, that is, with social situations such as "my father gives me problems," "I fought with my sister," or "my brother betrayed me." The only member of the family explicitly mentioned was the mother, and then to her praise. When I started to inquire more into this paradox, the answers I received included that it was not "appropriate for singers to talk about their family like that," "people would not like to listen to things like that," or "you have to show respect to your family."

## A Model of the Family

To understand raï songs and their reception in Algeria, it is necessary to appreciate an "ideal model" of Algerian family patterns, which are known from a number of writings on Middle Eastern societies.[5] The family is based on a single home where the members spend most of their time in the communal rooms, with little privacy. The kitchen is shared, and the other rooms—except the rooms for sleeping and for married couples—are not private. At the head of the table and of the hierarchy is the patriarch, who handles the resources of the family and is consulted whenever major decisions are made. Under him are his dependents, typically younger brothers or sons whose power of decision tends to follow their rank in a hierarchy of age. Among the other members of the family, further unequal relations tend to exist between older and younger siblings as well as between the sexes. Younger brothers, for example, have authority over their older sisters, and a wife is in general dependent on and subordinate to her husband.

Wealth and descendants follow the male line, which means that, in theory, an unlimited number of male descendants with their wives and children can live in a family. The preservation of a pure bloodline makes the protection of the women against intruders central. Of prime importance is the protection of the virginity of unmarried women in order to assure a future husband that his first-born child is of his own blood. This is also the basis of a man's interest in ensuring and perpetuating a division between the "public outside" of males and the "private inside" of women, the latter space being "veiled" from outsiders and serving as a base of privacy for men from which no news of any intimate nature emerges.

Thus a man will rarely mention the name of his wife, and the mother in the family will have no name either inside or outside the home. She will be the unnamed center for the procreation of the group. A major aim in the creation of a new unit in such a structure is to provide the family with new members. Marriage therefore transcends the will of individuals, their futures being interlinked with the future of the group and its general policies or strategies. The married couple is thus not supposed to be primarily linked through bonds of conjugal happiness and love, but rather through its contribution to the strengthening of the group vis-à-vis other families.

The patriarch's power over the family is on the one hand based on his control of resources, where his ascribed status can be maintained further through appropriate behavior. A man in power uses his resources. He displays his ability to provide and the value of generosity. Thus the wisdom of age—the accumulation of adequate knowledge of the values and norms of the society—is linked to the resources at the patriarch's disposal.

On the other hand the social organization of the family is maintained through the weaker members' deference toward the more powerful, primarily women's deference in front of men, but also juniors' deference toward seniors. If the family can basically be described as a place of intimacy, this latter notion must in itself be specified. The father tends to distance himself from the members of the family, who on their side respect the man—valued as a person of decision and strength—and behave modestly in his presence.

"*Qdar* [respect]," Zerdoumi writes, quoting an Algerian proverb, "is a word which marks great deference. In principle you ought to do everything to keep up respect, because if it disappears all life in common would collapse" (1982:166). And *ḥashūma* consists in feeling and showing modesty in a number of circumstances of individual, social, and family life. In the Muslim environment, it is the cornerstone of civility and good manners. Those who do not have *ḥashūma* are individuals "without religion, without shame, without modesty, without honour and mainly without dignity" (ibid.: 264). In this sense it is also associated with the notion of *ʿaql* (reason). A person without *ʿaql* is a person who does not show respect or display modesty. To have *ʿaql* is to act in a responsible, mature way. It is to be able to discern and react appropriately to the variety of social possibilities in any situation. It "is the ability of persons to control their needs and passions in recognition of the ideals of honor in order to perceive the social order and their place in it" (see Abu-Lughod 1986:108; see also Descloitres and Debzi 1964:47–48). To have no *ʿaql* is to have no control over the passionate, animal side of your nature or rather to be dependent on your animal side with no self-control in such activities as eating, drinking, defecating, and the satisfying of sexual needs (see Abu-Lughod 1986:91). Women are considered to have less *ʿaql* than men. Not only do their pregnancies make it difficult for them to hide their "passionate side," but also their menstruation makes them less in control over themselves insofar as it concerns a form of bodily waste which, like spit, hair, nasal mucus, nail parings, blood, urine, and excrement, is considered unclean (see Jansen 1987:51).

Having *ʿaql* is also, to use Eickelman's terms, a contextual rather than an absolute moral principle, as the reasonable person seeks "to discern accurately the contours of existing social and political realities and on that basis to calculate an effective course of action" (1985:312; see also Descloitres and Debzi 1964:48). Put another way, *ʿaql* is a quality linked to the contextual use of respect and modesty within a hierarchy of age, gender, and access to resources and power. For younger men it means behaving modestly in front of those who should be respected—that is, seniors, who are considered to possess more reason. It also means that they expect deference from those in a weaker position, primarily women. For women, in general, it means behaving modestly in the presence of men. Wives respect their husbands, daughters their fathers, and sisters their brothers. However, between mothers and sons, a different and more intimate relationship seems to exist.

In this ideal model of the North African family, the mother leaves her family and enters into a new one, taking few possessions with her. In the course of a lifetime she might succeed in improving her position. This is something related to her husband's life career and also to her sons and their future wives. Unlike the males of the family, a mother has no access to resources, but she is credited with having witnessed and cared for the male child when he was most vulnerable. The son's dependence can be perpetuated through affection, and the mother can maintain the relationship by being a mediator between her son and his father. She invests in her son's virility through bonds of affection. As a result, he becomes immersed in an emotional dependency which has as a side effect those conflicts between a wife and her mother-in-law that are so well known in North Africa (see Ben Jelloun 1977).

Altogether, the notions of *ʿaql, qdar,* and *ḥashūma* are an integral part of behavior within the family, where they function as mediators in relations of power. Inside the family, we discover what characterizes its relations to the outside: protection from and regulation of the unreasonable, the latter being associated with femininity rather than with masculinity. A man unable to master these elements in public and private is a man without self-control, a man without control of his femininity.

## Purity and Practice, Raï and Islam

Clearly, any "reification of the Algerian family" or any generalization of "Algerian listening patterns" is bound to be a hazardous affair. I have already hinted at a number of differences to be found between Algerian families, as well as to important changes that have historically taken place in the structure of the Algerian family. In the early 1990s in Oran, a number of cases did not conform to any of the ideals presented above. Many families lived under conditions in which the codes of respect were broken. One family I visited, with a forty-year-old son raised in France until the age of twenty, consisted of twelve people living in a three-room flat. The son would harass his father in a drunken state whenever the latter tried to make him leave the local bar. In another family, the son was an alcoholic, while his father owned a bar. A number of families, of course, allowed their female members to sing in public. Ali listened to raï in front of his father before starting his prayers, and in Kader's family, values regarding listening to raï did not seem necessarily to conform to hierarchies of age. The informal stories of raï singers' lives have already hinted at these diversities in family life. These examples indicate that one of the main sources in the success of raï's "moving lines about extraordinary situations" was that the situated approach to respect was frequently put to the test.

Nevertheless, in Oran the ideal model of the family did have relevance, since every time raï was brought up and the genre was discussed, the problem of the family and who could listen with whom would surface. Moreover, the contextual and situated practice of listening to raï, watching television, smoking, and drinking also appeared in relation to at least two other more formally sacred spheres of Algerian society, the holy month of Ramadan and the mosque.

One raï singer of Kabyle origin (with a membership card in the FIS) said to me, "Marc, you have to come here during Ramadan. That's when we are real Muslims. That's when there is the real Islam," echoing what I had heard several times already. Accordingly, I went to Oran and fasted the whole month of Ramadan. I was presented with a discourse which said it was good for the health, that it gave the body a rest for one month, that (besides teaching people solidarity with the poor of this world) the fast trained one not to depend on food and drink. It was exercise not only for the stomach, but also for the ear and the eye: In Ramadan you were not supposed to talk behind people's backs, gossip, bicker, or have sexual intercourse in the daytime. The latter prohibition was expressed in terms like, "You should not take an interest in women, look at them, or chase after them." "You should not watch X-rated films on French television, and if you did happen to see a woman in the street or a couple kissing on television, you should abstain from imagining anything of a sexual nature."

Everything was done as if the logic of morality in the family was applied to the daytime fast in Ramadan, since Ramadan was also known for the increase in food consumption that took place at night.[6] The men I knew referred to the daytime in Ramadan as comparable to the family, with no smoking, drinking, or expression of sensuality or sexuality, just as you were not supposed to do in the family. The same connection could be found in respect to the mosque.

Thus a number of acquaintances and friends who professed their faith in Islam, and even in the Islamist party, would identify with all the elements expressed above. Djillali did not pray, however, because he had "too many problems and was drinking alcohol," while a friend of his (newly married, a dealer on the black market), also a declared Muslim, was not praying because "I love to make love to my wife and it is too great a nuisance to have to wash all the time." A friend of Ali's had been praying, but had stopped because he "was chasing women and drinking alcohol." Another friend, however, had done the opposite. He "stopped listening to raï and chasing women, and was now praying." Kader told me that if he met a woman on his way to the mosque, and she excited him, his prayers would be invalid unless he washed. Hasni's cousin once spent a long time explaining a Muslim's duties to me, only to end up admitting that he did not perform them: "I am weak. I love women. When I get married, I can become a good Muslim." I heard this remark several times—that it is impossible to become a good Muslim when you have too many problems finding a wife, a house, and a job to support her.[7]

In all these examples, the men were referring to the mosque as if it were structurally parallel to the family. In the mosque you did not smoke, drink, or expose any sensuality or sexuality, just as you were not supposed to do within the family. To put it another way, when you entered the mosque or family, you were supposed to contribute to the purity of the environment. Thus, people were simultaneously referring to the key concept of impurity in Islam. "All that the body discards is impure and pollutes the body" (Boudhiba 1975:60). Before entering the mosque to pray, a purification must be made in order to approach God in the appropriate way. You make the minor purification, *uḍu,* or if you have had intercourse, the major purification, *ghusl,* since you are in *janāba,* strictly speaking, "alienated," being beside yourself (ibid.:62).

The purity of praying was compared to purity within the family. Altogether, therefore, there was agreement between the "moral logic" of the family, the mosque, and Ramadan in the sense that the nonconsumption of alcohol and regulated sexuality all belonged to the religiously sanctioned areas of what was prescribed as the duty of a Muslim, the *ḥalāl,* and what was forbidden, the *ḥarām.* Finally, the sociomoral scheme of the family was not only projected onto Ramadan and the mosque. A religio-doctrinal scheme of sacredness was projected onto the family, as is shown by the following verse of the Koran:

> Thy Lord hath decreed
> That ye worship none but Him
> And that ye be kind
> To parents. Whether one
> Or both of them attain
> Old age in thy life
> Say not to them a word
> Of contempt, nor repel them
> But address them
> In terms of honour.

(Koran, 17:23, from Yusuf's 1983 translation).

In Oran, there were many fuzzy boundaries between official Islamic doctrines and sociomoral everyday practice, for example, when a publisher invited me and another guest to share a bottle of whiskey with him while honoring us with a *bismillah,* "in the name of God," or when Hasni's friends extinguished their joints of hashish when FIS demonstrations passed by in June 1991 singing "*la illah il Allāh*" (there is no god but Allah), or when Kader, who would collect religious merits (*ḥassanats*) by giving money to beggars removing stones from the road he was passing along, and telling me not to read a newspaper in Arabic (God's language) in the toilet. There was the practice of drinkers giving up alcohol forty days before Ramadan in favor of hashish. There was Ali, who scolded Kader and his friends for going to the beach (which implied looking for women or simply the pleasure of looking at women) and attending Friday prayers at the same time, although Ali himself did not consider it contrary to Islam to have a steady girlfriend.

Many people in Oran would argue for an age-based understanding of the relation between the pure and impure. Thus a number of musicians, singers, and sellers of raï were adherents of the FIS (or were simply praying). They argued that they were in the business of making a future for themselves in which they would be able to respect Muslim doctrines. Several raï publishers had changed to other enterprises and would no longer talk about their former lives. Several raï listeners approved of the FIS but argued that they needed more time to become good Muslims and quit listening to raï.

But not only did there seem to be a fuzzy interdependence between the sociomoral organization of everyday life and the notion of the sacred. It also seemed as if, with the advent of the FIS, the concept of the contextualized sacred respect and modesty (involving power structures within the family) tended increasingly to be opposed to the concept of a sacred purity extended to all spheres and times. During my stay in Algeria, I followed young men, including singers, who started practicing doctrinal Islam, which meant giving up drinking and chasing girls, and which became the basic premise of going to the mosques which held political sessions. Many also went to the mosque only to subsequently stop praying because they could not succeed in managing their lives according to the totalizing concept of sacred purity.

In a fascinating essay, Benkheira (1982) has suggested that this tension became articulated in Oran in the late 1970s when an urban lifestyle dating back to the colonial period, centered around the *tbarna* (cantina or tavern), began to be replaced by a way of life symbolized by the mosque. The bars and "drinking salons" had fewer and fewer clients, while the mosques had more and more adherents. A new kind of sociality developed which was opposed not only to the bars, but also to the cafes (places for playing cards, sometimes for money) or teahouses and ice bars (where you could go with your family or meet single women).

Previously the consumption of alcohol was an initiation rite for youngsters, together with smoking and going to the brothel. To drink was a sign of virility and a proof of reaching adulthood. Drinking, however, was not done in the family, for this would be to mix the profane (the street) with the sacred (the home). Only after this youthful stage would drinkers become practicing believers, most often after marrying. Men stopped drinking because it became too expensive with a family to support, and they went to the mosque when they got old. The mosque was thus not only a place for "taming death" but also for sorting individuals into age groups. Youth was made for the pleasurable, old age for serious things.

According to Benkheira, the sacralization of public spaces had its origin in the dual organization of the colonial city. The colonial and the Muslim part each had their own kinds of cafes. In the former there were men, women, and alcohol, while in the latter there were only men, and no alcohol and no women. The Muslim cafe was a kind of representative of male society and part of a semisacred complex, represented by the *ḥammām* (the bathhouse), the market, and the mosque.

After independence, a process started in which the values of the Muslim cafe slowly invaded the basically impure, alcoholized, and sexually mixed European city.[8] Thus the development Benkheira described at the start of the 1980s was one of "purifying" public spaces, prohibiting women in men's spheres, prohibiting games in the cafes, women smoking in public, and the like. The price of alcohol was increased and campaigns against alcohol forced drinking to go behind closed curtains. In 1982 Benkheira could write that the interpenetration of the sacred with the secular was not total, but that it had gone very far (ibid.: 29). In 1991 it was still not total, though it was an increasingly present force.

In Nasser's family, the uncle, once he had returned from the United States as an Islamist, stopped kissing the female members of the family, and his wife stopped embracing and offering her hands to the male members. However, this reform practice stopped when the rest of the family refused to see them anymore. My French-bearded journalist friend (see chapter 4) was threatened with death one day by two young "Muslim-bearded" men while we were walking in his neighborhood, which, however forced his brothers in the FIS to find out who was targeting him. One day, Hasni went with his sister to the center of town and was followed all the way by a "brother" in order to check up on the nature of their relationship.

In 1991, I participated in the last mass meeting that occurred in Oran in the Fifth of July football stadium, held by by Abassi Madani and Ali Belhadj before their arrest. There were thousands of men present as well as about a thousand women in another part of the stadium, wearing the *ḥijāb*. The speaker's platform was facing away from the main stand, where hundreds of men were singing and shouting slogans—*Allāh akbar* (God is great), and so on—in a way which to me sounded like football supporters in the Copenhagen national stadium. During Madani's speech, I lit a cigarette and immediately was asked to extinguish it. I looked around and saw that I was the only person smoking in a crowd of normally fervent smokers. What I saw as a football stadium and a political meeting turned out to have been transformed into a sacred space.

## Clean and Dirty Raï, Weddings and Cabarets

When raï was on the rise in the 1980s, it provoked passionate debate. It was in this context that the expression of "clean raï" appeared initially among publishers. One of the first public uses of the expression was an interview with the top producers Rachid and Fethi, who said they were seeking to "purify a musical space that had been besieged for a long time by innumerable upstarts" (*Algérie Actualité,* April 18, 1984).

By the early 1990s, the expression "clean raï" or (in French) "*raï propre*" had become part of the common language. For example, a 1991 calendar featuring the well-known Houari Benchenet was accompanied by the motto "clean raï." When I made one of my first (official) interviews with a well-known singer, I asked him in French if he "*chantes tes propres chansons*" (in the sense of "do you sing your own songs"), to which he hastily replied, "*La, la nghanni ghīr nqāyan, des chansons pour la famille*" (No, no I only sing clean ones, songs for the family). Thus the singer understood the question to be, "Do you sing clean songs?" and he was eager to deny singing nonclean raï.

In fact, in public many singers denied any relationship with clubs, free women, or the consumption of alcohol. When the Festival of Oran music took place in October 1991, I had the opportunity to interview a number of less well known singers, most of whom I was meeting for the first time.

When I asked them what and where they sang, most of them stressed that they only sang clean raï, and only at weddings and concerts. When I was trying later to meet one of the top singers in raï, I contacted his father several times. He told me that his son would be home at the weekend or singing in a high-class restaurant. In fact he was performing in a well-known cabaret, but had chosen to cast a veil over the fact that he was associated with a nonclean milieu.

The expression "clean raï" established a semantic link between raï, the family, the mosque, and Ramadan—between everyday moral practice and official religious doctrine. In this sense, early raï became dirty, while more recent raï was clean (in fact, clean raï meant that songs about the competitive, conspicuous consumption of women were replaced by songs of love).

It is in this context that the problematic of early raï must be understood. As already mentioned, it was not the music as such that posed problems,[9] but the images and moods that raï suggested. For example, several people in Algeria told me that although they did not play raï at home, they did play Western music. They and their parents knew what the songs were about, but they did not understand them. Using the same line of argument (see, for example, chapter 2), proponents of raï have argued that the words of raï do not differ from the words of many Egyptian or *andalus* songs in the sense that if they were expressed in literary Arabic, they would be perfectly respectable. Thus words that were not expressed in the maternal language—or of which there was no practical experience—referred to other worlds and were felt differently. One of the most popular *tabrīḥas* in the early 1990s, heard at every wedding, was one that had already been quoted in 1985:

> I heard Sabah, the Lebanese, sing of love in all languages. She said in Italian: "Io te amo"; in French: "Je t'aime"; in English: "I love you"; in German: "ich liebe dich"; in Spanish: "te quiero." Well, we Algerians, we say: "Rabbak nabghik" ["for God's sake, I want you"]. (Ben Naoum 1986:13)

Ben Naoum writes that in 1985 the audience laughed when they heard this. In 1992, too, people laughed when they heard the Algerian expression, which was considered a rather direct one invoking both God and an immediate need for the other.

Words expressed in the maternal dialect were felt differently since they related to a local world, and feelings can endanger one's power over oneself and thus over others. In Oran, the fear of losing self-control could be seen in many cases. Djillali told me the story of a brother and sister in Arzew who had watched an X-rated film in each other's company, which resulted in an act of incest. Several heads of families tended to avoid being alone in the same room as their daughters-in-law. Victims of housing problems, or people commenting on housing problems, expressed it in terms of: "How can I change clothes in the presence of my mother and sister?" "What might happen if I were forced to lie beside my sister, back to back the whole night?"

I am, of course, not far from expressing the idea that if "sexuality is evoked," there was a fear that "sexuality there would be."[10] Nor am I far from well-known analyses of sexuality in Muslim countries which state that men fear that the power of women's sexuality might make them lose their self-control. These analyses insist on the fact that in Muslim societies, unlike Western ones, sexuality is viewed as a positive force as long as it is regulated, or channeled to take place within certain frames—basically, within marriage (see Boudhiba 1975; Camilleri 1973:202; Mernissi 1983). Both males and females are perceived as possessing an active sexuality. To maintain the male social order, it must be linked with women's virtue, because Muslim female sexuality, turned outward, is endowed with a fatal attraction which might erode the male's will to resist her. He can then only give in to her attraction, whence her identification with *fitna,* chaos, and with the antidivine and antisocial forces of the universe (Mernissi 1983:11). Out of this fear of a "fatal attraction" arises one of the rationalizations for veiling women and keeping them out of men's spheres.

However, an additional element has to be added in regard to raï. If the notion of respect was situationally constructed, then emotions were also directed at someone and connected with images of something (Abu-Lughod and Lutz 1990, Heller 1979, Langer 1953). The raï of the early 1980s produced concrete images of sexuality, love relations, or relations to a life with the *maryūlas*. The words denoted the circles from which they came. For those who knew raï well, images of the beach, the forest, the loose belt, and the railway were concrete images of immodest relations with women or of immodest behavior associated with consuming alcohol. All in all, early raï presented the cabarets as the specific representation of an impure, nonsacred, antifamily, and uncontrollable mode of life in Algerian society.

In this vein, the paradox of listening to raï at weddings can be understood. Elsewhere, it has been argued that events where raï is listened to can be seen as situations where feelings that otherwise should not be expressed in everyday life find an outlet (Guignard 1975:70, Yacine 1990:66), a context inverting the norms of everyday life which people judged by other criteria (Abu-Lughod 1986:189, Lortat-Jacob 1980:29). In Oran, the wedding party was an occasion for an outlet of energies that could not be expressed elsewhere. At parties people did dance in order to blow off steam, though not everyone, for certain people always stayed outside the circle of dancers the whole night. But frequently people got in the mood, going into the circle and dancing, sometimes for a moment, sometimes for much longer, until the urge disappeared. It might even be considered impolite not to participate in creating a festive atmosphere at a wedding.

It also seemed like people did not consider the wedding party to be opposed to daily life, but rather an integrated element of it. Weddings were part of the seasonal lives of people, of the life cycle of individuals and of the generational cycle of families. They were the points from which youngsters ideally established their households, and occasions for families and spouses to confirm, establish, and negotiate their position within the social structures of the society (see Boutefnouchet 1982:262). As such, they were thought of as being under the control of the collective, and furthermore they were framed (see Bateson 1972) to indicate this control. For example, when the procession set off to bring the bride or groom to the party, there was noise with car sounds, rhythm, with music, not only to show, as one member of a procession expressed it, "how many we are," but also "how happy we are," celebrating a wedding but under collective control. As such they showed that what was going on had to be judged by criteria other than nonwedding behavior. They allowed for new limits of enjoyment and for a liminal space where shame was not to be feared and where the norms and elements of everyday life could be expressed in a different order.

Thus everything happened as if the wedding instructed the participants in the important elements which made up the tissue of social life (see Kapferer 1979, Turner 1967), primarily the relationship between man and woman, husband and wife. When the party started, the husband often arrived on a fierce horse with guns blazing and hid his head in a cloak in order not to be made impotent by the antisocial forces of a jealous woman. He also entered the bridal chamber to display his virility in what came as close as possible to a public performance of the sexual act, the defloration of his wife. Finally, after this object lesson in the social idea of the wedding contract, the importance of the blood lineage is emphasized by having the blood-stained shirt shown in public. By then exiting the bridal chamber alone, leaving his wife to remain with the female members of his family, the groom demonstrates how male and female meet but are seldom together.

Wedding parties seemed to be very similar to raï performances in the cabarets in terms of several basic social elements. The same game of competition and exchange of words for money accompanying raï performances could be found in both places, in which people also "lost their heads." Both places also featured sexuality, in cabarets through men's contacts with "free women," at weddings through the consummation of the sexual contract between two families. At the same time, there were significant differences. At weddings, the formal purpose of the money invested in the game of dedications was to share expenses. In the cabarets, the dedications were used solely as a part of a competitive game among men (see Ziad 1983 : 18). Furthermore, in the cabarets, one would frequently hear dedications mentioning women by names, something unheard of at weddings. Naming women in public amounted to exhibiting women in public. Thus cabarets were places for competition among men featuring uncontrolled leisure and lust, where male and female roles were altered; the wedding party confirmed male unity in featuring regulated sexuality where male and female roles were confirmed. The wedding was thus in no way transgressive when compared to the cabarets.

However, bringing raï out of the collective control of the wedding party and into situations of everyday family life seemed to bring raï back to its association with the cabarets and thus to the danger of uncontrolled sexuality in the sacred realm of the family, exposing the weak side of those who should be strong. As such, early raï struck at the heart of a central Algerian institution at a time when it had been exposed to a number of threatening social, economic, and political changes.

Thus to the tension described above—between a situated moral practice and a totalizing one—we must add the fact that the totalizing version of Islam found today has its origins back at least as far as the 1930s, embedded in its ideological development of Islamic scriptural practices in opposition to the colonial regime and the West (see Colonna 1974, 1995; Merad 1967). To this we must also add additional demographic and social changes in postindependence Algeria: the advent (although limited) of working women to the public sphere, the democratization of the system of education, the growth of the cities, changes in the family structure, lengthening of the period of youth, and finally the development of an acute economic crisis. In the 1990s, these changes were paralleled by a large number of weddings taking place "*en famille.*" This basically meant that weddings were closed to the unrelated and allowed a mixing of genders; that is, couples or unmarried family members could be in each other's company. It also meant deemphasizing the blood performance and the separation of husband and wife after the consummation of the marriage. In a sense it brought the nuclear family to the forefront and stressed the fact that an impressive number of unmarried young men felt an urge not only to spend their leisure time with the opposite sex, but also to "separate what was united and unite what was separated" (see Alberoni [1980] 1992:20)—that is, an urge to fall in love, to separate themselves from their parents in order to choose a wife of their own.

Raï became an element in, and expression of, this urge. Not only did it suggest an Algerian image of the uncontrollable forces that defied established relations of authority, but its images of altered gender relations in the cabarets were set to a music which made references to the model of public consumption found in Western discos and parties.

Love is the topic of the next chapter, which ventures into the repertoire of "clean" raï. As already mentioned, it seems that after the official breakthrough of raï in the mid-1980s, raï songs changed slightly in order to reach wider circles. This was the major tendency, though of course there were exceptions such as the 1987 scandalous hit "Dārna l'amour fi l-baraka mrāniqa" (We made *l'amour* in a rotten hut). But nonetheless it still seems as though "clean" raï was accepted to a higher degree in the family because it dealt with love rather than lust. But how did raï become domesticated? What was the raï of love?

# 7

# The Raï of Love

Whereas many song lines in "dirty" raï led us into nature—to the woods, the beach, the wild olives—"clean" raï takes us into the city. Here you find streets, neighborhoods, doors, houses, post offices, telephones and cars, and frequently local business names.

*Khtu fi s-sonilak yaw rkabha l-hlāk*
His sister at Sonelec is in danger

Cheb Khaled, "Hayya nṣuddu" (Let's go) [Sonelec: Société nationale d'electricité. A series of raï songs evoked the national companies which from the mid-1970s started to employ women on a large scale.]

*El ʿAmriyya liya Būtlalis ʿalik*
Amriyya is for me and Boutlelis is for you

Cheb Khaled, "Gultlāk qilīni" (I told you to leave me alone) [two small towns in the Oran region. The line refers to the breakup of the couple.]

*Sh-shīra min Bal ʿAbbās w nakwa Akmīne*
The girl is from Sidi Bel Abbès and she lives [her identity is] in Eckmühl

Cheb Khaled, "Gāltli hāk" (She told me, that's yours) [Eckmühl is a local area of Oran where Khaled also lived.]

In addition, whereas dirty raï was populated by drinking and sexually active men and women, in the lines of clean raï are to be found one's father and mother, one's cousin, and not least the dual relation of "you and me," "me and her," or the triangle of "you, me, and the others."

Meetings between men and women were rarely described using the metaphors in which popular Maghrebin music is otherwise rich.[1] In fact, the wide consensus that there was nothing for young people in Oran to do and that there were no resources to draw on but only time to pass with women seemed to be replicated in the songs.

In general, while the lyrics in dirty raï could be interpreted as intending to arouse or affect people by mentioning "spheres of lust," the lyrics of clean raï could be seen as being based upon the idea that a man's deepest concern was love—his emotions or tensions when he was engaged in a relationship with a woman.

*Kwīt galbi bal kiyya min l-maḥna t-tālya*
My heart was burning because of my latest passion

Cheb Khaled, "Ma namshish mʿaāk" (I won't go with you)

*Minha hiyya ma ḥlāli n-nūm*
Because of her I don't sleep

Cheb Khaled, "Ma ḥlāli n-nūm" (Sleep doesn't come to me)

*Dhīk z-zarga salbatni nassātni ʿala kullshi*
This brunette seduced me and made me forget everything

Benchenet, "Ḥalli l-bāb" (Open the door)

Raï seldom specified qualities of the persons involved but offered open-ended descriptions, leaving the listeners to fill in the details themselves; and rarely did it describe specific conditions—"the where," "when," and "how long" of the love meeting, except for the following:

*Bāb ʿaand l-bāb w ana fi l-ʿadhāb*
Door to door and I am in pain

Cheb Mami, "Ana mazāl" (I am always)

*Khallūni minha kabrat mʿaāya*
Don't mention her anymore; she grew up with me

Mohammed Sghir, "Khallūni minha" (Don't mention her)

To obtain details, one had to look outside the songs.

## Love Stories

Salim, twenty-five years old, was an assistant in a shop owned by his father's cousin. Salim was the oldest of five sons. His mother needed a woman to help her around the house, and Salim married a girl of the family in an inexpensive wedding; soon afterward the couple had a child.

When I knew Salim, he was eager to promote the views of the FIS. He was also frustrated. He did not see how he could progress in the future, get a house of his own, and make room for his younger brother's marriage with the three thousand dinars he earned monthly. One day when I came to see him, he said that he was up to his neck in problems. His wife had left home without telling anyone. She had been stopped at the Moroccan border because she had taken the wrong passport. Now his father wanted him to divorce her, but he refused. He had talked to his wife and she had explained the problems she had had with his mother. Salim's aunt suggested that sorcery was involved, though Salim had never thought of such matters. He seriously considered using sorcery against his father in order to make him change his mind, even though, he said, the FIS condemned it as being *ḥarām*. Two weeks later, he left his family to live in the village of his wife's family. I never saw him again, and his father and uncles banned him from the family.

Brahim, Houari's older brother, had fallen in love with a girl from his school. They saw one another for several years without the knowledge of his parents. Brahim finally decided to ask his parents' permission to marry her. They refused because they did not want him to marry a girl he had met in "the street." Besides, at the time they had no room for a married couple. A year later the girl married another man, but she told Brahim that he would always be the man she loved.

Kader's eldest brother Mohammed (see chapter 4) had twice tried to marry women he loved, but it did not work; both times the mother of the girl refused his requests for marriage, saying that he came from an area of bad reputation. Finally, he asked his mother to find him a wife, which she did.

Hasni had forty-nine girls' names in his address book when I met him, and as already noted, one day he fell in love. He got to know the girl on the telephone at work. For two years they spoke together and one day the girl, the daughter of a widow in Relizane, came to visit him. She arrived with a friend, and Hasni was with his cousin. Together, they managed to borrow a house outside Oran. He told how they had spent a beautiful time together, the men playing cards, smoking hashish, some nights drinking whiskey. One night there were seven couples around the fire. One of the men asked Hasni's girlfriend who she would take if she had to choose between her mother and Hasni. In reply she kissed Hasni, but he said that she should not speak like that. For him, parents always came first; they were sacred, whatever they did. Hasni said that his girlfriend would do anything for him. She cried on the telephone when talking to him. They had also argued and he had slapped her face, but it was right to quarrel, to have things come out. They had slept together, but out of respect for her and both families, she still had her virginity intact. One night he said that he was afraid his parents would not accept her. She fainted when she heard that. She asked if he would throw himself into the sea with her if they could not get married. She wanted him to say yes, but he thought of his parents. She asked if they should stay celibate for the rest of their lives if they could not get married. He said yes. He finally said that if his parents refused, he would run away from home and go to live with her in Relizane or abroad.

Djelloul, twenty-three, worked for the municipality of Oran and lived with his parents in a crowded part of the city. He was shy and had never been with a woman except for a prostitute. For two years he had been in love with his neighbor's daughter, and he finally summoned the courage to ask his mother to ask for her hand. The mother came back with the reply that the girl cared a lot for Djelloul. She liked him as a brother, but she was still too young, and that the time was not yet right.

Djelloul spent hours trying to analyze what had happened. He did not trust his mother to have made the proposal in the right way. He knew that she did not care for his beloved. And often, while I knew him, his mother brought him photos of other girls she knew were ready for marriage, and she praised their qualities, their skills in housework, their full hips, their simple way of life. But Djelloul did not want to marry girls he had never met: he wanted his beloved. How was he to see her again to find out if his mother's version was true? In the two years he had been in love, he had not really had an opportunity to talk to her. He had developed a whole strategy of waiting at places and at times of the day when there was a possibility of her passing by. And the five or ten minutes they talked was enough to make him spend hours analyzing what she had really meant. The only time he told her he loved her, she had told him, "I don't do as they do on the other side" (i.e., France).

Djelloul had a friend, Hussein, twenty-six, a plumber, who had been in love with a girl for several years. Without having sexual intercourse, they had met regularly in the "lover's park" of Oran and outside the town. One day the girl asked him to wait for her, and some time later, he learned that she had been married in another town. This came as a shock to him. He told how he started drinking, smoking, going to brothels. The worst thing of all was that he did not know why this had happened. He and Djelloul had tried to find out why she had married. The most plausible explanation they could think of was that she had somehow lost her virginity, and her family had arranged a fake wedding (the girl later divorced and came back).

Youssef, twenty, a student at the university, was thoroughly depressed. His girlfriend had broken off their relationship. He had known ten girls before, but he had left them when he met her. They had made many plans together. Youssef said she had been influenced by her friends and some members of her family who were against him. Once the girl had come back and said she was sorry. But he said to himself that if she could break things off once, she could do it again. Being young, he preferred to take all the pain now.

Saïd, a twenty-eight-year-old teacher, did the same when his ex-fiancée came back and proposed that they start all over again. Saïd never knew why she had broken off their relationship. They had decided to marry, and he had received the blessing of his mother, a widow. He had succeeded in getting hold of an apartment, and they had chosen the furniture for their home together, but six weeks before the marriage, the girl came to his place and said she could not marry him.

Noureddine, thirty, Saïd's cousin, also a teacher, had tried to get a job abroad. He had no success and so decided to marry. Saïd knew an unmarried woman at his school. He described the girl to Noureddine and Noureddine to the girl. Before their first meeting, which was to last an hour, they had both already decided to say yes. Noureddine did not look the woman in the eye when they met, but only observed her when she looked away. He advised her to seek information about his personality in order to learn about his shortcomings. Otherwise, he said that she could say yes immediately or wait a week. Afterwards they asked their parents for their agreement. While they were waiting for the wedding, they met for an hour once a week. Nourri was a busy man and did not have time to take her out more often, though he said he was in love with his wife-to-be. It seemed they would get married.

## Love Stories and Raï

In raï songs there were a number of lines expressing the fact that relationships between men and women in general could become serious ones involving love:

*L-mūt lli taddīk—taddīni mʿaāk*
Death that takes you away, will take me away with you

Cheb Khaled and Cheba Zahouania, "Ha jaddak" (Oh the grandfather of yours)

*Lli bīk w biyya walli ḍarrek ḍarrni*
What's in you is in me, and what hurts you hurts me

Cheb Khaled, "Manish minna" (I am not from here)

But there were no lyrics dealing with the ability of some couples to find a way to marry out of love. No line in raï told about the shyness of men like Djelloul or about Noureddine's satisfied love, or the marriage of Kader's brother. These success stories did not reveal any significant tensions to sing about, and they generally showed men in control of their relationships (as Hasni also seemed to be sometimes). Instead the lines dealt with the examples of Djelloul, Hussein, Youssef, Saïd, Brahim, and Hasni in their difficult moments: that is, their message was that a man's relationship with women is basically one of suffering and great pain:

*Mūl l-mḥāyen yana w dīma ysūfri*
The man in love always suffers

Cheb Khaled, "Hayya nṣuddu" (Let's go)

*ʿAla l-mulāt l-khāna rāni nsūfri, ya rabbi*
I suffer because of the girl with the beauty spot, oh my God

Benchenet, "Ḥalli l-bāb" (Open the door)

*Dukhān w zallamīt, ana minha gdīt*
With cigarettes and matches, I burned of love

Cheb Khaled, "Shkūn addāk" (Who took you?)

*Rāni mrīḍ w majrūḥ w min l-ghrām bāyāt n-nūḥ*
I am ill and hurt. Because of my love I spent the night crying

Cheb Mami, "Faṭma, Faṭma" (Fatima, Fatima)

In raï, the love meeting was rarely brought to a happy consummation. I seldom found songs or lines praising happy love or telling about people together as a couple or getting married. Rather:

*Min lli ṭlagt anaya ya tzawwajti nti*
When I divorced, you married

Cheb Khaled, "ʿAndi mḥaīna" (I have a passion)

*Asmaʿa l-silāns bini w binha*
Listen to the silence between her and me

Benchenet, "Ṭilifun ḥrām" (The telephone doesn't work)

Thus the song lyrics seemed to be based on a notion of society in which no commercial success could be expected from men singing about their happy honeymoons.[2] As we shall see, public discourse in the streets of Oran was similar in the sense that while men's capacity to successfully love was sometimes recognized, the same power was rarely granted to women. In the songs, a love of love was expressed rather than love for a loved person (see de Rougemont 1956).

Another significant characteristic of clean raï was, as already mentioned, that one rarely found lines exploiting any tension within the private place of the family. Instead they expressed the sentiment of the ideal peace that is supposed to be found at home and the feelings of social identity and strength it might give.

*Ma dām ʿaandi l-mwīma ngayyal fi ḍlāl*
As long as I have my mother, I sleep in the shade [of our yard]
Cheb Khaled, "Dallāli, dallāli" (My guide, my guide)

*Sh-shadda fi Allāh w daʿawat l-walidīn mʿaāya*
I hold on to God, and the blessings of my parents are with me
Cheikh Naam, "Lli bini w binak māt" (What is between you and me is dead)

*La mma, la bba, ktāfha bardīn*
No mother, no father, and her shoulders [social relations] are cold
Cheb Khaled, "ʿAṭūni kwaghti" (Give me my personal papers)

Tensions that affected the family were rarely mentioned:

*Ṭrīg l-ʿumri ḥalwa w dīma nfūtha*
The road to my life [love] is sweet, I always take that way
Cheb Khaled, "Tastahel ya galbi" (You deserve it, oh my heart)

and at least got no closer than the door:

*Ḥalli l-bāb ʿalīya wulla nhaddam*
Open the door to me, or I'll break it down
Benchenet, "Ḥalli l-bāb" (Open the door)

*Ḥalli l-bāb ʿaliya, ana manīsh ʿaaduk*
Open the door for me, I'm not your enemy
Cheb Khaled, "ʿAlāsh ḥbībak tensih" (Why do you forget your boyfriend?)

And, if lines did admit of tensions within the sacred place of the Algerian family, it was by indirect means:

*Hatraft bīk l-bāraḥ w smʿaatni mma*
I dreamed of you yesterday, and my mother heard me
Zargui, "Ana ma nwallīsh" (I won't come back)

*Ma t'aayṭish fi dār d-daʿawa danjar*
Don't call home. The situation is dangerous

Cheb Hamid and Cheba Zohra, "ʿAyyaṭ fi ṭilifūn" (She called by telephone)

except for a rare occasion when, by giving us a small piece of information, a singer told us he had succeeded in transgressing the doorstep:

*Ma khūftsh rabbi nakdab, ḥawshkum fih dāliya*
If I lie I wouldn't be afraid of God. Surely in your house there are vines

Cheb Khaled, "Gāltli hāk" (She told me, that's yours)

But many lyrics related that what could really threaten the peace of the household and the social base of the man was the development of an independent relationship with a woman from the outside. As in dirty raï, this was expressed in terms of an irreconcilable split between the home and life outside, and as in dirty raï, it was primarily expressed as endangering a man's relationship with his mother:

*Ma ndīr maḥna w ma tkhaybini ʿala mma*
I won't take this passion. She will not make me deceive my mother

Cheb Khaled, "Dallāli, dallāli" (My guide, my guide)

*Ḍ-ḍurr liyya w ṣaḥḥa l-mwimti*
The pain is for me, and the well-being for my mother

Cheb Hasni, "Ana ndabbar rāsi" (I will manage on my own)

Clean raï thus played on the idea that what touched people particularly, beyond the evocation of the peacefulness of the home, was the evocation of the relationship between a man and his mother, the tension that might arise between a man and his mother if he engaged in relationships with women outside the home. This relationship was reflected in frequent statements like, "Your mother is the one you go to with your problems"; "your mother is the one who nurses you when you are ill"; "your mother is the one who suffered for you"; and "your mother is the one who will always love you."

As already mentioned, the value ascribed to one's mother was noteworthy in light of the fact that tensions between a young man and three other family members were left totally unexplored—those with his father, sister, and brother. His mother was the central figure in the parental couple. His sister was totally absent, and his brother was of no interest except for very serious events such as death.[3] If the father appeared, it was as the moral guardian of his daughters. But this was never the father of the "storyteller's" home but always the father of "others'" daughters or sisters (or as in line 6 in "Dablat galbi," [others' daughters' mothers]).

*Būha hlaf bal imīn w min d-dār ma jīsh*
Her father swore by his faith that she wouldn't come out of the house

Cheb Khaled, "Tastahel ya galbi" (You deserve it, oh my heart)

*Shūfu l-mankur, būha w gaṭṭaʿaha l-bḥar*
Look at the injustice; her father made her cross the sea

Cheb Khaled, "ʿAndi mḥaīna" (I have a passion)

This basically meant that the lines tended to transpose the sociomoral logic of family life into the lovers' meeting. In dealing with events outside the family, the songs assumed that listening to raï tended to take place outside the sacred family and that meetings between men and women did, too—in the same public sphere where the growing Islamist movement sought to segregate men and women.

## Street Life

Even though Oran was divided into gendered spaces, there were nevertheless places, hours, and possibilities for men and women to meet. The meetings took place in educational establishments or on students' way to and from school. Others took place in the afternoon rush hours, which were also times when women could make detours away from their proper business. Meetings also took place in vacant apartments or rooms at the backs of shops kept by young men. In the city center some tea shops, restaurants, and ice cream bars allowed "mixed couples" a free space. Otherwise lovers had to go to "nature"—the beach, the forest, or the few parks not reserved "for families," unless, of course, they possessed capital in terms of either money or social relations and had the means to rent a hotel room or a villa (preferably in another town) or borrow an apartment or a car that could take them away to a secluded place.

But although everybody noticed contacts being made, everything was done so as not to make them obvious. Couples distanced themselves from the public gaze, retiring to places known as being for lovers, where they could hold hands, talk, and steal a kiss. In the midst of street life they would make contact with subtle signs of the hand.

Houari, for example, had a date with a girl one day. He pointed her out to me as she passed by on the opposite sidewalk, looking as if she was taking no notice of us. Then she turned her head and looked over, and Houari made a sign with his hands blaming her for being late. She apologized, also with her hands, and he followed her further up the street to speak to her in a doorway. Then they went to a tea shop, he in front and she following a hundred meters behind.

When Hasni chased girls on the street, the idea was to catch the woman's eyes. When she had passed him, he would look back. If she turned to look at him, he made signs with his hands for her to stop and follow him at a distance to a tea shop or ice cream bar. One day, I was out in a tea shop with Hasni and Omar (someone from Hasni's district). Next to our table were two couples. Omar lowered his eyes and tried to catch the eye of one of the women. When they left the table she passed close to ours, and Omar quickly whispered his name and telephone number. He was proud afterward: he had *kaḥalhum,* "given them dark"; that is, dark eyes had met dark eyes without the man discovering anything. Had the man done so, it would have been "all over" for Omar.

It was not only men who took the initiative, but also women. The most famous raï singers received lots of love letters and pictures from female fans. The only time Kader had a date while I knew him, it was initiated by a woman who had spotted him and then bought him a flower one day at the black market. They went off alone for an hour together at the beach. But the opportunities for women to contact men were limited. Bechir, a twenty-seven-year-old office clerk, told me how a woman phoned him at one o'clock in the morning. Apparently she had dialed the number by chance in order just to speak to someone. Mustapha also received a phone call from a woman in his area who had found out who he was in order to date him. Hasni also received such phone calls and one day even a letter, with a photo of a girl he never had seen, asking for a date.

Several lines dealt with the fragility of the chances to meet in the street life of the city:

> *Dītha randivū, fi bāli nsāt*
> I made an appointment; I really think she forgot it
>
> Cheb Khaled, "Rrāy, ha rrāy" (Raï, oh raï)

> *Qāraʿat ʿala waḥda, thlāta fayta, ḥbibti gharatni*
> I waited till one o'clock; three hours passed. My love deceived me
>
> Cheb Khaled, "Rrāy, ha rrāy" (Raï, oh raï)

But more often, the lyrics exploited the tensions of an atmosphere in which contacts were constantly being made without being seen. Most often, meetings between men and women were expressed through the metaphor of the eyes. In fact, men could fall in love merely by glimpsing a woman's eyes.

*ʿAini shāfat fi z-zīn w galbi ʿashaq*
My eye saw the beauty and my heart fell in love

Cheb Khaled, "Hayya nṣuddu" (Let's go)

*Ṭābʿaak dhāk z-zīn w l-ʿaīnīn nāymīn*
The beauty is with you and your eyes are languishing

Zargui, "Ḍyāf rabbi" (The invited of God)

*ʿAinīk ma hannawak ma hannawni*
Your eyes did not leave either me or you in peace

Cheb Khaled, "Gultlāk qilīni" (I told you to leave me alone)

Some sentences hint at a social environment in which the eyes were the only medium of contact:

*ʿAīnīk gāluha w fummuk ma hdar*
Your eyes said it but your mouth doesn't speak

Cheb Khaled, "Ghīr ddūni lil dārna" (Just bring me to our house)

which is rather similar to the following:

*ʿAīnīk mʿaamrīn bal klām w fummuk ma hdar*
Your eyes are plenty of words and your mouth doesn't speak

Cheb Khaled, "Ḥasdūni fīk" (They were jealous of me because of you)

Another sort of line went into the emotions men could experience when challenging the peace and sacredness of other men's houses or simply when seeking to meet their lover without being discovered by her companions. This required a man to be guarded. He could use well-tested and ancient ways, as in the following:

*Narslak marsūli ʿandi ywaṣṣalni l-khbār*
I'll send you my messenger. He'll bring me the news

Cheb Hamid, "Ana qāsīt" (I suffered)

*Zalfaṭlak l-marsūl ḥatta lil dārkum, haya ʿumri*
I sent you a message to your home, oh my "life"

Zargui, "Ḍyāf rabbi" (The invited of God)

Or he could choose different techniques:

*Ktabt līha briyya, ma jāni jwāb*
I wrote her a letter, I got no reply

Cheb Khaled, "Wakhkha j'en ai marre" (Ah, I had enough)

Or he might use more recent means of contacting her, the most common being the telephone:

> *Ṭilifūn ḥram l-ḥitān darrgūh, takhruj ʿumri nakri e-busṭa*
> The telephone doesn't work, the walls are hiding it, my spirit goes out, I rent the post office
>
> Benchenet, "Ṭilifūn ḥram" (The telephone doesn't work)

> *Fi ṭilifūn nasmaʿaha w bal ʿaīni la*
> I hear her on the telephone, but not with my eye
>
> Cheb Hamid and Cheba Zohra, "ʿAyyaṭ fi ṭilifūn" (She called by telephone)

Rai lyrics, then, often revealed the tension that one would expect to find in young men who were making often futile efforts to contact women from outside their houses. The lines were part of a society in which independent relationships with women were an emotional, tense, problematic affair. And while no criticism of the family was allowed, this did not exclude many lines from reflecting certain daily events.

A common saying in Oran was that what divides men is either money or women. When preparing for a Thursday night out, men often preferred to keep to themselves even when the possibility of having female company arose; it might otherwise destroy the men's relationships with one another. While Hasni's friend seemed rather successful in "blackening" girls' eyes, things went worse for the friend of a musician, Mohammed, one night at the 1991 festival of raï. We were in the area reserved "for families," that is, for women and couples. Mohammed was in his finest clothes and started dancing happily, gradually getting nearer to a group consisting not only of men but also of women, too. Suddenly a man got up and told Mohammed to stop dancing. When he refused, a fight started. Mohammed's gold chain and shirt were torn to pieces, and the men were eventually taken away by the police.

Houari was more cautious when we went to an expensive restaurant for a raï evening during Ramadan. He saw a woman from work in company with a man. She pretended not to see Houari, and he did not try to contact her. Two brothers, friends of Hasni, were also prudent. They ran a small clothes shop in Medina Jdida. The eldest, Karim, was an experienced woman chaser. According to him, the way to success was to make the woman laugh. "I am Mark Knopfler," he would say, and maybe she would answer, "and I'm Elsa" [a French pop star], and contact was made. Karim's brother, Abdelhaq, explained how he had recently met a girl in Medina Jdida. He made contact, charming her by guessing her name. They became lovers and met in the forest near Canastel, but a friend of her brother's discovered them, and he had not seen her for three months. A similar thing happened to Mohammed, twenty-two, a student at the university, and a friend of Salim's. He and his girlfriend had been picked up in a police raid in the park of an open-air theatre (Théâtre de Verdure). They were brought to the police station, and the police had called her parents. Now she could not go out anymore and could phone him in secret only rarely.

The same thing happened again in the shop, which was in fact a meeting place for a group of young men and their ever-changing girlfriends. One day when I arrived, Abdelhaq was with a woman when a man came and introduced himself as her half-brother. The woman quickly took off the makeup she had put on after arriving at the shop, while her half-brother said that he had been warned by people in town that something was going on. He was a civilized man, not a *sufaj* (wild). He knew people did not marry out of "reason" anymore. Young people wanted to know one another before marriage, and he thought that it was all right that they met each other. He would even help in arranging meetings, but not that way, in public. "We live in a moral society. We all want to change, but someone has to take the first step."

Some lines in raï ventured into these conflicts. They could be interpreted as describing a social life embedded in a game of competition over a scarce commodity—women or relationships with femininity:

*Shafūni nabghīha dāru shunṭāj, bghaw newweḍha w ndīr ṭapāj*
They saw I wanted her. They blackmailed me, wanted me to wake
her and make noise

Cheb Abdelhaq, "Ntiyya sbābi" (You are the reason of mine)

*Mnīn gult narbaḥ nādhuli l-ʿarab*
When I said I was winning, the Arabs [people] rose against me

Cheb Hasni, "Si pa la pān" (It's not worth it)

*L-ʿaadyan ghīr rraktūb fi d-dnūb*
The enemies are collecting only evil

Cheb Hasni, "Āītu ma dīru binātna" (You will get tired of coming in between us)

Such lines exploited the tensions caused by a situation similar to the performative context of raï—in meetings outside, a man was never alone. But they added to this the fact that his life was not only embedded in constant social relationships with other men which embodied tension between equality and hierarchy and competition for the surplus in the redistributive Algerian state. Life was also embedded in a quest for access to the "other" world of women.

*Kull yūm nasmaʿa hadra lli ʿashaqtha gālu dāyra*
Everyday I hear talk [gossip] telling that the one I loved has "done it"

Benchenet, "Ḥalli l-bāb" (Open the door)

*L-maḥna bghāt l-maḥna w l-hadra ʿalāh*
The passion wanted the passion. Why all this gossip?

Zargui, "Ana ma nwallīsh" (I won't come back)

There are also sentences of this kind in "Dablat galbi" and in "Jibuhālu." Thus, in a number of lines, a man entering an "unregulated" relationship with a woman in the public spheres of the city came to possess a rare quality which, if exposed, made him fragile outside the circle of possible friends, bringing him into opposition with his social surroundings, which competed for and commented on this same quality. Many raï lines dealt with the feelings of men who possessed this rare quality of being victims of forces greater than themselves and with the feeling that these forces would have an effect on the object in their possession:

*L-ghalba tʿaammar rāsha w ma tḥī*
The "subduers" fill her head without any scruples

Cheb Abdelhaq, "Ntiyya sbābi" (You are the reason of mine)

*Smaʿati l-hadra w tqllaqti*
You listened to the gossip and you were in a hurry

Cheb Hasni, "Ma tabkīsh hadha maktubi" (Do not cry, this is my destiny)

In solving these problems, it seemed that raï preferred to express counterattacks rather than reflections on men's own personalities. Women, then, became the main topic in rationalizing the tensions and emotions of men. The focus on women—or on unregulated encounters with women—was a central aspect of male social life, producing action in a state of growing political and economic crisis. Sorcery was a major concern in Oran, and the "Algerian woman" even more so. Songs and discourse around these topics were focal points in the articulation of meanings and actions.

## Sorcery

One common statement in the public discourse in Oran was that women were not to be trusted. There are lines in raï dealing with the emotions connected with the experience of disloyalty:

*Nkhāf ndīrfīk kunfians tkhawnili galbi*
I am afraid of trusting you; you steal away my heart

Cheb Khaled, "Ḥasnu ʿaawni" (Bring me to sense)

*ʿAāyash mʿaak fi l-amān, nākra khad ʿaatuh*
He lives with you in trust; you, ungrateful, betrayed him

Cheb Khaled, "Ashḥāl bqātni nuṣbur" (How much can I endure?)

These statements of lack of trust could be understood as a reflection of the number of dates that were not kept either by women or men, and as a consequence, of what seems to have been the widespread practice for men and women not to reveal their personal backgrounds at first meetings. A number of men and women even seemed to have several "dates" running simultaneously in order to get the most credible or pleasurable one. However, in the early 1990s in Oran, it gradually became evident to me that part of men's distrust toward women was due to a fear of sorcery, *sḥūr*.

One day, one of Kader's friends told me he never accepted anything from the hand of a woman, an apple or the like, for fear of sorcery. Another young man, with whom I had most often discussed his trips to Denmark, later warned me not to give a woman my photograph or any of my personal belongings. A friend who spent most of his weekends in the cabarets told me how a female singer with whom he was having an affair once tried to get his mother to give her a sweater of his. At weddings, I began to notice how the groom hid his head in the wedding procession when entering the bridal chamber. At one particular wedding, the men in my company hurried away from the courtyard when they smelled wood embers burning on a balcony above. But particularly in the cabarets, according to musicians who had been bewitched, sorcery seemed to be a common phenomenon.

When they were bewitched, some men were said (and seen) to be losing their hair. Others lost weight, their skin turned yellowish, and they sat passively with lifeless eyes, showing no interest in communicating with their surroundings. Others avoided the company of their peer group. Some, it was said, even insulted their best friends. Others were unable to sleep, burned, or suffered at night from bodily pains.

Not all believed in sorcery or felt concerned by it since they had not experienced it themselves. Several explained such behavior with reference to the psychological constitution of the affected person, such as impotence on the wedding night, for example, obviously being due to bad nerves. Others claimed that sorcery existed as a scientific fact by making reference to verses in the Koran. In fact, quite a number did not seem to know very much about it except that they had heard it being talked about and had seen people behave in strange ways. On the other hand, several people without an apparent interest in or previous knowledge of sorcery did seem to be affected by it.

Nasser did not believe in sorcery until, for a period of two months after his mother returned to Nedroma, she began suffering depressions, becoming passive and not being able to sleep at night. She began quarreling with her husband and he was thinking of getting a divorce. However, one day, when coming home to their large villa, she surprised her housemaid watching television in their living room (where she was not supposed to be). Another time she found the housemaid's brother in their bathroom using the shower. Then one day at a women's party, she took out some small pieces of bread and saw what she would have thought was mold if an older, more experienced woman had not immediately identified it as sorcery. The following week they went to a diviner [*gazzāna*] who made *khaffīf* [lightness] to her. This is a widespread practice in the Middle East (Zubeida 1987:142) and consists of heating up lead, placing it between the patient's open legs, and pouring it through a sieve [*ghurbāl*] into a bucket of water. This treatment has two effects. First, it will make the person feel light. Second, the cooled lead will be transformed into figures in the water, which are used for predicting or diagnosing the situation of the patient, in this case the identity of the sorcerer. When the housemaid was subsequently sacked, Nasser's mother became well again. This story is one of sorcery in a highly educated family. The same elements are found in the following story from a different social setting.

Hasni, twenty-eight, was an employee in a state company and lived in a small, nice apartment in a heavily populated part of Oran. He was married with one child and was respected for his black belt in karate. However, whenever he came home to his wife, everything darkened before his eyes. At the smallest incident he would start beating her up and destroying the place. This state of affairs went on for a month, until one evening he heard a noise at the door. When he looked out, he saw an old woman spraying yellow water [urine] on the door of his house. Hasni then decided to move into a small room with his wife's family. Since that day he has stopped beating his wife.

However, most of the stories I heard were primarily related to women's acts of sorcery, with the purpose of either weakening men or attracting them. The following three stories were like this. The first is an extreme one.

Djillali knew a policeman who told him about an investigation in a village near Oran. A night watchman had seen a white object moving in a cemetery. He called for help, and they found an old woman veiled and sitting with the arm of a newly buried corpse around her neck in order to keep it upright. She was using the hand of the other arm to roll couscous on a plate. Balls of couscous made with hands of the dead are worth thousands of dinars. If you can get a man to eat them, he will be completely paralyzed up to his neck: he will not be able to move. I later heard this "classical" story (see Doutté 1908) several times in Oran. It did not say what people did to women discovered doing such things (they seemed to disappear), but it certainly dealt with the presumed force of women's sorcery in establishing control over men.

The second story—a particularly painful one—dealt with the wedding night at the moment the groom enters the bridal chamber. Before the wedding party, a jealous member of the family took a padlock to a sorcerer and paid him a huge sum of money in order to achieve a powerful result. The sorcerer first spoke some magic words over the padlock. Then he took a star lizard, killed it, put the padlock into its mouth, and closed it before it became stiff. Then the lizard was thrown into the sea, never to be found again. The effect was that the groom remained impotent for years, until he found a woman experienced in countermagic who wrote strange inscriptions on his penis. This story exists in several versions. Its main element is again the power of men, in this case their sexual potency at the most vulnerable moment in their sexual career.

The third story was told to me by a raï singer in the clubs, who at one time had worked in a factory in Oran. This deals with a third method of sorcery involving the use of something very personal from the victim, in this case a photograph, but it might equally be clothes or the name of the father and mother.

> I fell in love with a woman at work and spent days writing poetry to her. One day she asked me for my photo. It was after that that I began to feel strange. I always had her name in my head, I was always thinking of her. When I went out to see my friends, I ended up by instead going to her place. I started losing weight, and my mother began worrying about me. She took me to a *ṭālab,* who confirmed that sorcery was involved. Gradually I started getting better.

What is to be done about such sorcery? The following paragraphs are based on rather vague descriptions given to me by young men. Diagnosis and remedies were considered women's affairs.

The main elements involved were religious or magical (contacting a *ṭālab,* writings from the Koran, cabalistic sentences wrapped up in a small leather bag, writing on a piece of cloth blowing in the wind). Other elements were considered dirty or polluting (water used to wash the dead, couscous rolled with the hand of a dead person, a soiled sperm cloth, the saliva of Blacks, urine) or involved ambivalence (herbs, wild lizards, deeds of Jews or of old women; see Douglas 1966) or things taken from one's personal or intimate life (a hair, a sweater, a photograph, the name of one's mother, the name of one's mother and father, etc.). The active part of the sorcery consisted in using analogy (burning a candle, burning a sperm cloth, sticking needles into a candle to make a person burn, locking a padlock or a knife to lock the power of the intended victim), using ambivalence (placing writing in the doorway, pouring magic water on a door, closing a knife when a person enters a room), or putting something into the innermost part of the person, that is, his body (drinking magic water, eating grains of couscous, etc.). The cure for sorcery involved approximately the same elements, namely magico-religious means (going to a *ṭālab,* wearing a magic formula, drinking a magic formula) or elements considered unclean or polluting (writing a formula on a man's penis, eating nails and hair in a cake, drinking something to make one vomit, urinating on the bewitched object). Active cures used analogy (dissolving "heavy" lead to make people light), ambivalence (pouring lead through a sieve held between someone's legs, finding writing in doorways), or "went into" the person's body, that is, eating or drinking antisorcery prescriptions.

In Algeria many lines in raï mentioned acts of sorcery:

*Mashi ghalṭi dallāli, ghalbūni sḥūr*
It's not my fault, my guide. The witchcraft won me over

Cheb Abdelhaq, "Mashi ghalṭi" (It's not my fault)

*Sh-shīra wallāt tasḥār w takmi jmar*
Now the girls are practicing witchcraft and burning wood embers

Cheb Mami, "L-bnāt hāju" (The girls fly out)

*ʿAyīti ma taīḥargili w ʿayīti ma tkatbili*
You got tired of burning me [with witchcraft]. You got tired of writing me [talismans]

Cheikh Naam, "Lli bīni w bīnak māt," (What is between you and me is dead)

In this sense the lines might be understood as resulting from a state of insecurity (Ouitis 1984) in which sorcery became the (inefficient) weapon of women in their competition over men, a strategy of positioning themselves in the social system (Plantade 1988:139). They might also be understood as betraying men's fear of the power of women in the domain of sexuality, and also as referring to a struggle for power between men and women in a dual society in which the other half, the feminine side, possessed a power which was out of men's control—all in all, a separate social discourse with a reality of its own, morality reflecting on itself and expressing what could not be expressed otherwise in everyday social life (Jansen 1987:117–118, Rosander 1991:228).

However, the lines expressed more than this, playing on the tension that, through an unusual meeting with a woman, a man might involve himself with the most private aspects of his personal life. The fragility arising out of the love meeting might endanger his social life and physical being and bring him into contact with the impure and "external" social realms of life.

Sorcery could be seen as a consequence of any extraordinary involvement in the world of women. According to Houari, it was the result of love affairs. A man who had never experienced the sensation of falling in love would start thinking when he was alone. Maybe he would spend a lot of time in the woman's company, fetching her from school and making love to her in the evening. One day he might see her with another man, and yet still continue his relationship with her. Again he would start to think. Some of his friends would be getting at him, teasing him, asking him why he was always in the company of a woman. With all the social talk of sorcery going on, he might start doubting reality and think his overwhelming feelings were a result of sorcery rather than love.

One day I found Hasni and some of his acquaintances in the company of a man of twenty who had just arrived from Algiers. The reason for his visit was that his mistress, a twenty-eight-year-old married woman who lived next door to him, had come to Oran with her children in order to visit her family. The man had accompanied her to Oran to have the chance of being with her during the flight. He was now hoping she would manage to get some free time so that they could rent a hotel room and spend a lover's hour alone. This extraordinary event (worth singing about) was under discussion when I arrived. Was a young man spending a fortune to follow a married woman eight years his senior the result of real love or of *sḥūr*?

The fact that women could not be trusted, according to a number of young men, went along with the suspicion that men could lose their male power through unusual contacts with women. The symptoms of the results of sorcery were the same as descriptions of the antisocial behavior of men when they failed to be active, to be oriented toward public life, and to function well in peer groups.

Mistrusting women because of sorcery led to avoiding social contact with femininity. Raï, by singing of sorcery, reinforced the impression that men and women often did not really "meet." In this sense sorcery was one of the ways in which relations between men and women became socially regulated, which they would otherwise not be when outside domestic boundaries. That stories of sorcery were more frequent in the cabarets than elsewhere supports this idea.

## True Love, or the "Algerian Woman"

However, discussing the *nature* of Algerian women was important. Hasni's cousin explained to me one day how to find a really fine woman:

> You have a look in the streets. One in a group of girls might be all right. She looks down when men look at her. If they show her interest, she does not reciprocate. You observe her for some days as she walks by, and if she keeps up her ways, you find out where she lives. You ask her neighbors and acquaintances about her. If you are satisfied with the answers, you ask her to be with you. If she says no, you go away. With girls who are fine like this, you must be honest and show them who you are. Then it might happen that they drown in the ocean of love for you.

There are few lines in raï which describe women in this way; rather, they imply that this is how things ought to be. In the clean raï of the 1980s, a main topic was the tension resulting from unfulfilled gender encounters in meetings outside the sacred realms of society. As with sorcery, they dealt with forces that might be escaping from men's control—the world of women.

*Ḥasbu kullshi sāhal ma bqāsh l-ʿaqal*
They think everything is easy, they have lost their [reason] knowledge of right and wrong

Cheb Mami, "L-bnāt hāju" (The girls fly out)

*Khūtak murḍa w nti fi zunqa*
Your brother is ill, and you go around in the streets

Cheb Mami, "L-bnāt hāju" (The girls fly out)

*Lukān ṣbarti w khammamti, ḥjabti w ḥashamti*
If only you were patient and wise, if only you had veiled [stayed at home] and had kept your modesty

Cheikh Naam, "Lli bīni w bīnak māt," (What is between you and me is dead)

In Oran in the early 1990s, these lines reflected the major tensions young men expressed in describing women's activities in society. After being out chasing girls without success, Omar, a friend of Salim, the shop assistant, would say,

> The girls have no brain, no energy. They're like men. They smoke and drink. They're arrogant. They don't go for proper guys, but guys with cars. And there are those who only want to get laid. With those you really have to be careful.

According to another youth:

> The girls here do not date as they do in Europe, they go out to get pleasure for themselves. If you have an apartment they come, if you have money, if you have a car.

A third:

> All girls are materialists. We agreed to get married, and then she suddenly started asking me for presents. Is this love?

And a fourth:

> All girls are materialists—they want a rich man with a car to take them out dancing, so that they can have fun. When they discover that I've nothing, they disappear at once.

Mohammed, a thirty-two-year-old unmarried man working as an accountant for a lawyer, told how he thought of marrying a European girl:

> Algerian women are worth nothing. They have nothing in their heads. When you marry them, they put pressure on their husband, who wants to be with his mother, his brothers, their family. But a wife will not obey her mother-in-law, except the women wearing *ḥijāb*. Women are no good. They only seek material things from their men, not like European women, who attend to their husbands when they come home. Today you'll find women who are whores. They've had their adventures with men before marriage and they pretend to be serious. There are also women admitting they made

> a mistake, may God forgive them, but then they've tasted sex and cannot do without it anymore. There are also fine women, but they never go out and most of the time they are promised anyway.

A "colleague" of Kader's in the black market said:

> People want to live with their parents, ask for their advice and their blessing. But most women want their husbands to move away from home. They don't want to live with their mothers-in-law. Others want to move in order to be able to come and go as they please and live a life of glamor. They want freedom, but to do what?

A discussion with Djillali and two of his friends one day went approximately like this:

> Here you need a car to get a girl. They like cars. Never use a car when you go for a girl, because then you will know she is after the car. These girls are materialists. They see if you've got money, are nicely dressed, if you are handsome. They look down on you if you approach them, but if you talk to them they have inferiority complexes. They have nothing in their heads.

Or with Kader and his friend:

> Normally the man must control the woman. The woman follows the man. If there's no man, she will deviate from the proper path. There are many girls here, but they are materialists and they want a car. They have inferiority complexes. In Europe it's for love. It's for the rest of your life.

A young musician said:

> The girls here have inferiority complexes, not as in France. In France if you address a girl, she will approach you and talk to you. And if you fix a date with her, she'll be there.

The tensions expressed in these descriptions of women's activities suggested several generalizations: women (and their parents) sought to get money out of a future husband, asked too much of men, and approached marriage in a spirit of pure calculation. Women sought men with money (most often termed "men with cars"), that is, men who did not differ much from the *tshi-tshi* (see chapter 4). Thus, closely connected with the calculating woman was the sexually hungry woman, as in the story of a man who divorced his wife after a week because he saw her enter another man's car, or of another who divorced his wife after a month when she suggested having oral sex ("where had she learned that?").[4]

It is obvious that these images of women were to a certain extent the result of a male public discourse in reaction to women who were reacting against being treated like prey. Also, they might mirror a certain activism on the part of women in the field of contacts in the public sphere. Part of their involvement in love affairs and pleasure suggested that they were interested in evaluating which affair might lead to a reasonable marriage, economically and socially, in order not to end up as housewives in overcrowded apartments. It also seems plausible that part of the discourse was related to the increase in prostitution that had resulted from the growing social crisis in Algeria, a fact that was reported timidly in press articles during my stay in Algeria.

But there is certainly no question but that the improved education of women and their movement into wage labor has put them in public space more than ever before. The stereotyping of women provided a common way of describing class differences in terms of gender, for money was seen as having a feminine quality when it was used for pleasure and luxury, rather than as representing power and privilege (see Bourdieu 1992:36–38). Conspicuous consumption was also given female qualities in Oran. The *tshi-tshis*—Michael Jackson and men with earrings—were feminized, they were weak, as a man in power might become weak when confronted with cabaret images. In this sense, male images of women revealed acute sensitivity in identifying a link between the economic power to consume in general (including the consumption of leisure) and access to sexual pleasure. The whole of this was set up by the young men in a mood of resentment—"condemning the other for possessing what you want for yourself" (ibid.). As a result, the image of the "Algerian woman" in general was increasingly coming to resemble that of the transgressive *maryūla* in the cabarets. This image was constantly related to, on the one hand, the idea that the women of today were not like women before, and, on the other, the image of the decadent European girl.

The first time I noticed the existence of what you might call nostalgia (see Stewart 1992) for the woman of the past was one day shortly after my arrival in Oran, when Ali and I were heading for the city center. "Have you noticed, Marc," he asked, "have you noticed all the girls on the streets? It was not like that before." This was indeed not the last time I was to hear phrases like that, which came from a wide variety of people. Thus when I discussed "Jibuhālu" with Nasser, he expressed the following thoughts:

> A decade ago it wasn't the same. Today, there is a certain liberty. People marry as they like. . . . It couldn't have been done before because there was a certain dependence. Today, youngsters claim a certain liberty. Have you seen, during Ramadan? Before, you only saw guys in the main street, rarely girls. But the last few years, it's astonishing the number of girls who go out. Now, it's as if parents can't keep control over their children anymore. Before, parents demanded that you take care of the girls. Today, when the girl comes home, she knows she will get hell, and even then she takes the risk of going out. In Europe it's perfectly normal for a girl of seventeen or eighteen to go to the discos. That's the result of an evolution which has taken a long time, but here, are we really ready for that? Are we materially ready to experience such a radical change among the young? It's not possible to change so much in a time span of thirty years. The girls, of course, are fed up staying at home the whole day cooking, but I say they rush forward too fast.

I heard the same thoughts from Kader (whose social position otherwise differed totally from Nasser's), although he used different words. His discourse could be heard from several youngsters in his neighborhood and was probably close to formulations heard in a number of mosques:

> Boumedienne betrayed the Islamic government. If he had wanted Islam from the beginning, the women wouldn't be as they are today. He wanted debauchery when he sought to give freedom to women. Women want to be stronger than men. But what sort of talk is this? This is not what is in the Koran. What do they want this freedom for? To drink, to smoke, to date men and their cars? That's how Muslim women are. In Islam everybody acts according to his own responsibility. But the government wants the cabarets and so on.

In order to emphasize further the consistency of this nostalgic mode of thought and to show its variants, I quote from one of the most pirated raï songwriters of the early 1990s. Here he is not only referring to Ben Badis,[5] but also hinting at his adherence to the ideas of the FIS:

> The problem of women is an interesting one because if you can control women, you can have the whole world. It's the women who play the major role on this planet. If you control women, educate them, teach them how to live, how to love, how to educate their children, you can educate the whole society. If a woman isn't nor-

> mal, her children won't grow up normal. They'll become like wild animals and so on. In my songs I'm always against women, because I know that all our problems have been created by women. They have been given too much freedom, and the men have followed their ways. Everybody wants a beautiful Mercedes, a beautiful house, a video, a lot of money. Those are the problems men are living with and they come from the women.

But as already mentioned, these attacks on women were framed not only in a mode of nostalgia, but also in comparison with a notion of the European woman. Nasser refers partly to that subject in the quotation above, as does Kader. He "knew" of someone who had met a girl in Norway. He had problems with his residence permit and had to return to Algeria, but she loved him so much that she traveled to Oran to help him. He even said it was possible to find European girls who neither smoked nor drank, and that it did not matter if they were Christian. If you started by showing the girl respect, she might gradually come closer to Islam.

Among Kader's friends, stories went around about someone who had met an Irish girl in Spain. She had cried when he could not go with her to Ireland. Another had met a Dutch girl in London. She had started learning French to be able to communicate with him better. Another Algerian met a girl in London, but had to go home because his passport expired. The girl had told him that her body belonged to him. She sent him money and provided an attorney for him. He tried to reach her by traveling to Scotland, but he was registered with the immigration authorities. The girl succeeded in getting him to London, and the man's father had kissed her on the forehead (i.e., blessed her) when the couple visited him in Oran. It was true love. One of the most popular raï singers in Oran—versed in "sentimental raï" and a fan of Claude Barzotti and the *hijāz*[6]—explained the difference between Algerian and European girls like this:

> Girls today are worse than French or European girls. They have transgressed all borders. I myself would like to have a European woman and not live with an Arab woman, especially if I find a European who accepts my religion. That's something really beautiful, because a European girl is born with these things. Her mother, her father have been drinking alcohol. That's been her life. She can do nothing to change that. But if she loves a man, she can change, and if she starts understanding life, if she loves me, she can love my religion. But these girls here. It's not part of their manners;

> it is not part of their origins. A real Arab girl asks her father to investigate her future husband's habits: if he drinks, if he goes out with girls, if he works or not. Now it's the opposite. The man asks about the woman, if she goes out with men, how many men she has known. It's too much, too much. They don't suit me at all, girls like that. If I see a French girl do that, dating men and so on, it's perfectly normal. It's their life. They live like that. To them it's perfectly normal, even though it's weird for me . . . but it isn't weird to me because I know they are born into that environment. She has grown up in it . . . but to me, my sister, for example, if she does things like that, like a European girl does . . . my mother didn't do that. She married a husband and didn't even know what he was like. You see the difference between now and then? Before, wives didn't argue at all with their husbands. They didn't have the right to discuss anything. You're a woman. You keep the house, you shut up. You eat, you sleep. I'm the man. Now you have cases where the woman is giving orders, instances where the man gets into a fight, and she goes out and quarrels with the men. And you call that a woman? That's not a woman. So the best thing is to take a European girl who's open-minded, who understands. . . .

In North Africa, the existence of an image of the ideal Muslim woman set in relation to the West has been documented in a number of cases (Abrous 1988, Bennani-Chraïbi 1994, Bentahar 1989, Camilleri 1973, Chelig-Aïnad-Tabet 1982, Déjeux 1989, Mernissi 1983).[7] Although the notion of love relations may never have been absent in Algeria, nevertheless, at least since the period of modern national awakening in the 1930s, it has been posed in terms of the idea of an "original" Muslim gender identity which was conceptualized in terms of its opposition to gender identity in the West (see Baffet 1985, Berque 1962, Merad 1967). The question of feminism and the status of Muslim women became of acute concern in the early 1930s in the form of a reaction to the feminist movement in the West and the colonial attitude toward the "Muslim woman." The debate on women's position in Kemalist Turkey and Egypt was echoed in Algeria and intimately linked with a particular image of European morality (Ahmed 1991, Merad 1967:315–330). Thus, the question of gender in North Africa has been part of a larger game in which power and identity were at stake. For a long time, the sociopolitical conditions of modern North Africa have been described by men in terms of women.

However, the image of the Western woman seems to have undergone a slight change in the 1980s and 1990s; at any rate I have not seen it so described for previous periods in North Africa. When Madonna was interviewed by Michel Drucker on French TF1 in the spring of 1991 on a program seen by millions of people in Algeria, I expected the men I knew to condemn her as much as Algerian women, but they did not. Rather, they were impressed by her performance, not because of her "sexual merits," but because of her general behavior. In this sense, she was desexualized.

Thus in Oran in the early 1990s, it seemed to me that there existed an acute awareness that the Western woman belonged to another sphere of power than the Algerian woman. She was similar to the *maryūla* in the sense that she possessed some male qualities. She smoked, she drank, she ventured into male spheres in a way that could be seen as a transgression of gender roles. But she was also different from the *maryūla.* For a man to have a relation of pleasure with the calculating *maryūla* demanded capital and power—he did not receive something for nothing. But the European woman offered access to Europe; she had the power of love; that is, she could give without asking anything in return.[8]

Generally speaking, three major images of women existed among male youth, through which they expressed part of their quest to establish themselves as adults and thus their position within a larger social context. The first image was the *maryūla*—the "masculine" woman, close to men, a woman of pleasure and lust who might lead a man into contact with unregulated and impure parts of himself and of society. The second was the woman with *ḥijāb,* who would not be interested in the world outside the home, who would obey her family and husband, and who would not seek the freedom of the world of consumption. The third was the European or Western woman, the only one capable of loving, that is, a woman being "like a man" ought to be: intelligent, trustworthy, and not interested in material affairs. Raï lyrics portrayed these images, two of which were absent from public life: the "good" Muslim woman who did not mix with men and the European women who had left Algeria.

*Tmūti ʿala ṣ-ṣyāgha w jurri ḥāīkak*
You die for want of jewelry and you drag around your veil

Zargui, "Ana ma nwallīsh" (I won't come back)

*Mūl l-luṭu yklaksūni sh-shīra jāya tajri*
The car owner sounds his horn; the girl comes running

Cheb Mami, "Khallūni nabki" (Let me cry)

*La fille d'aujourd'hui tʿaamdda, shtā dīr bīk ma fīk fayda*
The girl of today acts with intentions. See what she will do with you. You are no use to her

Cheb Hasni, "L'amour c'est pas facile" (Love is not easy)

These lines also exposed a universe of calculating, strategic relations with women, as if men did not possess the strength to distance themselves from that world. Several lines repeated throughout the whole of the 1980s described the tensions and emotions involved in lacking the material or social power to control one's surroundings:

*Ma gūlt wālu w ghīr ʿaaṭuni kwāghti*
I said nothing, just give me my personal papers

Cheb Khaled, "Gāltli hāk" (She told me, that's yours)

*Rāni nqāraʿa winta l-maktūb yzūrni*
I am waiting for destiny to visit me

Benchenet, "Ḥalli l-bāb" (Open the door)

*Zahri twaddar klātuh ḥūta fi l-bḥar*
My luck was eaten by a fish in the sea

Zargui, "Ḍyāf rabbi" (The invited of God)

*Ha rrāy, ma ʿandi wālu*
Hey raï, I've got nothing

Sahrauoi and Fadela, "Ma ʿandi wālu" (I've got nothing)

Rarely did a raï song overtly venture into political matters,[9] yet raï nonetheless expressed possible resolutions to tensions. These were also phrased in terms of love and gender:

*Si pa la pān bāsh nwalli līk*
It's not worth it, that I come back to you

Cheb Hasni, "Si pa la pān" (It's not worth it)

*Ana kammalt mʿaāk w shaffina kullḥ sabātna*
I am all finished with you, all accounts are settled

Benchenet, "Ana kammalt mʿaāk" (I am all finished with you)

One idealized result to be found in some lines dealt with man's repentance and his retreat into the sacred life of the family:

*Galbi ʿaya min t-takhmām, bāghi ntūb sa fini*
My heart is tired of worrying; I repent; it's all over

Cheb Mami, "Khallūni nabki" (Let me cry)

*Ndīrha fi yadd allāh w rabbi kbīr*
I put her in the hands of God, and God is great

Cheb Khaled, "Ṣṣubri, ṣṣubri" (Have patience, have patience)

There were also lines pleading for the restoration of the father's authority in society, of a sacralized father above competition and strategies:

*Khālafti l-ʿaahd w ʿaand rabbi nḥāsbak*
You betrayed the pact. Before God I'll ask for judgment

Cheb Hamid, "Ana qasit" (I suffered)

*Rāni msāmḥāk guddām rabbi lli ma darti fiyya*
I forgive you before God, for all you didn't do for me

Benchenet, "Ana kammalt mʿaāk" (I am all finished with you)

Some lyrics described a man who upheld a sharp distinction in gender roles, who sought to sacralize the public sphere of society and who maintained his power by stigmatizing his sisters for being "free women":

*Allah yahdiīk, ḥashmi, khīr ma ghādi tandmi*
May God guide you. Have shame, otherwise you'll regret it

Cheikh Naam, "Lli bīni w bīnak māt" (What's between you and me is dead)

*Tāḥ qadrak ma bqalak shān*
Your honor has fallen. You have lost your rank

Benchenet, "Ana kammalt mʿaāk" (I am all finished with you)

Other song lines depicted other idealized solutions, like seeking elsewhere, outside society, to establish a material base for realizing an adult life with women, outside the power relations of Algerian society.

*Ya zīna manīsh ʿalik w rāni ʿala r-rumiyyāt*
Oh beauty, I'm not like you. I go for European women

Raïna Raï, "Zīna tdīri l-tay" (Beauty, make the tea)

*Samḥaliyya zarga mʿaāk malqīt fayda*
Sorry, brown-haired girl. With you I didn't find anything of interest

Cheb Hasni, "Bayḍa mon amour" (My blonde, my love)

In this sense, raï touched on matters of national and political concern. It provided a running commentary on society; the music integrated formulas with references to spheres of pleasure and consumption in the West, all of which came from young singers in Algeria with few resources. Thus raï reflected two major movements among Algerian youth in the early 1990s in terms of love and gender, one toward the mosque and the other toward the West, as well as concern for those who had chosen neither path.

# 8

•

# Postscript

In studying raï, he wants to find out what is going on in our skulls.

—owner of a recording studio commenting on my presence to a visitor

In 1981, in a study of the musical landscape in four small countries prior to the 1970s, the question was raised as to whether new musical currents had emerged in response to what seemed like the homogenization of music on a worldwide level. In spite of the transnational music industry, dominated by Anglo-American concepts and money, a move toward the "nationalization" of music was taking place in the nation states of the world. This trend had its origin in the European middle-class attitude toward music, which involved the creation of national music companies, national music educational systems, and national music festivals and competitions, all of which favored the bourgeois "stage show" concept of music (Malm 1981:175–188).

A few years later, it was shown how music industry technology had found its way into every corner of the world. The most spectacular change in the 1970s was the development and spread of music hardware and software (Malm and Willis 1984:272). No other technology had penetrated society so quickly, and the rate of penetration even appeared to be accelerating (ibid.:269). With the multinationals selling similar products in as many different countries as possible, a transnational form of culture hybridity could be seen to be developing.

The cassette had given millions of people the opportunity to hear more music than ever before. The accessibility of music industry technology had brought about another pattern of change which was particularly noticeable in smaller countries. Generally speaking, the transformation of the business side of the music industry into giant concerns did not stop small enterprises, often run by local music enthusiasts, from cropping up everywhere (ibid.: 270; see also Nettl 1985: 29).

In 1992, Malm and Willis confirmed that the growth of the multinational media giants in the 1980s was "at the forefront of a move towards global standardization of cultural products . . . a future involving a few giant organizations involved in several forms of entertainment and based on different continents" (Malm and Willis 1992: 7). But they also noted that the 1980s experienced a process of transculturation involving "the combination of stylistic elements from several forms of local music taking place in an industrial environment" (ibid.:215).

The modern story of raï does not seem to deviate greatly from the trends outlined above. After independence, Algeria was endowed with national institutions such as l'Institut national de musique (1968) and l'ONDA (l'Organisation des droits d'auteur), not to mention national radio and television. In 1964, *andalus* was declared the national classical music of Algeria, and after independence a number of official festivals featuring different musical styles were held all over the country, with music becoming an integrated activity in the party-controlled youth centers.[1]

However, this trend toward the nationalization of musical life was also countered, first by the constant presence of Anglo-American and French music, and second by independent "transcultural" musical styles. In the 1970s, a Kabyle (Berber) music revival integrated a Western "folk and protest" instrumentation into a repertoire stressing Kabyle identity. In the 1980s, raï became the de facto national music of Algeria in terms of the numbers of cassettes sold. It also traveled to the West to become part of the World Music complex.

So in this sense, there is nothing special in the story of raï. Indeed, many of the elements described in the preceding pages could hold for a number of other countries.[2] Common elements include musicians being entertainers as well as artists, piracy and lack of copyright, musical spheres that are transgressive with regard to gender, producers who seek maximum profits by taking minimal risks, "formulaic" songs of love listened to by young people.

But although raï belonged to a global transcultural musical trend and to worldwide features with regard to the influence of mass media, it was nevertheless simultaneously embedded in a field of power, interests, and interpretations of its own. These pages have dealt with what people have done to raï and how they have perceived it within the worldwide framework mentioned above.

The first place I went in my fieldwork was Paris, where I discovered that raï had become part of the World Music complex. The World Music label was originally created in 1987 by the heads of a number of small London-based record labels who found that their releases by African, Latin American, and other international artists were not finding rack space because record stores had no obvious place to put them (see Broughton et al. 1994, Fairley 1989). Since then, Paris (together with London, New York, and Los Angeles) has become a major cultural center for concerts, agents, and labels involved in World Music. As such the city is the center where different cultures are linked in an asymmetrical relationship to more "typical" world cities such as Oran, Cairo, and Dakar, where Occidental culture is translated, adapted, and reworked in local contexts and circumstances, after which it is sometimes transmitted back to the West (see Chambers 1994:76).

In Paris, raï first became (and still is) part of the promotion of World Music, which involves minor record labels, art mediators, music journalists, academics, state cultural organizations, private organizations, and Third World journalists and intellectuals who are connected with a huge market and area of musical production outside the Western world as well as among ethnic minorities in Europe and America. This musical production is weakly controlled by state regulation and official economic policies and guarantees that musical diversity will survive in the future.

The agents of World Music also act in effect as intermediaries for the multinational companies through their handling of specialized styles and as talent scouts for new performers (Feld 1994:262). Thus, through Barclay record company, Khaled became involved in Polygram (controlled by Philips), one of six European, North American, and Japanese multinational companies which control 93 percent of official music sales. Here, he was developed into a megastar through a musical and ideological transformation of his image that—to paraphrase Feld—appeared to resemble the visual-graphic process through which primitive crafts are transformed into aesthetically and commercially significant ethnic art forms through the rhetoric, sponsorship, and connoisseurship of Western artists, dealers, academics, and museums (ibid.:270)—a process in which long-term profit seems to favor the promoters.

Raï has thus been involved in an ongoing musical and economic process of elaboration in a world of increasing global contacts, a world where technological invention—the phonographic recording, and then later the radio, the tape recorder, and finally digital recording—has increasingly precipitated a separation of sound from its sources and has introduced elements from one musical context into other—even radically different—ones (see Stokes 1994:3). This process can be said to have led to a phantasmagoric separation of space from place, as places have become thoroughly penetrated by and shaped in terms of social influences quite distant from them: an anxiety-ridden process of relocation (ibid.: 3).

World Music and electric raï are examples of such relocations, of creating and adjusting musical performances, embodied habits, and meanings to one another. These forces have been at work in the transformation of raï both in the West and in Algeria. Musically, both examples can be said to have operated in a context of deferring, decentering, and appropriating Anglo-American commercial global cultural concepts (Chambers 1994). Raï has fluctuated between the apolitical arts image of Khaled—freed from all political constraints except that of creating art—and the image of raï as a powerful anti-establishment force. In Algeria, raï was initially linked with anti-regime and anti-Islamist aspirations. In the West, the fascination of raï singers' voices was associated with anti-authoritarian youth cultures. With these were linked a perceived freedom of expression and equality between genders by means of sexuality and alcohol, the whole again being linked to concrete political statements against both racism and fundamentalism.

The process of the making of raï in the West fostered the perception that merely speaking about raï music was a deliberate transgression of established powers. Something that smacked of revolt, of promised freedom, of the coming age of a different law slipped easily into this discourse (see Foucault 1990:7). In the West raï singers have been seen as setting the stage for a transgression of laws, a lifting of prohibitions, a reinstatement of pleasure within the constraints of everyday reality (ibid.: 6). But we might also say that the Western perception of raï has tended to imply that, outside the world of raï, people in Algeria were repressed and condemned to prohibition, nonexistence, and silence (ibid.)—the depersonalized victims of a monolithic fundamentalism.

## Raï and Society

Algerian social reality is far more nuanced and complex than it has normally been portrayed in the literature. Certainly, the characterization of raï as a "scream of revolt" must be dismissed as oversimplified. The same can be said of the notion that raï is surrealistic or that it is a representation of a fuzzy and ambivalent state of mind in its consumers. By this I do not mean to imply that the listeners of raï did not have problems or that some might not live contradictory lives, but rather that this could not be deduced from the songs. Most approaches to raï seem to have been based on "graphic" (written) transcriptions/translations of a performance rooted in orality.[3] Their failure to acknowledge the aesthetics of orality in raï has led to some of these errors in interpretating its social significance, for raï was never intended for the privileged gaze of the eye.

One of these errors has been to overlook the fact that each song line basically tells its own independent story, and that as such a song line imploring help from God followed by a song line praising the pleasures of the bottle is not necessarily contradictory. Furthermore, if raï songs were considered in light of the principle of *situated* modesty and respect (see chapter 7)—that what is proscribed in one situation might not be proscribed in another—rather than of a *totalizing* concept of the forbidden and allowed (in Islamic terms, the *ḥarām* and *ḥalāl*), most contradictions disappeared. The songs can then be seen as an expression of situated morality in a concentrated form. Also, they were sung by "guys from the local area" involved in a sometimes difficult sphere of musical production with few possibilities, ideals, or intentions of doing much more than selling hits. The singers made a living out of their voices, basically giving people in their songs the pleasure of recognizing what was in the air socially and musically. To a large extent, their art brought forth associations with tabloid press headlines and other products, termed "popular culture," that take the daily life of their customers as a point of departure while focusing on extraordinary stories from this life. If there was any confusion to be deduced from raï, it was at the level of production—the playing errors, the missing pieces of soundtrack, the cassette covers that promised the listener a song that was not on the tape—in which I include not only the social and material organization of playing but also the distribution and "marketing" of raï.

These aspects have been neglected in debates on raï. Put in another way, there has been a neglect in following raï in all its phases from production to consumption and in realizing how these relate to the musical product; this neglect is obvious in the press story of raï (chapter 2). Moreover, consumers' and producers' reflections on raï have not been taken into account.

In general, care should be taken when one is seeking to deduce non-poetic facts from songs. Any poetic performance must be related to its context (Colonna 1974, Herzfeld 1985) if one wants to break from a common-sense approach to understanding songs as constituting the unified expression of a unified identity. If we want to explore the dynamics to be found in the social and cultural space of production and consumption of songs, we must also be careful not to establish a statistical (and thus static) relation between the content of the songs and the active and participating consciousness of the songs' consumers (see Bourdieu 1979:12).

In Algeria, raï was both the outcome and the cause of a complex social dynamic. A variety of relations were presented as entertainment through raï. The songs contained several elements—the instrumental part, the text, the voice of the singers, the reference to primary scenes, and the sociocultural image of singers—that could be combined and apprehended in various ways. As such, there was room for numerous interpretations and attitudes toward raï.

At the same time, the songs integrated a number of references to possible meeting places between the sexes—the "modern" Western discos and parties, the "traditional" weddings, and the "obscene" cabarets (see Lefevre 1995:36)—that outside the songs referred to different, contradictory models of power relations in Algerian society. As such the songs opened a wide range of meanings to be discussed and imported from raï into social life at a time when significant social changes were taking place in Algeria.

Generally speaking, raï can be characterized as an open-ended game that moved people.[4] But its success was not only due to the multiple interpretations it could lead to. Another important reason was that the songs offered pleasure that was difficult to attain outside the game.

In Oran, the encounters of the sexes were often based on interest and calculation. In the cabarets the meetings were mediated by money and at the weddings by the family, while the ideal woman, the true Muslim woman or Western woman, stayed at home or had gone overseas.

As a musical game, raï was part of a celebration of the crossing of gender boundaries at parties with lines that dealt with a love of love. Generally speaking, if the elements in raï formally referred to unfulfilled love meetings outside the songs, the game itself gave expression to the emotions involved in meeting the eternal, female Other.

## Raï in Social Life

The recordings provoked pleasure among Algerians and became one focal point of a discussion of Algerian identity. Low culture versus high culture, purity versus impurity, Islam versus the West, and youth versus experience were mediating words that transformed the game into a debate in which the leisure activities associated with raï were perceived as possibly changing or defying the power relations that were constantly negotiated and fought over in Algeria. The young, as the main consumers of raï, stood at the center of this debate.

In dealing with this group, I sought inspiration in writings on Western youth cultures, but without seeking to impose these concepts directly on the Algerian context. In the West, the relation between youth cultures and music is primarily associated with post-World War II economic growth, the postwar baby boom, the democratization of the educational system, and the lengthening of the period of youth. Taken together, the significance of these factors has been that youth as a category independent of the parental generation has been able to establish significant space for its own concerns, acquiring the economic resources to become consumers—and thus becoming a target group for the entertainment industry.

Studies of British youth cultures have focused on how music is used by the young in order to express an independent identity in relation to the parental generation and in relation to other youth groups—to "stage" themselves through the consumption of leisure goods such as music and fashion. The young also seem to have used music as "wallpaper sound" in the creation of a space for youth identities and ways of signaling sexuality—with whom to mate or not to mate (see Frith 1983:235–249, Mortensen 1989:52). In this quest, Western sub- and countercultures seem to have identified with the music of "oppressed people," especially Black music.

In Algeria, the advent of electric raï in the 1980s can on the one hand be said to have taken place in a situation of relative surplus due to the oil price rise and public investment in jobs for men and women in the cities, and on the other hand to have been a function of the "baby boom" and the democratization of the system of education, which created separate spheres for independent youth concerns. And there is no doubt that the Algerian youth culture associated with electrified raï, which integrated sounds and musical formulae from the international pop music of the early 1980s, was similar to Western youth culture. Not only was the use of labels such as "pop raï," "raï reggae," and "disco raï" an indication of this, but so too was the way raï was described as being modern, civilized, and on par with universal pop, and—to a certain degree—the way the dress style was associated with clothes produced in the West. The social context, of course, differed from that of Western youth cultures.

First, economic development in Algeria did not follow the pattern of growth seen in postwar capitalism in the West, and, hence, most of the modern story of raï is linked to the economic recession in Algeria. Second, the technological change associated with raï had less to do with radio and television, as it did in the West, than with the disappearance of the record and the advent of the cheap cassette tape. Third, raï music has not sought inspiration in the music of the oppressed, but (partly, at least) in the music of Western groups. Finally, the social organization of the family in Algeria clearly differs from that of families in the West; in Algeria, the elements of purity, economy, modesty, and power are negotiated in situated encounters.

Due to the sexual segregation and social organization of the family, "street cultures" and peer groups functioning outside the home have involved not only youth culture in Algeria, but also male culture in general. Moreover, the negative stereotyping of groups associated with Western consumption and the tendency toward a positive view of the "Islamist style" indicate that the consumption of leisure and sexuality by Algerian listeners to raï has not been realized without provoking a critical view of Western youth and its values.

During my fieldwork, no one contested the basic values structuring the moral organization of the Algerian family. This holds for both the social organization of the contexts of listening and the song lyrics, as long as they are evaluated in the light of the situated approach to respect rather than in the light of a totalizing ideological system of what is forbidden. If the lines in cabaret songs seemed transgressive (and vulgar), the fact that they were often expressed in an indirect "tense" implied that even here a certain moral code was being upheld. Also, closely linked with the transgressive song lyrics were lines expressing regrets over leaving the proper path, which could be interpreted as an expression of distress at breaking family codes of respect and modesty.

The consumption of raï and of leisure was generally not perceived as a form of opposition to the parental generation. Rather, raï and leisure were experienced outside the family sphere altogether. It was the tensions there, outside, that raï exploited—the outcomes of young men engaging in relationships with the female world, and of young women entering the male world. In this sense, raï revealed how major contradictions existed between young people's aspirations to enjoy leisure and to establish themselves as individuals within a couple, while at the same time having to manage codes of respect. In the raï universe, the car became a symbol of those who had overcome this tension because it represented both success within the field of consumption and the ability to move away from the social environment while still respecting its codes.

In terms of the problems arising from attempts to create an independent space for meetings with the opposite sex, the main focus in raï was women. The *maḥna* (see chapter 5) became a male projection within a specific system of consumption and power which reflected dominant contradictions in young men's efforts to create lives for themselves. Here, I am thinking of men's basic dependency on women and femininity and their lack of recognition thereof.

In general, the boundaries between gender roles, related as they were to consumption and power, formed a central theme in raï that was found in dirty raï and in clean raï's critique of women's materialism. It was a theme closely related to the "deregulation" of gender behavior and thus to the changes in postindependent Algeria concerning family structure, the lengthening of the period of youth, and the arrival of women in the public sphere. Moreover, this theme could not be dissociated from the worsening economic conditions in Algeria throughout the 1980s. Access to material power was needed to create room for the concerns of Algerian youth—that is, the love meetings.

Thus, this analysis of raï music has examined national political matters expressed in terms of love and women. It does not isolate the young as an independent social category within Algerian society, nor does it see raï as a counter to Islamism, like the Western media views of raï tended to do. Rather, I hope this study has contributed to an understanding of raï as an expression of the crisis in Algerian society in the early 1990s through such images as cabarets, street girls, and Western women.

Raï is still alive in Algeria today. At the start of the school year in 1994, the GIA (Groupe islamique armé) threatened to burn down schools if girls and boys were not segregated and if music lessons and girls' gymnastics were not abolished (*Libération,* September 7, 1994:7). In fact, the GIA treated the schools as if they were cabarets. When a group of Islamists hijacked an Air France airplane in December 1995, they realized that they were going to die and chose to perform a final act of charity. However (according to *Libération,* December 30, 1994), they did not make their offering to the Algerian passengers or to the poorest people on the plane, but gave it to the stewardesses, the Western women, the uniformed symbol of another world in Algeria.

# Appendix 1

## Four Versions of "Ma ḍannitsh natfārqu"

(I didn't think we would separate)

### Version 1: Cheikh Naam

*Introduction to the musical theme*

CHORUS 1:

(a) *Ma ḍannitsh natfārqu min baʿad ʿaashratna*
I didn't think we would separate after our life together
(b) *Ya ḥabibi l-walf ṣʿaīb w l-frāq mabliyya*
Oh, my friend, the habit is hard and the separation is evil
(c) *ʿAandi mʿaāk dhrāri ṣghār ya lli nsitina*
I've had small children with you, oh you who forget us
(d) *Mʿaāk dhikrayāt ana ma nansāk ma tansini*
I've shared memories with you, I won't forget you and you won't forget me

*Musical interlude*

(1) *Ya ḥaṣrah l-iyyām lli mḍāt shḥāl kānet zīna*
Oh how beautiful were the days that passed away
(2) *Wīn rāh dhāk l-waqt lli kunt nabghīk w tabghīni*
Where has the time gone when I wanted you and you wanted me?
(3) *Fi kadha min marra ʿala l-frāq tʿaāhadna*
How many times did we promise one another not to separate?
(4) *Mahma lli yaṣra ghir la dfantak walla dfantini*
Whatever happened, until the time when I would bury you and you would bury me

Chorus 2:

(a) *Ma ḍannitsh natfārqu min ba'ad 'aashratna*
I didn't think we would separate after our life together
(b) *Ya ḥabibi l-walf ṣ'aīb w l-frāq mabliyya*
Oh, my friend, the habit is hard and the separation is evil
(c) *'Aandi m'aāk dhrāri ṣghār ya lli nsitina*
I've had small children with you, oh you who forget us
(d) *M'aāk dhikrayāt ana ma nansāk ma tansini*
I've shared memories with you, I won't forget you and you won't forget me

*Musical interlude*

*Fi khaṭr Schnurr . . . Muḥammad Tayar . . . w la famille Na'am . . . fi khaṭr 'Assam l-batteur, fi khaṭr Yāsīn nta'a studiu* (in honor of Schnurr . . . Mohammed Tayar . . . and the Naam family . . . in honor of Assem the drummer, in honor of Yacine in the studio)

(5) *Ḥatta fi l-mnām ṣurtak tahtaf 'aliyya*
Even in my dreams the image of you comes to me by surprise
(6) *Sma'at 'alīk hdūr ṭḥāyḥa rāki shaffitini*
I heard evil words on your behalf, you disappoint me [it makes me sorry]
(7) *Natmanna talqi n-nās lli khīr manni ana*
I hope you will meet people who are more worthy than me
(8) *Ya rabbi yastājab d-da'awti w ana Mālika ynassīni*
May God hear my wishes and make me forget Malika

Chorus 3:

(a) *Ma ḍannitsh natfārqu min ba'ad 'aashratna*
I didn't think we would separate after our life together
(b) *Ya ḥabibi l-walf ṣ'aīb w l-frāq mabliyya*
Oh, my friend, the habit is hard and the separation is evil
(c) *'Aandi m'aāk dhrāri ṣghār ya lli nsitina*
I've had small children with you, oh you who forget us
(d) *M'aāk dhikrayāt ana ma nansāk ma tansini*
I've shared memories with you, I won't forget you and you won't forget me

*Musical interlude*

*ʿAbdalwahab fi khaṭr Nūri . . .* (Abdelwahab in honor of Nourri . . .)

(9) *Natmanna talqi n-nās lli khīr manni ana*
I hope you will meet people that are more worthy than me
(10) *Ya rabbi yastājab l daʿawti w aliha ynassīni*
May God hear my wishes and make me forget her
(11) *Hadh sh-shi maktūb jmʿaana min bʿaad fraqna*
It is the destiny which made us meet again after our separation
(12) *Ya l-mra, yahdīk aʿadhrāni w fahamīni*
Oh woman, by God, please, excuse the feeble and understand me

Chorus 4:

(a) *Ma ḍannitsh natfārqu min baʿad ʿaashratna*
I didn't think we would separate after our life together
(b) *W l-kas idur ṣʿaīb w l-frāq mabliyya*
The drinking (the glass in a round) is hard and the separation is evil
(c) *ʿAandi mʿaāk dhrāri ṣghār ya lli nsitina*
I've had small children with you, oh you who forget us
(d) *Mʿaāk dhikrayāt ana ma nansāk ma tansini*
I've shared memories with you, I won't forget you and you won't forget me

*Musical interlude (repeated only once)*

(13) *Min l-yūm lli tfāraqna ma zadtshi shuft l-hna*
Since the day of our separation I have not succeeded in finding peace
(14) *ʿAyīt min ṭ-ṭubba ṭ-ṭulba, wullāh, ma nafʿaūni*
I am tired of visiting doctors and healers, by God, they did me no good
(15) *L-yūm rāna ʿaāyshān w ghadwa ygūlu mātna*
Today we are alive and tomorrow they will say we are dead, oh yeah
(16) *Hādhi d-danya khaṭra naḍḥak nūba tbakkini*
This is how life is—sometimes I laugh sometimes she makes me cry
(17) *Nhār ykūn mlīh w nhār tadyāq ʿalina*
One day may be fine and another day we will find ourselves in trouble

(18) *W l-waqt l-ghaddār, ya l-mra, rāh ghadrak w ghdarni*
And the times are treacherous, oh woman, it betrayed you and betrayed me
(19) *L-iyyām lli mḍāt muhāl tarjʿaa līna*
The days that have passed away will never return to us
(20) *W lli fāt khadʿani w lli jāy yxūfni*
What happened hurt me, what is coming gives me fear
(21) *ʿAlīk dart l-muḥāl, Mālika, w qsamt mʿaāk akbar māḥna*
For you I did the impossible, Malika, I shared with you the greatest suffering
(22) *Fi sh-shadda w ḍ-ḍiq ghīr anāya lli lqitīni*
In difficulties and in constraints, it was only to me you could come

CHORUS 5:

(a) *Ma ḍannitsh natfārqu min baʿad ʿaashratna*
I didn't think we would separate after our life together
(b) *Ya ḥbibi l-walf ṣʿaīb w*
Oh my friend, the habit is hard and

## Version 2: Cheb Fethi

*Spoken introduction to musical background*

*Edition Khalīfa tuqaddim shābb Faṭḥi. Fi khaṭr Muḥammad Tayar w Huwāri sans oublier la famille Saḥa . . . w Ḥajj Balasqa . . . w* (the publisher Khalifa presents Cheb Fethi. In honor of Mohammed Tayar and Houari, not forgetting the Saha family and Hadj Balasqa . . . and . . . )

(1) *Ki ṭafrat ʿalāsh nkhammam*
Since it happened, why do I ponder
(2) *Ah, ki ṭafrat ʿalāsh nkhammam*
Yeah, since it happened, why do I ponder?
(3) *Dārtha shuftha salakha*
I did it, saw her, I left her
(4) *Ana ḥṣalt mʿaāk hadh l-ʿaām*
This year I was tied up with you
(5) *Walfak ki ndīr nakhṭīhā*
My habit, how to leave it all behind
(6) *Waqīl khlāṣ ḥsābt thādam*
I think the plans [accounts] are all broken down

(7) *Nkhallīha w nshūf tālīha*
I'll leave her and see the next one
(8) *S-sās lli bnītha thādam*
The foundations I constructed are broken down
(9) *Shahni l-ghrām w fi dāri tamanītha*
I hoped to have her in my home, the need of love within me
(10) *Kunt ḥāsab tafham ki nafham*
I thought she would understand as I understood
(11) *Sʿaā fhamathā, fhamathā*
From time to time you understood it as you understood it [in your own way]
(12) *Dāt ṭrīg l-ʿawja*
She took the bad road
(13) *Ma bghāt tatṣaggam*
She didn't want to redo it
(14) *Ghar bihā l-gharār*
The flaw directed her toward the flaw
(15) *Wʿaadha yaḥfaḍha*
And it promised to take care of her
(16) *Wlīdak ki kūn meshḥūr msammam (tandam)*
Your child, when it is bewitched and poisoned
(17) *W yḍarrni ghīr lli ma jarrabha*
Only he who lives it through can understand and excuse her

CHORUS 1:

(a) *Ma ḍannitsh natfārqu min baʿad ʿaashratna*
I didn't think we would separate after our life together
(b) *Ya ḥabibi l-walf ṣʿaīb w l-frāq ṭayaḥni*
Oh, my friend, the habit is hard and the separation made me fall
(c) *ʿAandi mʿaāk s-sās kbār ya lli nsitina*
I've had a solid foundation with you, oh you who forget us
(d) *Mʿaāk dhikrayāt ana ma nansāk ma tansini*
I've shared memories with you, I won't forget you and you won't forget me

*Musical interlude*

(1) *Ya ḥaṣrāh l-iyyām lli mḍāt shḥāl kānat zīna*
Oh how beautiful were the days that passed away
(2) *Wīn rāh dhāk l-waqt lli kunt nabghāk w tabghīni*
Where has the time gone when I wanted you and you wanted me?

(3) *Fi kadha min marra ʿala l-frāq tʿaahadna*
How many times did we promise one another not to separate?
(4) *Mahma lli yaṣra ghir la dfantak walla dfantini*
Whatever happened, until the time when I would bury you and you would bury me

*Musical interlude*

(5) *Ḥatta fi l-mnām ṣurtak tahtaf ʿaliyya*
Even in my dreams the image of you comes to me by surprise
(6) *Smaʿat ʿalīk hdūr ṭḥāyḥa rāki shaffitini*
I heard evil words on your behalf, you disappoint me [it makes me sorry]
(7) *Natmanna talqi n-nās lli khīr manni ana*
I hope you will meet people who are more worthy than me
(8) *Ya rabbi yastājab d-daʿawti w ana Faṭiḥa ynassīni*
May God hear my wishes and make me forget Fatiha

*Musical interlude*

(9) *Hadh sh-shi maktūb jmʿaana min bʿaad fraqna*
It is the destiny which made us meet again after our separation
(10) *Ya l-mra, yahdīk aʿadhrāni w fahamīni*
Oh woman, by God, please, excuse the feeble and understand me
(11) *Min l-yūm lli tfāraqna ma zadtshi shuft l-hna*
Since the day of our separation I have not succeeded in finding peace
(12) *ʿAyit min ṭ-ṭubba ṭ-ṭulba, wullāh, ma nafʿaūni*
I am tired of visiting doctors and healers, by God, they did me no good

CHORUS 2:

(a) *Ma ḍannitsh natfārqu min baʿad ʿaashratna*
I didn't think we would separate after our life together
(b) *Ya ḥabibi l-walf ṣʿaīb w l-frāq ṭayaḥni*
Oh, my friend, the habit is hard and the separation made me fall
(c) *ʿAandi mʿaāk s-sās kbār ya lli nsitina*
I've had a solid foundation with you, oh you who forget us
(d) *Mʿaāk dhikrayāt ana ma nansāk ma tansini*
I've shared memories with you, I won't forget you and you won't forget me

*Musical interlude*

*Fi khaṭr Surāya* (in honor of Soraya)

(13) *Nhār ykūn mlīh w nhār tadyāq ʿalina*
One day may be fine and another day we will find ourselves in trouble
(14) *W l-waqt l-ghaddār, ya l-mra, rāh ghadrak w ghdarni*
And the times are treacherous, oh woman, it betrayed you and betrayed me
(15) *ʿAlik dart l-muḥāl, w qsamt mʿaāk akbar māḥna*
For you I did the impossible, I shared with you the greatest suffering
(16) *Fi sh-shadda w ḍ-ḍīq ghīr anāya lli lqitīni*
In difficulties and in constraints, it was only to me you could come

CHORUS 3:

(a) *Ma ḍannitsh natfārqu min baʿad ʿaashratna*
I didn't think we would separate after our life together
(b) *Ya ḥabibi l-walf ṣʿaīb w l-frāq ṭayaḥni*
Oh, my friend, the habit is hard and the separation made me fall
(c) *ʿAandi mʿaāk s-sās kbār ya lli nsitina*
I've had a solid foundation with you, oh you who forget us
(d) *Mʿaāk dhikrayāt ana ma nansāk ma tansini*
I've shared memories with you, I won't forget you and you won't forget me

*Musical interlude*

## Version 3: Houari Benchenet

*Musical introduction with a spoken dedication*

*Oran musique tuqaddim l-huwāri benshnet, fi khaṭr Ḥalim l-librar ntāʿa bulūji, fi khaṭr ʿamar w krishtāl* (Oran Music presents Houari Benchenet, in honor of Halim the bookseller from Boulanger [a local area], in honor of Amar and Kristel)

*Sung introduction*

(1) *Balāk ḥsabti nsīt ma mḍa ma fawwatna, ay*
Maybe you think I forgot what happened, what we went through

(2) *Wida l-jurḥ tkhayyaṭ rāh rjaʿa ḍurri dakhlāni*
If the wound is closed again, the evil has come to remain inside
(3) *ʿAlik dart l-muḥāl w qsamt mʿaāk akbar māḥna, ay*
For you I did the impossible, I shared with you the greatest suffering
(4) *Fi sh-shedda w ḍ-ḍīq ghīr anāya lli lqitīni, aya*
In difficulties and in constraints, it was only to me you could come, oh

Chorus 1:

(a) *Ma ḍannitsh natfārqu min baʿad ʿaashratna*
I didn't think we would separate after our life together
(b) *Ya ukhti l-walf ṣʿaīb w l-frāq ana bakkāni*
Oh, my sister, the habit is hard and the separation makes me cry
(c) *ʿAandi mʿaāk istwār kaḥla dhrāri ṣghār ya lli nsitina*
I've had a dark story with you, oh you who forget us
(d) *Mʿaāk dhikrayāt ana ma nansāk ma tansini, aya*
I've shared memories with you, I won't forget you and you won't forget me

*Musical interlude*

(5) *Ya ḥaṣrāh l-iyyām lli mḍāt shḥāl kānat zīna*
Oh how beautiful were the days that passed away
(6) *Win rāh dhāk l-waqt lli kunt nabghāk w tabghīni*
Where has the time gone when I wanted you and you wanted me?
(7) *Fi kadha min marra ʿala l-frāq tʿaāhadna*
How many times did we promise one another not to separate?
(8) *Mahma lli yaṣra ghir la dfantak walla dfantini, aya*
Whatever happened, until the time when I would bury you and you would bury me?

Chorus 2:

(a) *Ma ḍannitsh natfārqu min baʿad ʿaashratna*
I didn't think we would separate after our life together
(b) *Ya ukhti l-walf ṣʿaīb w l-frāq ana bakkāni*
Oh, my sister, the habit is hard and the separation makes me cry
(c) *ʿAandi mʿaāk dhrāri ṣghār dhrāri ṣghār ya lli nsitina*
I've had small children with you, oh you who forget us
(d) *Mʿaāk dhikrayāt ana ma nansāk ma tansini, aya*
I've shared memories with you, I won't forget you and you won't forget me

(9) *Ḥatta fi l-mnām ṣurtak tahtaf ʿaliyya*
Even in my dreams the image of you comes to me by surprise
(10) *Smaʿat ʿalīk hdūr ṭḥāyḥa rāki shaffitini*
I heard evil words on your behalf, you disappoint me [it makes me sorry]
(11) *Natmanna talqi n-nās lli khīr manni ana*
I hope you will meet people who are more worthy than me
(12) *Ya rabbi yastājab d-daʿawti w ana ʿaliha ynassīni*
May God hear my wishes and make me forget her

Chorus 3:

(a) *Ma ḍannitsh natfārqu min baʿad ʿaashratna*
I didn't think we would separate after our life together
(b) *Ya ukhti l-walf ṣʿaīb w l-frāq ana bakkāni*
Oh, my sister, the habit is hard and the separation makes me cry
(c) *ʿAandi mʿaāk istwār kaḥla dhrāri ṣghār ya lli nsitina*
I've had a dark story with you, oh you who forget us
(d) *Mʿaāk dhikrayāt ana ma nansāk ma tansini, aya*
I've shared memories with you, I won't forget you and you won't forget me

(13) *Min l-yūm lli tfāraqna ma zadtshi shuft l-hna*
Since the day of our separation I have not succeeded in finding peace
(14) *ʿAyīt min ṭ-ṭubba ṭ-ṭulba, wullāh, ma nafʿaūni*
I am tired of visiting doctors and healers, by God, they did me no good
(15) *L-yūm rāna ʿaayshān w ghadwa ygūlu mātna*
Today we are alive and tomorrow they will say we are dead, oh yeah
(16) *Hādhi d-danya khaṭra naḍḥak nūba tbakkini*
This is how life is—sometimes I laugh sometimes she makes me cry

Chorus 4:

(a) *Ma ḍannitsh natfārqu min baʿad ʿaashratna*
I didn't think we would separate after our life together
(b) *Ya ukhti l-walf ṣʿaīb w l-frāq ana bakkāni*
Oh, my sister, the habit is hard and the separation makes me cry
(c) *ʿAandi mʿaāk mḥāyn kbār dhrāri ṣghār ya lli nsitina*
I shared times of great pain with you, oh you who forget us

(d) *Mʿaāk dhikrayāt ana ma nansāk ma tansini, aya*
I've shared memories with you, I won't forget you and you won't forget me

(21) *L-yūm rāna ʿaāyshān w ghadwa ygūlu mātna*
Today we are alive and tomorrow they will say we are dead, oh yeah
(22) *Hādhi d-danya khaṭra naḍḥak nūba tbakkini*
This is how life is—sometimes I laugh sometimes she makes me cry
(23) *Nhār ykūn mlīh w nhār tadyāq ʿalina*
One day may be fine and another day we will find ourselves in trouble
(24) *W l-waqt l-ghaddār, ya l-mra, rāh ghadrak w ghdarni*
And the times are treacherous, oh woman, it betrayed you and betrayed me

Chorus 5:

(a) *Ma ḍannitsh natfārqu min baʿad ʿaashratna*
I didn't think we would separate after our life together
(b) *Ya ukhti l-walf ṣʿaīb w l-frāq ana bakkāni*
Oh, my sister, the habit is hard and the separation makes me cry
(c) *ʿAandi mʿaāk istwār kaḥla dhrāri ṣghār ya lli nsitina*
I've had a dark story with you, oh you who forget us
(d) *Mʿaāk dhikrayāt ana ma nansāk ma tansini, aya*
I've shared memories with you, I won't forget you and you won't forget me

(25) *Balak ḥsabti nsīt ma mḍa ma fawwatna, ay*
Maybe you think I forgot what happened, what we went through
(26) *Wida l-jurḥ tkhayyaṭ rāh rjaʿa ḍurri dakhlāni*
If the wound is closed again, the evil has come to remain inside
(27) *ʿAlīk dart l-muḥāl w qsamt mʿaāk akbar māḥna, ay*
For you I did the impossible, I shared with you the greatest suffering
(28) *Fi sh-shadda w ḍ-ḍīq ghir anāya lli lqitīni, aya*
In difficulties and in constraints, it was only to me you could come, oh

Chorus 6:

(a) *Ma ḍannitsh natfārqu min baʿad ʿaashratna*
I didn't think we would separate after our life together

(b) *Ya ukhti l-walf ṣ'aīb w l-frāq ana bakkāni*
Oh, my sister, the habit is hard and the separation makes me cry

**Version 4: Cheb Hamid**

*Musical introduction*

*Édition Nouvelle Étoile tuqaddim shābb Ḥamid. . . . Nūri w Karīm. . . .*
(New Star presents Cheb Hamid . . . Nourri and Karim . . .)

(a) *Ma ḍannitsh natfārqu min ba'ad 'aashratna*
I didn't think we would separate after our life together
(b) *Ukhti walf ṣ'aīb ana walft w nti walftini*
My sister, the habit is hard, I got used to you and you got used to me
(a) *Ma ḍannitsh natfārqu min ba'ad 'aashratna*
I didn't think we would separate after our life together
(b) *Ukhti walf ṣ'aīb ana walft w nti walftini*
My sister, the habit is hard, I got used to you and you got used to me

*Musical interlude*

(1) *Jībt m'aāk dhrāri ṣghār ya lli nsitina*
I had small children with you, oh you who forget us
(2) *M'aāk dhikrayāt ana ma nansāk ma tansini, aya*
I've shared memories with you, I won't forget you and you won't forget me
(3) *Jībt m'aāk dhrāri ṣghār ya lli nsitina*
I had small children with you, oh you who forget us
(4) *M'aāk dhikrayāt ana ma nansāk ma tansini, aya*
I've shared memories with you, I won't forget you and you won't forget me

(a) *Ma ḍannitsh natfārqu min ba'ad 'aashratna*
I didn't think we would separate after our life together
(b) *Ukhti walf ṣ'aīb ana walft w nti walftini*
My sister, the habit is hard, I got used to you and you got used to me

*Musical interlude*

(5) *Ḥatta fi l-mnām ṣurtak tahtaf 'aliyya*
Even in my dreams the image of you comes to me by surprise
(6) *Sma'at 'alīk hdūr ṭḥāyḥa rāki shaffitini*
I heard evil words on your behalf, you disappoint me [it makes me sorry]

(7) *Ḥatta fi l-mnām ṣurtak tahtaf ʿaliyya*
Even in my dreams the image of you comes to me by surprise
(8) *Smaʿat ʿalīk hdūr ṭḥāyḥa rāki shaffitini*
I heard evil words on your behalf, you disappoint me [it makes me sorry]

(a) *Ma ḍannitsh natfārqu min baʿad ʿaashratna*
I didn't think we would separate after our life together
(b) *Ukhti walf ṣʿaīb ana walft w nti walftini*
My sister, the habit is hard, I got used to you and you got used to me

*Musical interlude*

(9) *Fi kadha min marra ʿala l-frāq tʿaāhadna*
How many times did we promise one another not to separate?
(10) *Mahma lli yaṣra ghir la dfantak walla dfantini*
Whatever happened, until the time when I would bury you and you would bury me
(11) *Fi kadha min marra ʿala l-frāq tʿaāhadna*
How many times did we promise one another not to separate?
(12) *Mahma lli yaṣra ghir la dfantak walla dfantini*
Whatever happened, until the time when I would bury you and you would bury me

(a) *Ma ḍannitsh natfārqu min baʿad ʿaashratna*
I didn't think we would separate after our life together
(b) *Ukhti walf ṣʿaīb ana walft w nti walftini*
My sister, the habit is hard, I got used to you and you got used to me

*Musical interlude*

(13) *Ḥatta fi l-mnām ṣurtak tahtaf ʿaliyya*
Even in my dreams the image of you comes to me by surprise
(14) *Ya rabbi smaḥli, ʿawni ʿaliha*
My God, listen to me; help me get rid of her
(15) *Ḥatta fi l-mnām ṣurtak tahtaf ʿaliyya*
Even in my dreams the image of you comes to me by surprise
(16) *Ya rabbi smaḥli, ʿawni ʿaliha*
My God, listen to me; help me get rid of her

(a) *Ma ḍannitsh natfārqu min baʿad ʿaashratna*
I didn't think we would separate after our life together
(b) *Ukhti walf ṣʿaīb ana walft w nti walftini*
My sister, the habit is hard, I got used to you and you got used to me

*Musical interlude*

(17) *Jībt mʿaāk dhrāri ṣghār ya lli nsitina*
I had small children with you, oh you who forget us
(18) *Mʿaāk dhikrayāt ana ma nansāk ma tansini*
I've shared memories with you, I won't forget you and you won't forget me
(19) *Jībt mʿaāk dhrāri ṣghār ya lli nsitina*
I had small children with you, oh you who forget us
(20) *Mʿaāk dhikrayāt ana ma nansāk ma tansini*
I've shared memories with you, I won't forget you and you won't forget me

(a) *Ma ḍannitsh natfārqu min baʿad ʿaashratna*
I didn't think we would separate after our life together
(b) *Ukhti walf ṣʿaīb*
My sister, the habit is hard . . .

# Appendix 2

## Four Raï Songs

**"Dīri dār"** (Make a home)

*Musical introduction*

(1) *W ma darti dār ma darti dhrāri sghār*
You didn't make a home; you didn't have small children
(2) *'Aajbāk r-rikār, ya 'umri, taḥwās l-bulvār*
You like Ricard, oh my life, and walk the streets [boulevards]
(3) *Khallu l-maḥna t - tṣawwag ya washta ḥāzkum*
Let my passion do what she wants, why do you interfere?
(4) *Lli bīk biyya walli lli ḍarrak ḍarrini*
What's in you is in me, and what hurts you hurts me

CHORUS 1:

*Ah khla dār muk, kaytak, dīri dār dār*
Ruin of your mother's house, get it, make a home, a home
(5) *Ma ndīr l-maḥna ma tasbaghli gwāymi*
I won't take that passion; you will not make me change [paint my bones]
(6) *Ma ndīr l-maḥna ma tji l-'aawda tlūmni*
I won't take that passion; the mare will not be able to make complaints to me
(7) *Ma ndīr l-maḥna ma tfashshli l 'aḍam*
I won't take that passion; you won't weaken my bones

(8) *Khallu l-maḥna tṣawwag ya washta ḥāzkum w ya*
Let my passion do what she wants; why do you interfere, oh?

Chorus 2:

*Ah khla dār muk, kaytak, dīri dār dār*
Ruin of your mother's house, get it, make a home, a home
(9) *La dārhalak zīnek walla ḥdāydak*
Was it your beauty that did it to you or your jewelry?
(10) *La dārhalak zīnek . . .*
Was it your beauty that did it to you . . . ?
(11) *La dārhalak zīnek walla ṣaḥḥitak*
Was it your beauty that did it to you or was it your health [state of being]?
(12) *Yana bḥar ʿaliyya w ntiyya la*
I will manage, but you, no

Chorus 3:

*Ah khla dār muk, kaytak, dīri dār dār*
Ruin of your mother's house, get it, make a home, a home
(13) *L-factur yṭabṭab w jāb l-maḥna mṭabgwa*
The postman knocks at the door; he brings my passion enveloped
(14) *Jātni briyya w lli qrāha ndab w ya*
A letter came to me; the one who reads it cries in pain
(15) *Jātni briyya w nās jzaāyer ʿaayyṭu*
A letter came to me; the people of Algiers are calling
(16) *Khallu l-maḥna tṣawwag ya washta ḥazkum w ya*
Let my passion do what she wants, oh, why do you interfere, oh?

Chorus 4:

*Ah khla dār muk, kaytak, dīri dār dār*
Ruin of your mother's house, get it, make a home, a home
(17) *W bāyat natgallab yana dāruli l-ḥrīg*
I spent the night turning in my bed; they burned me with sorcery
(18) *Yana bḥar ʿaliyya qlālat ṣaḥḥti w ya*
I will manage; my health deteriorated
(19) *Nabghīk baghu rabbāni, walla dartili s-sḥūr*
I love you with a God-given love, or was it sorcery you made?
(20) *Khallu l-maḥna tṣawwag ya washta ḥāzkum w ya*
Let my passion do what she wants, oh, why do you interfere, oh?

CHORUS 5:

*Ah khla dār muk, kaytak, la māzo*
Ruin of your mother's house, get it, the "maison"
(21) *Naddīk, naddīk bla nabda ʿalik*
I will take you; I will take you with you having to cry in pain
(22) *Naddīk, naddīk bla katbaʿalīk*
I will take you; I will take you; without you having to make talismans
(23) *Naddīk, naddīk bla sabba njīk*
I will take you; I will take you; I will take you without hidden motives
(24) *Khallu l-maḥna tṣawwag ya washta ḥāzkum w ya*
Let my passion do what she wants, oh, why do you interfere, oh?

CHORUS 6:

*Ah khla dār muk, kaytak, dīri dār dār*
Ruin of your mother's house, get it, make a home, a home

Spoken dedication

*Fi khaṭr Édition Royale w Kwīder Banṣʿaid* (in honor of Edition Royale and Kouider Bensaïd)

(25) *W jbāl wahrān dargu ybānet marsāy*
The mountains of Oran vanished and Marseilles appeared
(26) *Khallu l-maḥna tṣawwag kima bghāt*
Let my passion do what she wants
(27) *Lli bīk biyya walli ḍarrek ḍarrini*
What's in you is in me, and what hurts you hurts me
(28) *ʿAīn l-kbīra tuktal walla tmūt, ya Muhammad*
The great eye kills or you die, oh Mohammed

CHORUS 7:

*Ah khla dār muk, kaytak, dīri dār dār*
Ruin of your mother's house, get it, make a home, a home
(29) *Ma shuft shufa ki maḥḥanti dāyra*
I saw a look, in the way of my passion
(30) *ʿAīnīk ki ʿaīniyya ʿaīnīk nāymīn w ya*
Your eyes are like mine; your eyes are languishing

(31) *ʿAīnīk ki ʿaīniyya ya ʿaīnīk ya naʿasīn*
Your eyes are like mine; your eyes are languid
(32) *La klīt zahri mʿaa maḥḥanti l-uwla*
I didn't have a chance [I ate my chance] with my first love

CHORUS 8:

*Ah khla dār muk, kaytak, dīri dār dār*
Ruin of your mother's house, get it, make a home, a home
(33) *Bashshar jāni walla Nurmandi ʿaayṭat*
Good news came to me, or is it Normandy calling?
(34) *Yana bḥar ʿaliyya w ntiyya la w ya*
I will manage, but you, no
(35) *ʿAadbatni min maḥḥanti ma ndīr ḥadd*
She made me suffer; I swore not to take another
(36) *Wa ḥlaft ma nṣhabshi, ma ʿaandi zhar Muḥammad ya khuya*
I swore not to get tied up; I don't have any luck, Mohammed, my brother
(37) *W ma darti dār ma darti dhrāri sghār*
You didn't make a home; you didn't have small children
(38) *ʿAajbāk r-rikār, ya ʿumri, taḥwās l-bulvār*
You like Ricard, oh my life, and walk the streets [boulevards]
(39) *Khallu l-maḥna t - tṣawwag ya washta ḥazkum*
Let my passion do what she wants, why do you interfere?
(40) *Lli bīk biyya walli lli ḍarrak ḍarrini*
What's in you is in me, and what hurts you hurts me

CHORUS 9:

*Ah khla dār muk, kaytak, la māzo*
Ruin of your mother's house, get it, the "maison"

**"Sʿaīda bʿaīda"** (Saïda is far away; first version)

(1) *Ya w māni mhanni . . . w maḍṭirab w ya*
I am not at peace . . . I am disturbed
(2) *Rabbi, rabbi ki ngūl nāsi* [the sound disappears]
My God, my God, what shall I tell my people . . . ?
(3) *Rabbi, rabbi ki ngūl nāsi, khllītha w jīt b-rāsi*
My God, my God, what shall I tell my people, I left her and came back alone

(4) *Rabbi, rabbi ki ngūl nāsi, khllītha w jīt b-rāsi*
My God, my God, what shall I tell my people, I left her and came back alone

*Musical interlude*

(5) *W ʿalash l-ḥbībi yʿaādi . . .*
Why does the friend get angry . . .
(6) *Ya ḍrāri, waṣṣīt l-ʿaawd w yak ma ya yanhamsh*
Oh my sufferings, I told [advised] the horse not to neigh . . .
(7) *Ya ḍrāri, waṣṣīt l-ʿaawd w yak ma ya yanhamsh*
Oh my sufferings, I told [advised] the horse not to neigh . . .
(8) *Ya ḍrāri, waṣṣīt l-ʿaawd w yak ma ya yanhamsh*
Oh my sufferings, I told [advised] the horse not to neigh . . .

*Musical interlude*

(9) *Wṣ ʿaīda bʿaīda w l-mashīna ghālya w ya*
Saïda is far away and the train is expensive, oh yeah
(10) *Taḥwās l-ghāba . . .*
Walking in the wood . . .
(11) *W ya ḍrāri taḥwās l-ghāba . . . sh-shābb yʿaallam l-bujādi, wah, wah*
Oh my sufferings, the walks in the wood . . . the youth loses his innocence, oh yeah, oh yeah
(12) *W ya ḍrāri taḥwās l-ghāba . . . sh-shābb yʿaallam l-bujādi, wah, wah*
Oh my sufferings, the walks in the wood . . . the youth loses his innocence, oh yeah, oh yeah

*Musical interlude*

(13) *Ya w māni mhanni . . . w maḍṭirab w ya*
I am not at peace . . . I am disturbed
(14) *W ya ḍrāri . . .*
Oh, my sufferings . . .
(15) *W ya ḍrāri . . .*
Oh, my sufferings . . .
(16) *W ya ḍrāri . . .*
Oh, my sufferings . . .

*Musical interlude*

(17) *W ʿalāsh l-ḥbībi yʿaādi . . .*
Why does the friend get angry . . .

(18) *W ya ḍrāri . . .*
Oh, my sufferings . . .
(19) *W ya ḍrāri . . .*
Oh, my sufferings . . .
(20) *W ya ḍrāri . . .*
Oh, my sufferings . . .

*Musical interlude*

(21) *Ya w māni mhanni . . . w maḍṭirab w ya ya w māni mhanni . . .*
I am not at peace . . . I am disturbed
(22) *Bnāt l-yūm ki ḥyūṭ r-ramla*
The girls of today are like walls of sand
(23) *W ya ḍrāri w bnāt l-yūm ki ḥyuṭ r-ramla walli shādd fihum yrīb*
Oh, my sufferings, the girls of today are like walls of sand, the one who leans on them collapses
(24) *W ya ḍrāri w bnāt l-yūm ki ḥyuṭ r-ramla walli shādd fihum yrīb*
Oh, my sufferings, the girls of today are like walls of sand, the one who leans on them collapses

*Musical interlude*

(25) *Ya w māni mhanni . . . w maḍṭirab w ya*
I am not at peace . . . I am disturbed
(26) *Rabbi, rabbi ki ngūl nāsi, khallītha w jīt b-rāsi*
My God, my God, what shall I tell my people, I left her and came back alone, rabbi
(27) *Rabbi, rabbi ki ngūl*
My God, my God, what shall I tell?

**"Sʿaīda bʿaīda"** (Saïda is far away; second version)

(1) *Ya w māni mhanni w ma glaybi w maḍṭirab w ya ya*
I am not at peace and my heart is disturbed
(2) *Rabbi, rabbi ki ngūl, nāsi* [the sound disappears] . . .
My God, my God, what shall I tell my people . . . ?
(3) *Ya, ḍrāri, rabbi, rabbi ki ngūl, nāsi, khallītha w jīt b-rāsi, āli ah*
Oh my sufferings, my God, my God, what shall I tell my people? I left her and came back alone
(4) *W ya l-mwīma, rabbi, rabbi ki ngūl, nāsi, khallītha w jīt b-rāsi, āli ah*
Oh, mother, my God, my God, what shall I tell my people. I left her and came back alone

*Musical interlude*

*Wah, wah* (Oh yeah, oh yeah)

(5) *Ya w ʿalāsh l-ḥbībi yʿaādi walla la nti w yah*
Why do the friends [lovers] get angry at one another and [why] not you?
(6) *Ya ḍrāri, waṣṣīt l-ʿaāwd w yak ma ya yanhamsh*
I told [advised] the horse not to neigh
(7) *Ya ḍrāri, waṣṣīt l-ʿaawd w yak ma ya yanhamsh ghirā khaym l-maghbūna*
Oh my sufferings, I told [advised] the horse not to neigh until we came to the lover's tent
(8) *Ya ḍrāri, waṣṣīt l-ʿaawd w yak ma ya yanhamsh ghirā khaym l-maghbūna, āli, wah, wah*
Oh my sufferings, I told [advised] the horse not to neigh until we came to the lover's tent, my Lord, oh yeah, oh yeah

*Musical interlude*

(9) *W ṣʿaīda bʿaīda w l-mashīna ghālya w ya*
Saïda is far away and the train is expensive
(10) *Taḥwās l-ghāba rgāda l-khallāj*
Walking in the woods and sleeping in the bushes
(11) *W ya ḍrāri taḥwās l-ghāba rgāda, sh-shābb yʿaallam l-bujādi, āli, ʿaawni, khuya, ʿaawni*
Oh, my sufferings, walking in the wood [in the sense of a jungle] and sleeping, the youth loses his innocence, my God, help me brother, help me
(12) *W ya ḍrāri taḥwās l-ghāba rgāda, sh-shābb yʿaallam l-bujādi, āli, ah, wah*
Oh, my sufferings, the walking the woods and sleeping, the youth loses his innocence, my God, oh, yeah

*Musical interlude*

*Wah, wah* (yeah, yeah)

(13) *Ya w māni mhanni w marra glaybi w maḍṭirab w ya ya*
I am not at peace and sometimes my heart is disturbed
(14) *Ya dhrāri, gatluh sallam w ma bghāshi sallam*
She told him to kiss her, and he didn't want to

(15) *Ya dhrāri, gatluh sallam w ma bghāshi sallam ḍallīt dārkātah mahna*
Oh my sufferings, she told him to kiss her, and he didn't want to, the passion and pain took him
(16) *Ya dhrāri, gatluh sallam w ma bghāshi sallam ḍallīt dārkātah ghumma wah Muḥammad, wah*
Oh my sufferings, she told him to kiss her and he didn't want to, he was left suffocating, yeah, Mohammed, yeah

*Musical interlude*

(17) *Ya w ʿalāsh l-ḥbībi yʿaādi walla la nti w yah*
Why do the friends get angry at one another and not you, oh yeah?
(18) *Sallāk salma hak l-sānak ʿaaḍḍa*
Take a kiss with bites in the tongue
(19) *W ya ḍrāri sallāk salma hak l-sānak ʿaaḍḍa khayti saʿa yaya*
Oh my sufferings, take a kiss with bites of the tongue, my sisters, she will come back
(20) *W ya l-mwīma sallak salma hak l-sānak ʿaaḍḍa fi ʿars wullāh waʿada nakhalafha*
Take a kiss with bites of the tongue at the wedding or at the *waada*. I will get revenge on her

*Musical interlude*

(21) *Ya w māni mhanni w marra glaybi w maḍṭirab w ya*
I am not at peace and sometimes my heart is disturbed
(22) *W bnāt l-yūm ki ḥyūṭ r-ramla*
The girls of today are like walls of sand
(23) *W ya ḍrāri w bnāt l-yūm ki ḥyūṭ r-ramla walli shādd fihum yrīb*
Oh my sufferings, the girls of today are like walls of sand. The one who leans on them collapses
(24) *W ya ḍrāri w bnāt l-yūm ki ḥyūṭ r-ramla walli shādd fihum yrīb, ah līl, wah, wah*
Oh my sufferings, the girls of today are like walls of sand. The one who leans on them collapses, oh night, oh yeah, oh yeah

*Musical interlude*

(25) *Ya w māni mhanni w marra glaybi w maḍṭirab w ya*
I am not at peace and sometimes my heart is disturbed

(26) *Rabbi rabbi ki ngūl nāsi w ya ḍrāri rabbi rabbi ki ngūl nāsi khallītha w jīt b-rāsi, āli*
Oh my sufferings, my God, my God, what shall I tell my people? I left her and came back alone, my God
(27) *W ya l-mwīma rabbi rabbi ki ngūl . . .*
Oh, mother, my God, my God, what shall I tell . . . ?

**"Dablat galbi"** (Ruin of my heart)

*Istikhbār*

*Amān, amān, amān . . .*

*Musical prelude*

(1) *Ma nūrgad la yjīni n-nūm ya dāri khālya, wah, ya dāri khālya, wah*
I don't sleep; dreams do not come; my house is empty, yeah, my house is empty, yeah
(2) *Mnīn tkūni bʿaīda ʿaliyya ya yarkābni l hbāl, wah ya yarkābni l hbāl, wah*
When you are far away from me, I am caught in madness, yeah. I am caught in madness, yeah

CHORUS 1:

*W yah dablat galbi w yah dablat ʿumri*
Oh, ruin of my heart, oh yeah, ruin of my life
*W yah dablat galbi w yah dablat ʿumri*
oh, ruin of my heart, oh yeah, ruin of my life

*Musical interlude*

(3) *W skantili l-galb ki l-ʿaashsh fārsha, wah, ki l-ʿaashsh fārsha, wah*
You stayed in my heart like a bird's nest in a tree, yeah, like a bird's nest in a tree
(4) *Ya kalmtak jarḥatni ya l-khudmi la, wah w l-khudmi la, wah*
Oh, your words wounded me, not the knife, yeah, not the knife

CHORUS 2:

*W yah dablat galbi w yah dablat ʿumri*
Oh, ruin of my heart, oh yeah, ruin of my life
*W yah dablat galbi w yah dablat ʿumri*
Oh, ruin of my heart, oh yeah, ruin of my life

*Musical interlude*

(5) *Gūlu l-ṣayyād yakhṭīni, ya yakhṭī ḥmamti wah, ya yakhṭī ḥmamti wah*
Tell the hunter to let, let my pigeon alone, yeah, let my pigeon alone, yeah

(6) *L-ḥāssād ma bghāw yqilūni ya zādatni l-muk ya zādatni l-muk wah*
The jealous didn't want to let me be and your mother did it worse to me; your mother did it worse to me, yeah

CHORUS 3:

*W yah dablat galbi wah dablat ʿumri*
Oh, ruin of my heart, oh yeah, ruin of my life
*W yah dablat galbi w yah ma tashtani*
Oh, ruin of my heart, oh don't hurt [crush] me

*Musical interlude and singing*

*Waaah, yaaaa, waaaah* (Yeah, oh yes, yeah)

(7) *Dartu fiyya rrāykum rabbi wkīlkum wah, ya rabbi wkīlkum wah*
You treated me according to your own plans. God will look after you, yeah; God will look after you, yeah

(8) *Yana bghīt maḥḥanti ya shkūn ysālni wah, ya shkūn ysalni wah*
I wanted my love; who has the right to question that? Yeah, who has the right to question that? Yeah

CHORUS 4:

*W yah dablat galbi w yah dablat ʿumri*
Oh, ruin of my heart, oh yeah, ruin of my life
*W yah dablat galbi w yah dablat ʿumri*
Oh, ruin of my heart, oh yeah, ruin of my life

*Musical interlude with singing and a spoken dedication*

*Ya mma ya līl ya mma* (Oh mother, oh night, oh mother) . . . *Fi khaṭr . . . Kamal w Ḥammudi* (in honor of [not understandable] . . . Kamel and Hammoudi)

(9) *Yana bḥar ʿaliyya ya w l-maḥna la wah ya w l-maḥna la ah*
I will manage but my passion no, yeah, my passion no, oh

(10) *Khalad w Ḥamīd ya Rashīd waṣṭa wah Rashīd waṣṭa wah*

Khaled and Hamid, oh, Rashid is in the middle; yeah, Rashid is in the middle, yeah

CHORUS 5:

*W yah dablat galbi w yah dablat ʿumri*
Oh, ruin of my heart, oh yeah, ruin of my life
*W yah dablat galbi w yah dablat ʿumri*
Oh, ruin of my heart, oh yeah, ruin of my life

*Musical interlude*

(11) *Ma nūrgud ma yjīni n-nūm w nti ghāyba, wah, w nti ghāyba, wah*
I don't sleep; dreams do not come when you are away, yeah, when you are away
(12) *Gullah w ydabbar rāsah lli ḍāʿalah wah lli lli ḍāʿalah wah*
Tell him to manage on his own with what he lost, yeah, with what he lost
(13) *W lli ʿabd l-maḥna ya rabbi yʿaawnah wah ya rabbi yʿaawnah*
The slave of passions, may God help him, yeah, may God help him

CHORUS 6:

*W yah dablat galbi w yah dablat shiri*
Oh, ruin of my heart, yeah, ruin of my "chérie"
*W yah dablat galbi wah yah dablat ʿumri wah wah*
Oh, ruin of my heart, yeah, ruin of my life, yeah, yeah

*Musical interlude with a spoken dedication*

*Fi khaṭr l-parsunal ntaʿa Zianīd, fi khaṭr ʿAzzdīn w ʿAbdalmūla* (in honor of the staff at the Hotel Zianide, in honor of Azzedin and Abdelmoula)

(14) *Liyah liyah w mūl l-maḥna tsārru wah, l-maḥna tsārru wah*
Why, why do you destroy the man of passion, yeah, destroy the passion, yeah?
(15) *Ya ʿamawli ʿaīniyya w zāduli l-galb wah, zāduli l-galb wah*
Oh, they blinded my eyes and did the same to my heart, yeah, did the same to my heart, yeah

CHORUS 7:

*W yah dablat galbi w yah dablat ʿumri*
Oh, ruin of my heart, oh yeah, ruin of my life
*W yah dablat galbi w yah dablat ʿumri*
Oh, ruin of my heart, oh yeah, ruin of my life

*Musical postlude*

"Jibuhālu" (Bring him to her)

*Musical introduction*

CHORUS 1:

*Jibuhālu ya bni ʿammu jibuhālu*
Bring him to her, oh cousins; bring him to her
*Jibuhālu kuntra ʿalli ysāluhālu*
Bring him to her against those who interfere

*Musical interlude*

(1) *Yabki w ynūḥ xāyaf la z-zarga la trūh*
He cries and weeps; he's afraid that the brunette will leave [him]

CHORUS 2:

*Jibuhālu ya bni ʿammu jibuhālu*
Bring him to her, oh cousins; bring him to her
*Jibuhālu kuntra ʿalli ysāluhālu*
Bring him to her against those who interfere

*Musical interlude*

(2) *L-kurtaj qallaʿa w anaya galbi nglaʿa*
The cortège [procession] went off and my heart was torn to pieces

CHORUS 3:

*Jibuhālu ya bni ʿammu jibuhālu*
Bring him to her, oh cousins; bring him to her
*Jibuhālu kuntra ʿalli ysāluhālu*
Bring him to her against those who interfere

(3) *Wih, mʿa l-bayḍa yamshi ʿala z-zarga ymūt*
He is dating the blonde and dies of want for the brunette

CHORUS 4:

*Jibuhālu ya bni ʿammu jibuhālu*
Bring him to her, oh cousins; bring him to her
*Jibuhālu kuntra ʿalli ysāluhālu*
Bring him to her against those who interfere

(4) *Wīh, l-layla tzawwaj huwa ṭallagti nti*
The night he married and you divorced

CHORUS 5:

*Jibuhālu ya bni ʿammu jibuhālu*
Bring him to her, oh cousins; bring him to her
*Jibuhālu kuntra ʿalli ysāluhālu*
Bring him to her against those who interfere
(5) *W lli ḥaḍru fi twḥālit harribu*
Those who assisted at the end, they will escape

CHORUS 6:

*Jibuhālu ya bni ʿammu jibuhālu*
Bring him to her, oh cousins; bring him to her
*Jibuhālu kuntra ʿalli ysāluhālu*
Bring him to her against those who interfere
(6) *Wīh rāni ngūl nkammal rabbi yaktab*
I say to myself carry it out [do it (the marriage)] and God has written it

CHORUS 7:

*Jibuhālu ya bni ʿammu jibuhālu*
Bring him to her, oh cousins; bring him to her
*Jibuhālu kuntra ʿalli ysāluhālu*
Bring him to her against those who interfere
(7) *Lli dāruhālu ya ḥbābi ghīr min jmāʿatu*
The ones who did it to him, my friends, they cannot but be part of his group

CHORUS 8:

*Jibuhālu ya bni ʿammu jibuhālu*
Bring him to her, oh cousins; bring him to her
*Jibuhālu kuntra ʿalli ysāluhālu*
Bring him to her against those who interfere
(8) *W jmāʿaa fi Karma taswa ḥaqqiha*
And the group of Karma is worth its weight in gold

CHORUS 9:

*Jibuhālu ya bni ʿammu jibuhālu*
Bring him to her, oh cousins; bring him to her
*Jibuhālu an sukri ʿalli ysāluhālu*
Bring him to her "en secret" against those who interfere
(9) *Wīh w shaṭnuha ʿaliyya w khḍa rrāyhum*
They put me in an impossible situation [because of gossip] and he believed their sayings

Chorus 10:

*Jibuhālu ya bni ʿammu jibuhālu*
Bring him to her, oh cousins; bring him to her
*Jibuhālu kuntra ʿalli ysāluhālu*
Bring him to her against those who interfere
*Wīh, ʿaadyān galbi w fi twāli ykhāllișu*
The enemies of my heart at the end they will pay

Chorus 11:

*Jibuhālu ya bni ʿammu jibuhālu*
Bring him to her, oh cousins; bring him to her
*Jibuhālu kuntra ʿalli ysāluhālu*
Bring him to her against those who interfere

# Notes

## Chapter 1

1 See, for example, Berkaak 1993; Fornäs et al. 1984; Frith 1983; Hebdige 1979, 1987; Willis 1978.

2 I use the concept of popular music without any intention of venturing into a "ritual" opening discussion of the pros and cons of mass culture and popular culture versus high culture and folk culture (see, e.g., Frith 1983; Malm and Willis 1984, 1992; Manuel 1988, 1993; Mukerji and Schudson 1991, etc.). I take the popular to be opposed to the "rare"; as such it is a relative concept. The consumers of what is defined as popular by others will tend not to use this expression, but rather talk about the singers, songs, football players, and movie stars they like.

3 See Henni 1990 for an economist's approach to the parallel economy in a redistributive state.

4 Earnings from wage labor rose from 5.8 billion dinars ($900 million) in 1967 to 33.4 billion ($5.6 billion) in 1977. In the same time period, the number of wage labor jobs increased from 1,177,000 to 2,193,000.

5 For example, from 1987 until the revolt of October 1988, per capita consumption in Algeria fell by 7.6 percent, income by 8 percent, and purchasing power by 15 percent (Addi 1990).

6 In the Muslim world, adolescence refers to the age from fasting to wedding (see Davis and Davis 1989; Pascon and Bentahar 1969).

7 In 1987, 47.9 percent of Algerians were living in nuclear families (i.e., a couple with or without children) while 52.1 percent were living in extended families (Messaoudi 1990:200).

8 On the Islamist movement see Al-Ahnaf et al. 1991, Burgat 1988, Khelladi 1992, Labat 1995, and Rouadjia 1990.

9 For documentation see, for example, Mouffok 1996, Reporters sans frontières 1995.

10 For discussion of the birth of the World Music concept in 1987, see Fairley 1989.

11 See also recent books by Daoudi and Miliani (1996) and Virolle-Souibès (1995).

12 On the rules of the art of *malḥūn,* see Tahar 1975. For examples of translations of *malḥūn* into French, see Azza 1979, Belhalfaoui 1982b, Boubakeur 1990, and Sonneck 1902.

13 Of course within the *badawi* style, there are several genres as well as several types of *gaṣbas.*

14 Two of the best known poets in the Oran area are Mostfa Ben Brahim and Mohammed Belkheir (see Azza 1979, Boubakeur 1990), both of whom lived well into the second half of the nineteenth century. Among interpreters remembered today are Cheikh Khaldi, Cheikh Hamada, Cheikh Madani, Cheikh Bourras, Cheikh Mohammed Relizane, and Cheikh Abdelmoula, who have all recorded a considerable number of songs.

15 The best known *shīkha* today is Cheikha Remitti (from the French *reméttez,* give me [one more drink]), who could still be heard performing in 1992. Her first recordings came out in the early 1950s; her first great hit was in 1954, "*Sharrak gaṭṭaʿa*" (Tear in pieces, cut), an allusion to virginity (see Virolle-Souibès 1993). Before Remitti, the best known names were Cheikha Kheira Gendiil, who recorded in the early 1930s, and Fatma el Khadem, Fatma Wahraniya, and Mama el Abbasiya from the 1930s and 1940s. Later followed Cheikha Ouashma (the "tattooed"), Cheikha Habiba el Kebira, and Cheikha Hab Lahmar ("red buttons"), while among the new generation we find Cheikha Djenia (the "she-devil"), who also sings in the electrical form of raï.

16 That is, they sing with simple phrases (the melody rarely extending beyond a fifth), a simple dance rhythm, and the use of response choruses.

17 The best known are Chaba Zahouania, Chaba Fadela, Chaba Zohra, and Chaba Amina.

18 The names of Ahmed Wahby and Blawi el Houari, and secondarily Ahmed Saber and Mohammed Benzerga, are closely related to *wahrāni.* Together, they represent a repertoire of over one thousand songs.

## Chapter 2

1 This history has been pieced together from meetings with Algerian and French radio and newspaper journalists, producers of raï, musicians who

have been involved with raï since its early days, and a number of people who took part in organizing the first raï festivals in Algeria.

2 See Jansen 1987, Mebarki and Naceri 1983, Miliani 1983, Miliani and Belkadem 1981, and Ziad 1983.

3 For an early version of this section, see Schade-Poulsen 1996. References to the press articles can be found in Schade-Poulsen 1995a.

4 See Virolle-Souibès 1988a and Mazouzi 1990 for similar thoughts that later were quoted in the Western press.

5 I am using a metaphor—in line with the arguments of Bruner's 1986 article—characterizing Arabic music in which each musician in a group plays variations on a common theme.

6 For an early report, see Bariki 1986.

7 A number of LPs produced for the Western market have camels or veiled women as cover motifs, which, of course, are never used in Algeria.

8 "The warm voices develop rapid subtleties"; "a scream which breaks your heart in two and tears out your guts"; "an emotive, wailing Islamic voice"; "a spirited nasal wail"; "a singing that evokes a state of perpetual pleading and lamentation"; "a voice that might as well be diffused from the round towers of the minarets"; "a passionate pleading vocal"; "a grainy, urgent, minutely ornamented vocal." See, respectively, *Le Monde,* January 24, 1986; *Le Nouvel Observateur,* June 26–30, 1986; *New Musical Express,* December 20–27, 1986; *Q Magazine,* December 1986; *The Independent,* July 22, 1988; *Aktuelt,* August 14, 1988; *Folk Roots,* May 1989; *The New York Times,* August 10, 1989.

9 See Appaduraï 1990:299.

10 An article by Regev (1989) indicates that Western-based raï may function as a mediator between Oriental and Western sociomusical spheres in Israel.

11 In doing so, the record company has privatized part of Algerian oral folklore and the work of musicians and popular song makers in Algeria.

## Chapter 3

1 See Schade-Poulsen 1995b for the Arabic text. Names that might be identified have been abbreviated.

2 See Bourdieu 1980, Crapanzano 1980, Eickelman 1976, 1989, Geertz 1979, 1983, and Rosen 1984, for thoughts which can be related to the *barrāḥ*'s game. Here I follow mainly the version in Crapanzano 1980: 77–81. See Waterman 1990 for similar comments on a game in Nigeria.

3 These concepts taken together are known in literature as "honor." I do not intend to go into further discussion of the complex notion of honor here, since to focus on it would obscure the fact that the concept of honor

is a "floating signifier" demarcating wider spheres of interests that I deal with later; in this I follow Abu-Lughod 1986, 1993, Bourdieu 1966, and Peters 1967.

4 One was unemployed, one was a shop assistant in a supermarket, two were hairdressers, one was an unskilled worker, one was a carpenter, one was an itinerant retailer, and one was a school attendant.

5 It was a remunerative activity to distribute master tapes at a time when the value of basic goods in Algeria was calculated on the basis of prices in Europe and the black market for foreign currency in Algeria.

6 An elaborated genre from Algiers dating from the 1920s and 1930s; see Hadj Ali 1979, Saadallah 1981.

7 I have inquired into the backgrounds of fifty-three active singers, some of whom have recorded cassettes, others being singers in the cabarets or at weddings. It is not possible to say how great a percentage of the total number of singers they constitute. This is first because being a singer is relative. Some may sing only during the summer for very small returns and may be characterized as unemployed. Second, an inquiry I carried out at the Union nationale des arts culturels d'Oran (the artists' union in Oran) revealed that 4,663 individuals were registered as artists. Since it was well known that a good many of these musicians obtained or paid for a professional card in order to qualify for a visa to go to Europe, I asked how many were considered active musicians. The answer was seven hundred, a figure including both male and female instrumentalists. Virolle-Souibès (1988b: 218) obtained the figure of five hundred *maddāḥas* and *shīkhas,* which would leave very few male musicians in the whole area. Thus it is difficult to estimate the number of male singers. However, it is not completely unreasonable to estimate my sample as constituting at least one third of the singers in the Oran area, and at least two thirds of the full-time professionals.

8 The latter phenomenon is documented in Brita Landof's (1993) film *Lite för mit hjärta och lite för min gud* (A little for my heart, a little for my God).

9 Daoudi and Miliani's 1996 book, which constitutes an exception to the official story of raï, has significantly contributed to a better understanding of raï.

10 This claim was solidly disavowed in *El Moudjahid* (May 22, 1992) by Amar Belkhodja, who produced a fine inquiry into the *malḥūn* in spring 1992.

11 Names of popular rhythmic patterns are *haddi, barruāli, wahrāni, trāb, ʿallawi,* forms of rumba, *maddāha,* etc.

## Chapter 4

1 The names of the seven men have been changed.

## Chapter 5

1 Elements of the present analysis of "Diri dar" can be found in Schade-Poulsen 1993.

2 The mare in the *malḥūn* is a metaphor describing the woman in more romantic terms than those offered here in the context of an Algerian in the 1990s (see Tahar 1975:9).

3 Cheb Khaled, "Tastahel ya galbi" (You deserve it, oh my heart).

4 My initial understanding of the text was as indicated in Appendix 2, version 1.

5 "Hadha rrāykum" (This is your opinion).

6 The text of "Hadha rrāykum" has been reproduced at least twice in English (probably from Virolle-Souibès' 1988a:196 French translation)—not with any musical considerations, but rather as an example of raï singers' comments on society (M. Rosen 1990:22) or as an example of the sensibility of the singers "in favour of free expression in love" (McMurray and Swedenburg 1991:40).

7 I choose to preserve the anonymity of the singer Mustapha refers to here, as well as that of "Y," below.

8 For similar examples from the Middle East, see Lambert 1989, Racy 1986. The condemnation of popular music professionals is of course not exclusive to the Middle East.

9 An algerianization from the French for "pimp" or "mafioso." Poitiers 1955:23 noted that they were called *chiqueurs* ("tobacco chewers").

10 Some of the raï songs in chapters 6 and 7 are from the early 1980s and thus help stress that the chronological order I have imposed in my discussion of raï songs depends on one major tendency alone.

## Chapter 6

1 The selection of song lines in this and the following chapters is from a sample of 120 songs covering the whole period of modern raï—including raï songs in the hit parade on Channel 3 from 1985 to 1987—but with a definite emphasis on the most prominent of the singers, Cheb Khaled. Secondary themes have been left out of the analysis, such as songs about saints, songs of migration, songs of nostalgia, and songs about divorcées. Some were initially deciphered and translated by Amina ben Salah. A series of them were then discussed in detail with raï listeners in Oran. However, the responsibility for the interpretation of the lyrics rests solely with me.

2 As in the song "Saknat Marseilles," which describes a *maryūla* as a *bint l-blādi*—that girl of ours, who has fun, does crazy things, but with a charming innocence.

3 See Dwyer 1982:195–212 for an account of a pleasure party with female singers in Morocco.

4 A former pimp of the town told how there existed a code of honor among men in the brothels. In drinking sessions, no man was allowed to leave the group before all the wine offered was consumed. In the state-controlled brothels a newcomer had to be "married," and the groom would be the man in the strongest position. The prostitute would not take clients if "her man" were present. In the private brothels or "*maisons honnêtes,*" the prostitute's favors had to be "won."

5 Here I am relying on Abu-Lughod 1986, Ben Jelloun 1977, Boudhiba 1975, Bourdieu 1980, Boutefnouchet 1982, Camilleri 1973, Davis and Davis 1989, Descloitres and Debzi 1964, Dwyer 1978, Eickelman 1976, Jansen 1987, Mernissi 1983, Rosander 1991, L. Rosen 1984, and Zerdoumi 1982.

6 This description does, of course, leave out several features of Ramadan: the religious experience, the family gatherings, the late evenings with friends, etc.

7 It is also an important notion in Islamist ideology. See chapter 1 and Schade-Poulsen 1988.

8 At that time, music in mass circulation had been a part of the soundscape of the larger Algerian cities since the first recordings at the beginning of the century (see Gronow 1981), producing cherished names such as El Anqa, Guerrouabi, Ahmed Wahby and Blawi el Houari, Ghaffour, etc., who were heard on the radio in most families.

9 Camilleri 1973:202 has argued in the same vein.

## Chapter 7

1 See, for example, Dernouny and Zoulef 1980, 1982.

2 See Carey 1972 for this theme in Western pop. One hit from the late 1980s sung by most raï singers, "Yallāh bina," has lines like "*Alik rāni nghanni ya sbāb fārḥi*" (Because of you I sing, oh, you are the reason of my happiness), but the song was one of the exceptions that proved the rule. It was further well known that it originated from Lebanon, and that one reason for its success was that it showed that raï knew songs from the Machreq.

3 Cheb Khaled, "*Mālu khūya mālu ma jāsh*" (What is the matter with my brother; why didn't he return?).

4 Several stories indicated that the immigrée, the Algerian woman living in France, was also stereotyped in the same way.

5 The founder of the Islamist reformist movement in Algeria (see Benkheira 1990; Merad 1967:330).

6 A mode widely used in the call to prayers from the mosques.

7 Similar (or related) images can also be found in Mediterranean societies; see Archetti 1991, 1994; Bowman 1989; Brandes 1981; Herzfeld 1985; Loizos 1994.

8 In large part, my argument here emerged from a discussion of a previous paper (Schade-Poulsen 1994b) with Hassan Nissar. Bowman 1989 has discussed the relationship between Palestinian men and European women in terms of wider issues of power. However, he does not relate it to men's relationships with Palestinian women.

9 One song, "Harba wīn" (Where to flee), has been mentioned several times as an example of the political content of raï (see, e.g., Gross, McMurray, and Swedenburg 1992:42, M. Rosen 1990). It was released in 1988 not long before the October revolt and was played and sung by youngsters during the revolt. But this song is an exception in raï. According to my information, the text was written by a poet who was a member of the ruling FLN. The tune "Zwit, rwit" was originally sung by the Kabyle singer Idir ("A vava inou va"; see chapter 1) and was closely associated with the Kabyle political and cultural revival of the 1970s and 1980s. Thus it seems that "Harba wīn" was a clever attempt by a faction within the ruling party to use raï for the purpose of encouraging a popular revolt in Algeria.

## Chapter 8

1 For an early debate, see Bureau du colloque sur la musique 1964.

2 See Berkaak 1993; Denisoff 1972; Frith 1983; Hennion 1983, 1989; Hirsch 1991; Manuel 1988, 1993; Robinson 1991; Stokes 1992; Waterman 1990.

3 In using the term *graphic,* I allude to the French translation of the title of Goody's book, *La raison graphique* (see Goody 1977), in which the differences between orality and literacy are explored.

4 In Huizinga's words a game is "a voluntary activity or occupation freely accepted but absolutely binding, having its aim in itself and accompanied by a feeling of tension, joy, and the consciousness that it is 'different' from 'ordinary' life" (1970:47; see also Bateson 1972; Caillois 1958; Geertz 1973, 1983).

## Glossary

| | |
|---|---|
| *andalus* | the classical city music of North Africa originating from Muslim Andalusia. |
| *badawi* | Bedouin musical style. |
| *banndīr* | a tambourine-like drum with a wire that makes a humming sound. |
| *barrāḥ* | public announcer or party entertainer. |
| *darbūka* | vase-shaped hand drum. |
| *drabki* | darbūka player. |
| *gallāl* | cylindrical drum with a wire that makes a humming sound. |
| *gaṣba* | reed flute (several kinds in use). |
| *gawri* | a foreigner. |
| *ghayta* | an oboe-like woodwind instrument. |
| *ḥalāl* | licit. |
| *ḥarām* | illicit. |
| *ḥawsh* | a courtyard. |
| *ḥijāb* | type of veil originally associated with the women of the Islamist movement. |
| *istikhbār* | introduction to a song. |
| *khaffīf* | light (as opposed to heavy). |

| | |
|---|---|
| *maddāḥa* | female singer. |
| *maḥna* | passion, woman. |
| *malḥūn* | sung poetry. |
| *mariyūl* | a man who enjoys the pleasures of life. |
| *mariyūla* | a woman who enjoys the pleasures of life. |
| *nakwa* | identity card. |
| *nāy* | reed flute used primarily in city music. |
| *nqī* | clean. |
| *qanūn* | classical Arabic stringed instrument resembling the sitar. |
| *qarqabu* | iron castanet. |
| *qaṣīda* | a poem. |
| *rbāb* | local bowed string instrument. |
| *shābb* | a young man. |
| *shābba* | a young woman. |
| *shʿaabi* | an elaborated genre based in Algiers. |
| *shiʿar* | poetic verses. |
| *shīkh* | singer of the *malḥūn*. |
| *shīkha* | female singer. |
| *sḥūr* | sorcery. |
| *Sīdi Bīlal* | religious brotherhood associated with African practices south of the Sahara. |
| *snī* | a tray. |
| *tabrīḥa* | a dedication. |
| *tqīl* | heavy. |
| *trāb* | earth, soil. |
| *tshi-tshis* | rich, spoiled youngsters. |
| *ṭālab* | a religious student, a magician. |
| *ṭbal* | large drum, beaten with two sticks. |
| *ṭbīla* | a small clay drum beaten with a stick. |
| *wahrāni* | elaborated musical style from Oran. |
| *waʿada* | religious festival. |
| *ʿuud* | the Arabic lute. |

# Bibliography

Abrous, D. 1988. L'honneur et l'argent des femmes en Algérie. *Peuples Méditerranéens* 44–45: 49–65.

Abu-Lughod, L. 1986. *Veiled Sentiments: Honor and Poetry in a Bedouin Society.* Berkeley and Los Angeles: University of California Press.

———. 1993. *Writing Women's Worlds: Bedouin Stories.* Berkeley and Los Angeles: University of California Press.

Abu-Lughod, L., and C. Lutz. 1990. Introduction: Emotion, Discourse and the Politics of Everyday Life. In *Language and the Politics of Emotion,* edited by L. Abu-Lughod and C. Lutz. Cambridge: Cambridge University Press.

Addi, L. 1990. La crise structurelle de l'économie algérienne. *Peuples Méditerranéens* 52–53: 187–195.

Ahmed, L. 1991. *Women and Gender in Islam.* New Haven and London: Yale University Press.

Al-Ahnaf, M., B. Botiveau, and F. Frégosi. 1991. *L'Algérie par ses islamistes.* Paris: Karthala.

Alberoni, F. 1992 [1980]. *Forelskelse og kærlighed.* Copenhagen: Lindhardt og Ringhof.

Appadurai, A. 1988. Introduction. In *The Social Life of Things,* edited by A. Appadurai. Cambridge: Cambridge University Press.

———. 1990. Disjuncture and Difference in the Global Cultural Economy. In *Global Culture,* edited by M. Featherstone. London: Sage.

Archetti, E. 1991. Argentinian tango—Male sexual ideology and morality. In *The Ecology of Choice and Symbol,* edited by R. Grønhaug et al. Bergen: Alma Mater.

———. 1994. Models of Masculinity in the Poetics of the Argentinian Tango. In *Exploring the Written Anthropology and the Multiplicity of Writing,* edited by E. Archetti. Oslo: Scandinavian University Press.

Azza, A. 1979. *Mestfa Ben Brahim: Barde de l'oranais et chantre des Beni 'Amer.* Algiers: SNED.

Baffet, R. 1985. *Tradition théâtrale et modernité en Algérie.* Paris: L'Harmattan.

Bariki, S. 1986. Les effets culturels de l'émigration, un enjeu de luttes sociales. In *Nouveaux enjeux culturels au Maghreb.* Paris: CNRS.

Barth, F. 1989. The Analysis of Culture in Complex Societies. *Ethnos* 54 (3–4): 120–143.

Barthes, R. 1987. The Grain of the Voice. In *Image, Music, Text,* edited by S. Heath. London: Fontana Press.

Bateson, G. 1972. *Steps to an Ecology of Mind.* New York: Ballantine Books.

B'Chir, B., and R. Zghal. 1984. Les jeunes et le temps libre: Reproduction ou transformation de la société. In *Jeunesse et Changement Social.* Tunis: CERES.

Beaussier, M. 1958 [1887]. *Dictionnaire pratique arabe-français.* Algiers: Maison des livres.

Belhalfaoui, M. 1982a. Khaira Es-Sebsajiyya: Poétesse chanteuse de Mostaghanem et Oran. In *Litterature orale—Actes de table ronde.* Algiers: O.P.U.

———. 1982b. *La poésie arabe maghrébine d'expression populaire.* Paris: Maspéro.

Benestad, F. 1976. *Musikk og tanke.* Oslo: Aschehoug.

Ben Jelloun, T. 1977. *La plus haute des solitudes.* Paris: Seuil.

Benkheira, H. 1982. *Alcool, religion, sport.* Oran: University of Oran.

———. 1986. De la musique avant toute chose: Remarques sur le raï. *Peuples Méditerranéens* 35–36: 173–177.

———. 1990. "Machisme," nationalisme et religion. *Peuples Méditerranéens* 52–53: 127–145.

Bennani-Chraïbi, M. 1994. *Soumis et rebelles: Les jeunes au Maroc.* Paris: Editions CNRS.

Ben Naoum, A. 1986. Le raï, délit d'opinion? *Internationale de l'Imaginaire* 5: 5–16.

Bentahar, M. 1989. *La jeunesse arabe à la recherche de son identité.* Rabat: Al Kalam.

Berkaak, O. A. 1993. *Erfaringer fra risikosonen—Opplevelse og stilutvikling i rock.* Oslo: Universitetsforlaget.

Berque, J. 1962. *Le Maghreb entre deux guerres.* Paris: Seuil.

Bertherand, A. 1857. De la prostitution en Algérie. In *De la prostitution en France.* Paris: Baillière and sons.

Boubakeur, Cheikh S. H. 1990. *Trois poètes algériens.* Paris: Maisonneuve and Larose.

Boudhiba, A. 1975. *La sexualité en Islam.* Paris: PUF.

Bourdieu, P. 1966. The Sentiment of Honour in Kabyle Society. In *Honour and Shame,* edited by J. Peristiany. Chicago: University of Chicago Press.

———. 1979. *La distinction.* Paris: Editions Minuit.

———. 1980. *Le sens pratique.* Paris: Editions Minuit.

———. 1992. *Les règles de l'art—Genèse et structure du champ littéraire.* Paris: Seuil.

Boutefnouchet, M. 1982. *La famille algérienne.* Algiers: SNED.

Bouzar-Kasbadji, N. 1988. *L'Emergence artistique algérienne au XXe siècle.* Algiers: OPU.

Bowman, G. 1989. Fucking Tourists: Sexual Relations and Tourism in Jerusalem's Old City. *Critique of Anthropology* 9 (2): 77–93.

Brabrant, J. 1975. Migrations et integration urbaine: L'origine géographique de la population d'Oran. *Actes du colloque de démographie maghrébine.* Oran.

———. 1977. Du sous-emploi dans la société urbaine algérienne: Une étude du changement social sur l'espace urbain oranais. *Recherche géographiques à Strasbourg* 3: 125–150.

Brandes, S. 1981. Like Wounded Stags: Male Sexual Ideology in an Andalusian Town. In *Sexual Meanings: The Cultural Construction of Gender and Sexuality,* edited by S. Ortner and H. Whitehead. Cambridge and New York: Cambridge University Press.

Bromberger, C. 1995. *Le match de football.* Paris: Editions de la Maison des Sciences de l'homme.

Broughton, S., M. Ellingham, D. Muddyman, and R. Trillo, eds. 1994. *World Music: The Rough Guide.* London: Penguin.

Bruner, E. 1986. Ethnography as Narrative. In *The Anthropology of Experience,* edited by E. Bruner and V. Turner. Urbana and Chicago: University of Illinois Press.

Bureau du Colloque sur la Musique. 1964. *Colloque national sur la mu-*

*sique algérienne*. Algiers: FLN, Commission centrale d'orientation, section des affaires culturelles.

Burgat, F. 1988. *L'islamisme au Maghreb*. Paris: Karthala.

———. 1990. Algérie—Les élections locales. *Maghreb Machrek* 129: 5–23.

Burrows, D. 1989. Singing and Saying. *Journal of Musicology* 7 (3): 390–402.

Caillois, R. 1958. *Les jeux et les hommes*. Paris: Gallimard.

Camilleri, C. 1973. *Jeunesse, famille et développement*. Paris: CNRS.

Carey, J. T. 1972. Changing Courtship Patterns in the Popular Song. In *The Sound of Social Change*, edited by S. Denisoff and R. Peterson. Chicago: Rand McNally.

Carlier, O. 1995. *Entre nation et jihad*. Paris: Presses de Sciences Po.

Chambers, I. 1994. *Migrancy, Culture, Identity*. London: Routledge.

Chellig-Aïnad-Tabet, N. 1982. La femme musulmane moderne vue par les lycéens algériens. *Annuaire de l'Afrique du Nord* 1979: 147–163.

Clifford, J. 1986. Introduction: Partial Truths. *Writing Culture*, edited by J. Clifford and G. Marcus. Berkeley and Los Angeles: University of California Press.

———. 1988. On Ethnographic Authority. In *The Predicament of Culture*, edited by J. Clifford. Cambridge: Harvard University Press.

Colonna, F. 1974. Cultural Resistance and Religious Legitimacy in Colonial Algeria. *Economy and Society* 3 (3): 1–20.

———. 1976. Questions à propos de la littérature orale comme savoir. *Revue de l'Occident Musulman et de la Méditerranée* 22: 17–26.

———. 1995. *Les versets de l'invincibilité*. Paris: Presses de Sciences Po.

Comité d'Organisation du 1er Festival. 1985. *1er Festival de la chanson "ray."* Wilaya d'Oran: Republique algérienne démocratique et populaire.

Cornwall, A., and N. Lindisfarne. 1994. Dislocating masculinity: Gender Power and Anthropology. In *Dislocating Masculinity*, edited by A. Cornwall and N. Lindisfarne. London: Routledge.

Crapanzano, V. 1980. *Tuhami: Portrait of a Moroccan*. Chicago and London: University of Chicago Press.

Danielson, V. 1988. The Arab Middle East. In *Popular Musics of the Non-Western World*, edited by P. Manuel. New York and Oxford: Oxford University Press.

———. 1991. Female Singers in Cairo During the 1920s. In *Women in Middle Eastern History*, edited by N. Keddie and B. Baron. New Haven and London: Yale University Press.

Daoudi, B., and H. Miliani. 1996. *L'aventure du raï.* Paris: Seuil.

Daumas, E. [1869] 1983. *La vie arabe et la société musulmane.* Geneva and Paris: Slatkine Reprints.

Davis, S., and D. Davis. 1989. *Adolescence in a Moroccan Town.* New Brunswick and London: Rutgers University Press.

Déjeux, J. 1989. *L'image de l'étrangère.* Paris: La boîte à documents.

Delphin, G. 1886. *La poésie et la musique arabe dans le Maghreb algérien.* Paris: Ernest Leroux.

———. 1891. *Receuil de textes pour l'étude de l'Arabe parlé.* Paris and Algiers: Leroux and Jourdan.

Denisoff, R. ed. 1972. *The Sounds of Social Change.* Chicago: Rand McNally.

Dennouni, H. 1986. Les dispositions du code algérien de la famille. *Annuaire de l'Afrique du Nord* 1984: 711–726.

Dernouny, M., and B. Zoulef. 1980. Naissance d'un chant protestataire: Le groupe marocain Nass el Ghiwane. *Peuples Méditerranéens* 12: 3–31.

———. 1982. L'identité culturelle au Maghreb: A travers un corpus de chants contemporains. *Annuaire de l'Afrique du Nord* 1983: 1021–1051.

Descloitres, R., and L. Debzi. 1964. Système de parenté et structure familiales en Algérie. *Annuaire de l'Afrique du Nord* 1963: 23–59.

Douglas, M. 1966. *Purity and Danger.* London: Kegan Paul.

Doutté, E. 1908. *Magie et religion dans l'Afrique du Nord.* Algiers: Jourdan.

Dwyer, D. H. 1978. *Images and Self-Images: Male and Female in Morocco.* New York: Columbia University Press.

Dwyer, K. 1982. *Moroccan Dialogues: Anthropology in Question.* Baltimore and London: Johns Hopkins University Press.

Eickelman, D. 1976. *Moroccan Islam.* Austin and London: University of Texas Press.

———. 1989. *The Middle East: An Anthropological Approach.* Englewood Cliffs, N.J.: Prentice Hall.

El-Boudali, S. 1949. La musique arabe en Algérie. *Documents Algériens,* 36: 1–5.

Fabian, J. 1978. Popular Culture in Africa: Findings and Conjectures. *Africa* 48 (4): 315–334.

Fairley, J. 1989. Out of the Archive and into the World of Music. *Popular Music* 8 (1): 101–107.

Feld, S. 1994. From Schizophonia to Schismogenesis. In *Music Grooves,* edited by S. Feld and C. Keil. London and Chicago: University of Chicago.

Fodil, A. 1987. Ménages et logements dans la ville d'Oran. Ph.D. diss., University of Paris V.

Fornäs, J., U. Lindberg, and O. Sernhede. 1984. *Ungdomskultur: Identitet-motstand*. Stockholm: Akademilitteratur.

Foucault, M. 1990. *The History of Sexuality: An Introduction*. New York: Vintage.

Frith, S. 1983. *Sound Effects: Youth, Leisure, and the Politics of Rock*. London: Constable.

———. 1991. Critical Response. In *Music at the Margins*, edited by D. C. Robinson. London: Sage.

Gaudefroy-Demombynes, M. 1901. *Les cérémonies du mariage chez les indigènes de l'Algérie*. Paris: Maisonneuve.

Gaudry, M. 1961. *La société féminine au Djebel Amour et au Ksel*. Algiers: Société algérienne d'impressions diverses.

Geertz, C. 1973. Deep Play: Notes on the Balinese Cockfight. In *The Interpretation of Culture*. New York: Basic Books.

———. 1979. Suq: The Bazaar Economy of Sefrou. In *Meaning and Order in Moroccan Society*, edited by C. Geertz, H. Geertz, and L. Rosen. New York: Cambridge University Press.

———. 1983. Art as a Cultural System. In *Local Knowledge*. New York: Basic Books.

Gilsenan, M. 1982. *Recognizing Islam*. London: Croom Helm.

Goody, J. 1977. *The Domestication of the Savage Mind*. Cambridge: Cambridge University Press.

Gronow, P. 1981. The Record Industry Comes to the Orient. *Ethnomusicology* 25 (2): 251–284.

Gross, F., D. McMurray, and T. Swedenburg. 1992. Raï, Rap and Ramadan Nights. *Middle East Report* (Sept.–Oct.): 11–16.

Guettat, M. 1980. *La musique classique du Maghreb*. Paris: Sindbad.

Guignard, M. 1975. *Musique, honneur et plaisir au Sahara*. Paris: Geuthner.

Hadj Ali, B. 1979. El Anka et la tradition Chaabi. *Annuaire de l'Afrique du Nord* 1978: 905–1111.

Hammoudi, A. 1988. *La victime et ses masques*. Paris: Seuil.

Hannerz, U. 1987. The World in Creolization. *Africa* 57: 546–559.

———. 1989. Notes on the Global Ecumene. *Public Culture* 1 (2): 66–75.

———. 1992. *Cultural Complexity*. New York: Columbia University Press.

Hasnaoui, M. 1990. *Les principes fondamentaux de la pensée musicale orientale.* Algiers: Stencil.

Hebdige, D. 1979. *Subculture, the Meaning of Style.* London: Methuen.

———. 1987. *Cut 'n' Mix: Culture, Identity and Caribbean Music.* London: Comedia.

Heller, A. 1979. Towards an Anthropology of Feeling. *Dialectical Anthropology* 4: 1–20.

Henni, A. 1990. Qui a légalisé quel trabendo. *Peuples Méditerranéens* 52–53: 233–245.

Hennion, A. 1983. The Production of Success: An Antimusicology of the Pop Song. In *Popular Music 3,* edited by R. Middleton and D. Horn. Cambridge: Cambridge University Press.

———. 1989. *J'aime Bach.* Paris: Stencil.

Herzfeld, M. 1985. *The Poetics of Manhood.* Princeton: Princeton University Press.

Hirsch, P. 1991. Processing Fads and Fashions: An Organizing-Set Analysis of Cultural Industry Systems. In *Rethinking Popular Culture,* edited by C. Mukerji and M. Schudson. Berkeley and Los Angeles: University of California Press.

Hoggart, R. 1971. *The Uses of Literacy.* London: Chatto and Wintus.

Huizinga, J. [1949] 1970. *Homo Ludens.* London: Temple Smith.

Jansen, W. 1987. *Women without Men.* Leiden: E. J. Brill.

Kapferer, B. 1979. Mind, Self, and Other Demonic Illnesses: the Negation and Reconstruction of Self. *American Ethnologist* 6 (1–2): 110–133.

Kerrou, M., and M. Kharoufi. 1994. Maghreb: Familles, valeurs et changements sociaux. *Maghreb Machrek* 144: 26–40.

Kerrou, M., and M. M'Halla. 1993. La prostitution dans la médina de Tunis au XIX^e et XX^e siècles. In *Être marginal au Maghreb,* edited by F. Colonna and Z. Daoud. Paris: Editions CNRS.

Khelladi, A. 1992. *Les islamistes algériens face au pouvoir.* Algiers: Editions Alfa.

Labat, S. 1995. *Les islamistes algériens.* Paris: Seuil.

Lambert, J. 1989. Du "chanteur" à l'"artiste": Vers un nouveau statut du musicien. *Peuples Méditerranéens* 46: 57–76.

Langer, S. 1953. *Feeling and Form.* New York: Charles Scribner's Sons.

Lefebvre, H. 1995. *The Production of Space.* Cambridge, Mass.: Blackwell.

Lefevre, L. 1986. Si le raï m'était conté. *Afrique Asie* 368.

Lepoil, M. 1947. *Faut-il abolir la prostitution?* Algiers: V. Heintz.

Lesbet, D. 1994. Effets de la crise du logement en Algérie. *Maghreb Machrek* 143: 212–221.

Lespes, R. 1938. *Oran, étude de géographie et d'histoire urbaine*. Paris: Alcan.

Loizos, P. 1994. A Broken Mirror: Masculine Sexuality in Greek Ethnography. In *Dislocating Masculinity,* edited by A. Cornwall and N. Lindisfarne. London: Routledge.

Lord, A. B. 1960. *The Singer of Tales.* Cambridge: Harvard University Press.

Lortat-Jacob, B. 1980. *Musique et fêtes au Haut-Atlas.* Paris: Mouton.

Malm, K. 1981. *Fyra musikkulturer.* Stockholm: Almquist and Wiksell.

Malm, K., and R. Willis. 1984. *Big Sounds from Small Peoples: The Music Industry in Small Countries.* London: Constable.

———. 1992. *Media Policy and Music Activity.* London and New York: Routledge.

Manuel, P. 1988. *Popular Musics of the Non-Western World.* New York and Oxford: Oxford University Press.

———. 1993. *Cassette Culture: Popular Music and Technology in North India.* Chicago and London: University of Chicago Press.

Marcus, G., and M. Fischer. 1986. *Anthropology as a Cultural Critique.* Chicago and London: University of Chicago Press.

Mariet, F. 1978. La constitution du goût musical. *Musique en Jeu* 33: 60–73.

Mazouzi, B. 1990. La musique algérienne: et la question raï. *La Revue Musicale,* nos. 418–420.

McMurray, D., and T. Swedenburg. 1991. Rai Tide Rising. *Middle East Report* (March–April): 39–42.

Mead, G. H. 1934. *Mind, Self and Society.* Chicago and London: University of Chicago Press.

Mebarki, Y., and K. Naceri. 1983. *Introduction à l'étude du "mahdar": La chanson "raï" dans les festivités de mariage à Oran.* B.A. thesis, University of Oran.

Merad, A. 1967. *Le réformisme musulman en Algérie.* Paris: Mouton.

Mernissi, F. 1983. *Sexe, idéologie, islam.* Paris: Tièrce.

Messaoudi, A. 1990. Chômage et solidarités familiales. *Peuples Méditerranéens* 52–53: 195–219.

Mezouane, R. 1992. Génération raï. *Autrement* 60: 64–70.

Miliani, H. 1983. *Culture populaire et contradictions symboliques.* G.R.F.A. working paper no. 9. Oran: University of Oran.

———. 1986. Parcours symboliques de la chanson raï. *Internationale de l'Imaginaire* 5: 17–21.

Miliani, H. and S. M. Belkadem. 1981. *Les représentations de la femme dans la chanson populaire oranaise dite raï*. G.R.F.A. working paper no. 8. Oran: University of Oran.

Mortensen, L. B. 1989. *"At være eller ikke være": tyrkisk ungdom i København og Ankara*. Cultural sociology series no. 27, Copenhagen: Akademisk Forlag.

Mouffok, G. 1996. *Être journaliste en Algérie*. Paris: Reporters sans frontières.

Mukerji, C., and Schudson, M. eds. 1991. *Rethinking Popular Culture*. Berkeley and Los Angeles: University of California Press.

Nattiez, J. J. 1973. Analyse musicale et sémiologie: Le structuralisme de Lévi-Strauss. *Musique en Jeu* 12: 59–79.

Nettl, B. 1985. *The Western Impact on World Music*. London: Collier Macmillan.

Nieuwkerk, K. van 1992. Female Entertainers in Egypt: Drinking and Gender Roles. In *Alcohol, Gender and Culture*, edited by D. Gefou-Madianou. London and New York: Routledge.

Office national des statistiques. 1988. Armature urbaine 1987. *Les collections statistiques*. Algiers.

Ortner, S. 1970. On Key Symbols. *American Anthropologist* 75 (5): 1338–1446.

Ouitis, A. 1984. *Possesion, magie et prophétie en Algérie*. Paris: L'Arcantère.

Pascon, P., and M. Bentahar. 1969. Ce que disent 296 jeunes ruraux. *Bulletin Economique et Social du Maroc* 21: 1–143.

Passeron, J. C. 1991. L'usage faible des images: Enquêtes sur la réception de la peinture. In *Le raisonnement sociologique*. Paris: Editions Nathan.

Peters, E. 1967. Some Structural Aspects of the Feud among the Camel-Herding Bedouin of Cyrenaica. *Africa* 37: 261–282.

Plantade, N. 1988. *La guerre des femmes*. Paris: La boîte à documents.

Poitiers, P. 1955. *Considérations sur la prostitution en Algérie*. Ph.D. diss., Paris: Impr. R. Foulon.

Racy, A. J. 1986. Words and Music in Beirut: A Study of Attitudes. *Ethnomusicology* 30 (3): 413–427.

Rafik, F. 1980. *La prostitution féminine à Essaouira (Maroc)*. Ph.D. diss., University of Paris V.

Regev, M. 1989. The Field of Popular Music in Israel. In *World Music, Politics and Social Change*, edited by S. Frith. Manchester and New York: Manchester University Press.

Reporters sans frontières. 1995. *Le livre noir de l'Algérie*. Paris: Reporters sans frontières.

Robinson, D. C., E. B. Buck, and M. Cuthbert, eds. 1991. *Music at the Margins*. London: Sage.

Rosander, E. 1991. *Women in a Borderland: Managing Muslim Identity Where Morocco Meets Spain*. Stockholm: Stockholm Studies in Social Anthropology.

Rosen, L. 1984. *Bargaining for reality*. Chicago and London: University of Chicago Press.

Rosen, M. 1990. Undertone. *Artforum* (Sept.): 22–23.

Rouadjia, A. 1990. *Les fréres et la mosquée*. Paris: Karthala.

Rouanet, J. 1920. La musique arabe dans le Maghreb. *Encyclopédie de la musique et dictionnaire du conservatoire*. Paris.

Rougemont, D. de 1956. *L'amour et l'Occident*. Paris: Union générale d'éditions.

Saadallah, R. 1981. *El-Hadj M'Hamed El-Anka maître et renovateur de la musique chaabi*. Algiers: La Maison des livres.

Safir, E. B. 1949. La musique arabe en Algérie. *Documents Algériens* 36.

Salvador-Daniel, F. 1986. *Musique et instruments de musique du Maghreb*. Paris: La boîte à documents.

Sari, D. 1990. L'indispensable maîtrise de la croissance démographique en Algérie. *Maghreb Machrek* 129: 23–47.

Schade-Poulsen, M. 1988. *Troens veje—et perspektiv på den islamiske vækkelse'*. Copenhagen: Institute of Anthropology.

———. 1993. Essai d'analyse d'une chanson raï—côté hommes. In *Être marginal au Maghreb*, edited by F. Colonna and Z. Daoud. Paris: Editions CNRS.

———. 1995a. *Men and Music in Algeria: An Analysis of the Social Significance of Raï Music*. Ph.D. diss., University of Copenhagen.

———. 1995b. The Power of Love: Raï Music and Youth in Algeria. In *Youth Cultures*, edited by V. Amit-Talai and H. Wulff. London and New York: Routledge.

———. 1996. Which World? On the Diffusion of Algerian Raï to the West. In *Siting Culture*, edited by K. Hastrup and K. Olwig. London: Routledge.

Seeger, A. 1987. *Why Suyá Sing*. Cambridge: Cambridge University Press.

Semmoud, B. 1986. Politique d'habitat et accès au logement en Algérie: L'exemple de l'Oranie. *Annuaire de l'Afrique du Nord 1986*: 127–139.

Sonneck, C. 1902. *Chants arabes du Maghreb*. Paris.

Soufi, F. 1994. Oran, un urbanisme sans histoire: Détruire pour construire. *Maghreb Machrek* 143: 204–211.

Stewart, K. 1992. Nostalgia: A Polemic. In *Rereading Cultural Anthropology*, edited by G. Marcus. Durham and London: Duke University Press.

Stockmann, D. 1991. Interdisciplinary Approaches to the Study of Musical Communication Structures. In *Comparative Musicology and Anthropology of Music*, edited by B. Nettl and P. Bohlman. Chicago and London: University of Chicago Press.

Stokes, M. 1992. *The Arabesk Debate: Music and Musicians in Modern Turkey*. Oxford: Clarendon.

———. 1994. Introduction. In *Ethnicity, Identity and Music*, edited by M. Stokes. Oxford and Providence: Berg.

Tahar, A. 1975. *La poésie populaire algérienne (melhun)*. Algiers: SNED.

Thompson, M. 1979. *Rubbish Theory*. Oxford: Oxford University Press.

Tinthoin, R. 1953. *Le peuplement musulman d'Oran*. Bulletin abstract. Oran: Société de géographie et d'archéologie.

Turner, V. 1967. *The Forest of Symbols*. Ithaca and London: Cornell University Press.

Tyler, S. 1986. Post-modern Ethnography: From Document of the Occult to Occult Documents. In *Writing Culture*, edited by J. Clifford and G. Marcus. Berkeley and Los Angeles: University of California Press.

Vigreux, P. 1985. *La derbouka*. Aix-en-Provence: Édisud.

Virolle-Souibès, M. 1988a. Ce que chanter rray veut dire: Prélude à d'autres couplets. *Cahiers de Litterature Orale* 23: 177–209.

———. 1988b. Le ray, coté femmes. *Peuples Méditerranéens* 44–45: 193–220.

———. 1989 Le Raï entre résistances et récupération. *Revue du Monde Musulman et de la Méditerranée* 1 (51): 47–62.

———. 1993. Déchire, lacère et Rimitti revaudra! *Liber* (Sept.): 16–20.

———. 1995. *La chanson raï*. Paris: Karthala.

Waterman, C. A. 1990. *Juju: A Social History and Ethnography of an African Popular Music*. Chicago and London: University of Chicago Press.

Westermarck, E. [1914] 1972. *Marriage Ceremonies in Morocco*. London: Curzon.

Wikan, U. 1977. Man Becomes Woman: Transsexualism in Oman as a Key to Gender Roles. *Man*, n.s., 12 (2): 304–319.

Willis, P. 1978. *Profane Culture*. London: Routledge.

Yacine, T. 1990. *L'izli ou l'amour chanté en kabyle*. Algiers: Bouchène-Awal.

Yafil, N. n.d. *Répertoire de musique arabe et Maure*. Yafil collection. Algiers.

Yusuf A. 1983. *The Holy Qur'an: Text, Translation and Commentary*. Brentwood, Md.: Amana Corp.

Zerdoumi, N. 1982. *Enfants d'hier: l'Éducation de l'enfant en milieu traditionnel algérien*. Paris: Maspéro.

Zghal, A. 1984. Note pour un debat sur la jeunesse arabe. In *Jeunesse et Changement Social*. Tunis: CERES.

Ziad, S. 1983. *Essai d'analyse de la chanson dite "raï."* B.A. thesis, University of Oran.

Zubeida, S. 1987. Components of Popular Culture in the Middle East. In *Mass Culture, Popular Culture and Social Life in the Middle East*, edited by G. Stauth and S. Zubeida. Boulder: Westview Press.

# Index